T0323796

'*TA 100 Key Points* is a must-read for all transactional analysis practitioners, both beginning and advanced. The book provides a refreshing and holistic account of transactional analysis and its connections with cutting-edge science and the theory of psychotherapy and related fields. Mark Widdowson masterfully integrates the wisdom of early transactional analysts with current developments in TA psychotherapy theory and practice. The book is full of practical wisdom and clinical insights and will serve as a guide into the complexities of the psychotherapy journey from the initial session to the end of psychotherapy. I highly recommend it.'

Gregor Žvelc, *PhD, TSTA, Professor of Clinical Psychology, Department of Psychology, University of Ljubljana*

'In *Transactional Analysis: 100 Key Points and Techniques*, Mark Widdowson offers a powerful and richly described account of how a master therapist pursues their craft. While providing a comprehensive overview of Transactional Analysis theory and practice, this book is also highly relevant to both experienced practitioners, and new trainees, in any approach to counselling and psychotherapy. The focus on key choice-points in therapy makes it possible for the reader to learn new options and strategies in relation to supporting clients through the therapy journey. Important aspects of this book include an engaging account of how TA has evolved since the pioneering work of Eric Berne, Claude Steiner and their colleagues, alongside an appreciation of the significance of responding in a respectful and empowering way to socio-cultural difference, marginalisation and oppression. Thoughtful links are consistently made to ideas and techniques from other therapy traditions, and current research evidence. The first edition of *Transactional Analysis: 100 Key Points and Techniques* was a best-seller, whose value was recognised by counsellors and psychotherapists from a wide range of theoretical orientations and areas of practice. This new edition is even better, and is warmly recommended as essential reading for anyone interested in deepening and broadening their capacity to work resourcefully with clients.'

John McLeod, *Emeritus Professor of Counselling, Abertay University*

'Dr. Mark Widdowson provides an excellent book on transactional analysis. Of particular note is how contemporary it is. Full of very up-to-date information and ideas on TA and the relationship to many other approaches and ideas. An excellent and highly recommended read for students, TA trainers and people with a wide range of expertise and knowledge.'

Nataliia Isaieva, *PTSTA -P-EATA/ITAA, Ukraine,*
Honorary Member of the Ukrainian
Society of Transactional Analysis USTA

TRANSACTIONAL ANALYSIS

The second edition of *Transactional Analysis: 100 Key Points and Techniques* synthesizes developments in Transactional Analysis (TA) and psychotherapy research, making complex ideas accessible and offering therapists practical guidance on refining TA psychotherapy skills.

Divided into seven parts, the 100 key points cover:

- The philosophy, theory, methods and critique of the main approaches to TA
- New developments and approaches in TA
- TA perspectives on the therapeutic relationship
- Client assessment, diagnosis and case formulation
- Contracting and treatment planning using TA
- A troubleshooting guide to avoiding common pitfalls
- Refining therapeutic skills

Specific updates incorporate emergent approaches in TA, recent developments in the understanding of neurodiversity and current best practice thinking.

This book is essential reading for trainee and beginner TA therapists, as well as experienced practitioners looking to update their field knowledge for a skilful and mindful application of this cohesive system of psychotherapy.

Mark Widdowson is a UKCP registered psychotherapist, based in Manchester. He is a senior lecturer in counselling and psychotherapy at the University of Salford, Associate Director of The Berne Institute and Director of Manchester Psychotherapy Foundation.

100 Key Points and Techniques
Series Editor: Windy Dryden

ALSO IN THIS SERIES:

COGNITIVE BEHAVIOUR THERAPY: 100 KEY POINTS
AND TECHNIQUES, 2ND EDITION
Michael Neenan and Windy Dryden

RATIONAL EMOTIVE BEHAVIOUR THERAPY: 100 KEY
POINTS AND TECHNIQUES, 2ND EDITION
Windy Dryden and Michael Neenan

EXISTENTIAL THERAPY: 100 KEY POINTS AND
TECHNIQUES
Susan Iacovou and Karen Weixel-Dixon

PERSON-CENTRED THERAPY: 100 KEY POINTS AND
TECHNIQUES, 2ND EDITION
Paul Wilkins

SINGLE-SESSION THERAPY (SST): 100 KEY POINTS AND
TECHNIQUES
Windy Dryden

ACCEPTANCE AND COMMITMENT THERAPY: 100 KEY
POINTS AND TECHNIQUES
Richard Bennett and Joseph E. Oliver

GESTALT THERAPY: 100 KEY POINTS AND
TECHNIQUES
Dave Mann

SINGLE-SESSION THERAPY (SST): 100 KEY POINTS AND
TECHNIQUES, 2ND EDITION
Windy Dryden

TRANSACTIONAL ANALYSIS: 100 KEY POINTS AND
TECHNIQUES, 2ND EDITION
Mark Widdowson

TRANSACTIONAL ANALYSIS

100 KEY POINTS AND TECHNIQUES

Second Edition

Mark Widdowson

Routledge
Taylor & Francis Group

LONDON AND NEW YORK

Second edition published 2024
by Routledge
4 Park Square, Milton Park, Abingdon, Oxon OX14 4RN

and by Routledge
605 Third Avenue, New York, NY 10158

Routledge is an imprint of the Taylor & Francis Group, an informa business

© 2024 Mark Widdowson

The right of Mark Widdowson to be identified as author of this work has been asserted in accordance with sections 77 and 78 of the Copyright, Designs and Patents Act 1988.

All rights reserved. No part of this book may be reprinted or reproduced or utilised in any form or by any electronic, mechanical, or other means, now known or hereafter invented, including photocopying and recording, or in any information storage or retrieval system, without permission in writing from the publishers.

Trademark notice: Product or corporate names may be trademarks or registered trademarks, and are used only for identification and explanation without intent to infringe.

First edition published 2009, Routledge

British Library Cataloguing-in-Publication Data
A catalogue record for this book is available from the British Library

Library of Congress Cataloging-in-Publication Data
Names: Widdowson, Mark, 1973- author.
Title: Transactional analysis : 100 key points and techniques / Mark Widdowson.
Description: Second edition. | Milton Park, Abingdon, Oxon ; New York, NY : Routledge, 2024. | Series: 100 key points and techniques | Includes bibliographical references and index.
Identifiers: LCCN 2023021542 (print) | LCCN 2023021543 (ebook) | ISBN 9781032452043 (hardback) | ISBN 9781032452036 (paperback) | ISBN 9781003375890 (ebook)
Subjects: LCSH: Transactional analysis.
Classification: LCC RC489.T7 W53 2024 (print) | LCC RC489.T7 (ebook) | DDC 616.89/145--dc23/eng/20230710
LC record available at https://lccn.loc.gov/2023021542
LC ebook record available at https://lccn.loc.gov/2023021543

ISBN: 978-1-032-45204-3 (hbk)
ISBN: 978-1-032-45203-6 (pbk)
ISBN: 978-1-003-37589-0 (ebk)

DOI: 10.4324/9781003375890

Typeset in Aldus
by MPS Limited, Dehradun

CONTENTS

Preface to the second edition   xiii
Acknowledgements   xvii

Introduction   1

Part 1
APPROACHES IN TRANSACTIONAL
ANALYSIS PRACTICE   5

1   Schools and approaches in TA   7
2   The classical school: foundations   11
3   The classical school: methods   14
4   The redecision school: foundations   16
5   The redecision school: methods   19
6   The cathexis school: foundations   22
7   The cathexis school: methods   25
8   Radical psychiatry   28
9   Eco-TA   32
10 Integrative TA: foundations   36
11 Integrative TA: methods   40
12 Psychodynamic TA 1   43
13 Psychodynamic TA 2: intensive
    transactional analysis psychotherapy   47
14 Psychodynamic TA 3: interpretive
    dynamic transactional analysis
    psychotherapy   50
15 Relational TA: foundations   53
16 Relational TA: methods   58
17 Co-creative TA   60

Part 2
THE THERAPEUTIC RELATIONSHIP 65

18	The initial sessions	67
19	Therapeutic enquiry	71
20	The centrality of empathy	73
21	Accounting for the impact of diversity in the therapeutic relationship	77
22	Conceptualizing the therapeutic relationship	81
23	Strengthening the working alliance by attention to tasks, goals and bonds	84
24	Considering Adapted Child responses as indicators of alliance rupture	87
25	The therapeutic alliance: rupture and repair	90
26	Understanding transference and countertransference	94
27	The drama triangle as a tool to explore countertransference	99
28	Transference and countertransference: an aide-mémoire of TA models	102
29	Ending TA therapy	105

Part 3
ASSESSMENT, DIAGNOSIS AND CASE
FORMULATION IN TA 109

30	The importance of observation	111
31	Conducting a structured intake assessment	115
32	Assessing suitability for TA therapy	119
33	Using Berne's four methods of diagnosis	122
34	Developing a conversational interviewing technique	126
35	Using pro-formas for rapid script diagnosis	129

36 Using functional and structural analysis of
   ego states   133
37 Accounting for internal ego state
   dialogue   138
38 Accounting for Cultural and Religious
   parent   141
39 Accounting for intersectionality and
   oppression   145
40 Accounting for neurodiversity   149
41 Building up the script system   152
42 Exploring drivers   157
43 Analysing games   160
44 Escape hatches as a framework for
   understanding client safety   163
45 Suicidal ideation: a brief introduction   167
46 Diagnosis checklist   171

Part 4
CONTRACTING   **177**

47 Contracting for the tasks and goals
   of therapy   179
48 Doing goal-oriented and
   process-oriented TA therapy   182
49 Using a standard written business
   contract   185
50 Contracting with the unsure client   190
51 Using homework and behavioural
   contracts   193
52 Dealing with resistance or
   non-compliance with homework
   and behavioural contracts   196
53 The 'good enough' contract   201
54 Contracting: preparing for conflict and
   negative transference   204

Part 5
TREATMENT PLANNING 207

55 Comparative treatment sequences 209
56 Formulating individualized treatment
   plans 212
57 Monitoring and revising treatment planning 216
58 Accounting for the impact of trauma 220
59 Treatment planning for experiential
   disconfirmation 224
60 Tackling 'the splinter' and 'the bent
   penny' 230
61 Awareness, spontaneity, intimacy,
   autonomy and homonomy 233

Part 6
AVOIDING COMMON PITFALLS 237

62 Being realistic about treatment length 239
63 Directionality and avoiding therapy drift 242
64 Reducing the risk of iatrogenic shaming 245
65 Avoiding 'racket OKness' 249
66 Avoiding marshmallowing 253

Part 7
REFINING THERAPEUTIC SKILLS 257

67 Balancing challenge and support 259
68 Developing emotional awareness and
   granulation 261
69 Soothing the Child ego state with
   emotion regulation techniques 264
70 Deepening affect 267
71 Promoting healthy expression of
   emotion 271

72	Tracking where the client is open, and where they are defended on a moment-by-moment basis	274
73	Encouraging journaling to promote self-awareness and self-reflection	276
74	Differences between decontamination and deconfusion	279
75	Disconfirming script beliefs	283
76	Using alliance rupture and repair for deconfusion	286
77	Using metacommunicative transactions	289
78	Therapy of games	291
79	Therapy of injunctions	294
80	Interventions and approaches to therapy of injunctions and injunctive messages	296
81	Escape-hatch closure revisited	300
82	Client protection	303
83	Potency and permission	306
84	Impasse theory revisited	309
85	Using chair work in TA: some guidelines	313
86	Using visualiszation and mental imagery in TA	318
87	Working with the Child ego state to resolve trauma	321
88	Revisiting discounting: incorporating cognitive biases into TA theory	324
89	Confrontation	328
90	Evaluating your clinical effectiveness	331
91	Using deliberate practice to enhance therapeutic skills	334
92	Writing clinical notes in TA therapy	338
93	Strengthening the Adult by cultivating mindfulness	341
94	Script development: an ongoing process	344
95	Helping clients identify and build on their strengths	347
96	Exploring the therapist's motivations	350

97	Using self-disclosure and authenticity	354
98	The Adult ego state revisited	359
99	TA as an existential psychotherapy	362
100	Analysing transactions	365

| **References** | **367** |
| **Index** | **393** |

PREFACE TO THE SECOND EDITION

CHANGES TO THE SECOND EDITION

Although the overall structure of the seven parts of the book remains the same, in terms of the content of the book, considerable changes have been made. The majority of the 100 key points have been completely re-written, (or written, where I have replaced a point from the first edition). Some have had moderate changes and the rest have certainly had more than one or two tweaks.

One major difference between the first edition and the second is a huge shift in emphasis towards research. The majority of points from Part 2 onwards include some level of engagement with research. The research I have drawn on comes primarily from the fields of psychotherapy, neuroscience, mental health/ psychopathology and the broader field of psychology. As such, many of the statements in this book are not just my opinion; they can be backed up with solid scientific research.

The positive feedback I received on the first edition completely blew me away (and still does). I knew I had written something important and had filled a number of gaps in the literature, however, every few weeks I get another email from a TA therapist thanking me for writing it, and telling me how useful it was to them in their training and in preparing for their Certified Transactional Analyst examinations. They tell me how it has influenced how they work with their clients, too. What a privilege I have to be able to have such a positive effect on people's practice and their career. Even now, every time I get such an email, I experience tremendous joy. Knowing I have helped someone to get better at their job and the impact this has on their clients truly makes the long hours well worth it.

I also received some constructive criticism (which I welcome, please do send me your constructive feedback if you have it to give), and I will take it on board. So, you will see more case examples and discussions of specific techniques which replace some of the more theoretical material, and there is also an index in this current edition (truthfully, I was too tired when I had finished the first edition – my first full book – to even begin to contemplate indexing the manuscript).

REFLECTIONS ON THE FIRST EDITION AND THE JOURNEY TO WHERE I AM NOW

When I re-read the first edition to prepare the manuscript for this edition, it was immediately obvious that my thinking had changed on many things, and, in some cases, radically so. Probably the most significant part of the journey that I have been on in the intervening years has been my own journey as a psychotherapy researcher. Around the time the first edition was published, I embarked on my PhD, which examined the process and outcome of TA therapy for depression (spoiler alert- I generated sufficient evidence to make the first evidence-based claims about the effectiveness of short-term TA therapy for depression). As is typical in a doctorate programme, I had to do a deep dive into the psychotherapy research literature. What I found astonished me. As I read, I kept on (and still do) finding jewels of information, guidance and insights which have changed the way I think and the way I practise, for the better. I said back in 2012 that my goal was for TA to have sufficient evidence for it to be considered an evidence-based therapy. That goal was achieved. It is important here to acknowledge here the incredible efforts of Dr Biljana van Rijn and Dr Enrico Bennelli, as they have continued to take TA research forward from strength to strength. There is still a long way to go in terms of building up the amount of evidence that would be needed for TA to be as widely recognized as it deserves to be.

At the time of writing the first edition, I was in full-time practice, largely doing long-term therapy. That has now changed dramatically, because of my engagement with research and also because I believe I have become a better and more efficient therapist. I also think my teaching and my writing have become richer from the various research-based sources I now draw upon in my work.

Over the years, I have found that one of the things I enjoy most about the process of writing and teaching, is delving into the available research and seeing where that leads me. I also get great satisfaction from the creative process of weaving different research findings into TA – either by finding research which has clear relevance to either support or critique TA theory (mostly it seems to be research which supports it in some way, albeit usually with a different name), or by finding research which can illuminate or enhance some aspect of the practice of TA psychotherapy. My aim has now shifted towards this integration of research into TA so that we are supported in the mastery of our art, drawing on the best current knowledge in the field and grounding TA practice firmly in research.

At the time I wrote the first edition, my practice was primarily long-term therapy with a definite psychodynamic theme. That too has changed. This is not because my clients group are any easier, in fact, in many ways my current client group present with more difficulty and complexity than my former client group. Instead of providing long-term therapy as the standard and default setting, my work is now almost exclusively short-term therapy (of up to 20 sessions), This change came about because of the research I read on the dose-response effect (i.e., how much therapy is needed to produce significant change) and because of what I found in my own research, where the therapy was limited to 16 sessions. I have come across hundreds of tips, suggestions and pieces of guidance that can be relatively seamlessly integrate into practice, increasing efficiency. I have found that I am a better therapist because of these change in how I practise. Also, this is not a groundless claim; I have kept detailed records of my clients' rate of improvement using a number of outcome measures for many years now, so I can see just from visual inspection of the data I have that I have improved in my clinical effectiveness. I do not think this is simply a matter of more experience. In fact, I largely attribute my professional growth to my engagement with and use of research embedded through and within how I work. So, to that end, I have included some of what have been to me the most productive adjustments to practice. I genuinely hope that you too will benefit from the pearls of research-based wisdom I have stitched into the fabric of this book. I also hope that you will see the positive effects of drawing on and using research in your work quickly.

ACKNOWLEDGEMENTS

In terms of contribution to this book, I would like to thank Ales Zivkovic for his invaluable contribution to Point 14 on Interpretive Dynamic TA and Giles Barrow for his input to Point 9 on Eco-TA. I would also like to thank Matt Taylor, for his encouragement and for being an 'accountability buddy' and helping me to keep on target with deadlines. As I have written this second edition, my thoughts have often turned to a dear colleague and friend, Alison Ayres, for many reasons, but mostly regarding all the help and support she generously gave me while I wrote the first edition. I would also like to express my thanks to Ian Stewart, Adrienne Lee and Keith Tudor for the central role they each played in my professional and personal development. All three offered me acceptance and provided me with the encouragement I needed to find my way and develop into the transactional analyst I became. I would also like to express my deep and enduring gratitude to my two PhD supervisors, Professor Sue Wheeler and Professor John McLeod, their wisdom, insight, support and challenge have left an indelible mark on my career and set me off in an entirely new and wonderful trajectory.

Finally, I would like to thank my husband, Philip McNally, for looking after me, for making me laugh, for being him, and for being mine.

INTRODUCTION

Transactional Analysis (TA) has a thriving international community made up of a dynamic body of practitioners who are developing their theory and innovating in practice. TA has developed into a therapy that is now proudly psychodynamic, and yet also fiercely humanistic. TA therapists consider many of their methods to be similar to those of cognitive-behavioural therapy. TA is also viewed as being an existential psychotherapy. I introduce some concepts from existential psychotherapy in this book, and invite the reader to explore how they can inform our use of TA and how we think about various TA concepts, and, more importantly, how we relate to our clients. The history of TA reveals the origin of this range of approaches – Berne developed TA from his knowledge as a psychoanalyst. His development of the theory of the Adult ego state, and concepts such as contamination also enabled him to develop a cognitive approach to therapy which did not exist at the time of Berne's innovations (Schlegel, 1998).

There is the most incredible diversity among TA psychotherapists, and in how we use TA. We share a common body of theory that has shown in this diversity its wonderful versatility. To me, what defines a transactional analyst is not what they do (which may be indistinguishable from other types of psychotherapy), but rather why they do what they do and how they think. Transactional analysts of all types use the concepts of ego states and scripts as their most basic thinking structures. Part 1 of this book discusses some of the many different ways in which TA practitioners work and I hope gives the reader a sense of the diversity of TA practice.

DOI: 10.4324/9781003375890-1   1

A word about the level of this text: this is not an introductory book, and I assume that the reader has a familiarity with TA concepts and methods. For those readers who do not have that knowledge, I would advise reading the following books first:

Lapworth, P. and Sills, C. (2011) *An Introduction to Transactional Analysis*. London: Sage.
Stewart, I. and Joines, V. (1987) *TA Today*. Nottingham: Lifespace.

Expecting the reader to have such background knowledge enables me to move directly into an intermediate level of discussion without the need to explain the basics, which are adequately covered in other books. This book is calibrated at an intermediate level, to bridge the gap between introductory texts and advanced texts and will be particularly useful to TA students who have completed their foundation year. I hope that more experienced practitioners will also find the book to be interesting and stimulating.

Part 1 covers the philosophy, theory, methods and some critique of the main approaches and schools of TA in practice. Readers who are not so interested in this theoretical background can go directly to Part 2. Part 2 deals with the therapeutic relationship. Psychotherapy research has consistently shown that the therapeutic relationship is critical to the outcome of the therapy, and is a precondition for effective therapy work (Norcross & Lambert, 2019). In line with this research, this part includes material on the effective 'ingredients' of the therapeutic relationship including empathy, transference and countertransference and also alliance rupture and repair. It has been my intention to make some of these complex concepts more accessible to newcomers. Parts 3, 4 and 5 take the reader through the process of diagnosis, contracting and treatment planning from a TA perspective. Part 6 deals with common pitfalls in TA practice, suggesting ways of avoiding them. The book concludes with Part 7, the longest part, which is on refining therapeutic skills. Each part contains new and original material that I hope will be of immediate practical use to the reader. The majority of the points in this book are firmly grounded in evidence-based practice, and are supported by psychotherapy research as being 'effective ingredients' in psychotherapy. Psychotherapy research demonstrates the effectiveness of empathy, attention to alliance rupture and repair, skilful transference interpretation, accounting for the client's cultural context, wider relationships and strengths, developing a personally tailored treatment approach for each client, goal consensus and collaboration, appropriate self-disclosure, and all are empirically supported. The discussion of such research is beyond the scope of this book, and the interested reader is recommended to read *Psychotherapy Relationships That Work*, edited by John Norcross and Michael Lambert (2019).

It has been my intention throughout to write a book that is practical and promotes the development of thinking, rigorous clinicians. I hope that the ideas in this book will encourage the reader to be creative and rigorous in their practice. In many ways this book is similar to a Greek meze, or Spanish tapas meal. Readers may find some of the 'appetizers' particularly 'tasty' and want more. I invite those readers to pursue the references given in the points they particularly like where they can find more material to digest at their leisure.

The material in this volume is gathered from my experience. My experience is collected from my client work, but also from my work as a trainer and supervisor of psychotherapists where I can see common mistakes or misconceptions 'secondhand'. One of the advantages that a trainer and supervisor has is a degree of distance from the direct interpersonal encounter. This distance gives us the space to make our observations and frame our comments. Some of the insights or ways of working I present here I have had to learn the hard way. While there is a place for learning the hard way in life, I think it has a limited place in learning psychotherapy, where clients can be given a disservice on the basis of a therapist 'needing' to learn the hard way. This is especially so when experience is available for them to learn from in a more comfortable, and all-round desirable fashion. I hope that this book both helps you learn the easy way and reminds you that the work of a psychotherapist is not easy. It requires deep and complex thought, a robustness, flexibility and openness of emotion. It requires a curiosity and receptivity to experience, immense patience and a willingness to sit and hear of profound distress and of the many horrors that humans can inflict upon each other and yet not lose faith in humanity or the tenacity of the human spirit.

A WORD ON TERMINOLOGY

For ease of reading, I use both 'he' and 'she' interchangeably throughout this book, and trust the reader will make the necessary changes to suit their own particular situation. I often refer to 'you' throughout the text. When I do so, I am referring to you, the reader. I am using this conversational writing style in order to invite you, the reader, into thinking and reflection.

Part 1

APPROACHES IN TRANSACTIONAL ANALYSIS PRACTICE

SCHOOLS AND APPROACHES IN TA

Although the core theoretical concepts of TA were developed by Eric Berne and the members of the San Francisco Transactional Analysis Seminars, as transactional analysis grew and developed, different theorists introduced new concepts and ways of working to promote change and growth. Over time, a number of these coalesced to form clear and distinct variations in transactional analysis theory and practice. Graham Barnes (1977) first identified these as different schools of TA. After Berne's premature death, a power vacuum existed within the TA world and a number of influential transactional analysts rose to prominence, each offering a different way of viewing the individual and their problems and specific methods to overcome these problems. A spirit of competitiveness emerged within TA, which is still evident to this day (although, in my view, is seldom acknowledged). Many authors turned to Berne's original writings to justify their theories and positions. However, Berne's thinking had evolved over a number of years and some of his early theories are different from some of his later work. There were also inconsistencies with the way he described some concepts, which means that authors with very differing views can accurately and legitimately cite Berne's writing to support their arguments. Whilst this creates a fertile ground for varied theoretical stances (and conflicting opinions) to emerge, it has turned out to be a great strength in TA, as it allows scope for a wide range of ways of thinking about and using TA in practice.

Each school/approach to TA has its own strengths and limitations and none have the monopoly on truth. Despite this, individual practitioners may be drawn into erroneously believing that their preferred approach is 'the superior and right way' of doing therapy, thus limiting options, instead of seeing 'the diversity of TA approaches as something to be appreciated' (ibid.: 12). The choice of whether to describe a type of TA as a school or approach is merely a matter of semantics and is of little consequence. As such, I will use the two terms interchangeably throughout the rest of this book.

In many respects, the notion of schools of TA is nowadays a redundant concept, as almost all transactional analysts use the concepts and methods developed by the classical school of TA and those from relational TA as the basis for their work. Theories and techniques from other approaches are integrated into their work according to their own personal preferences, the type of clients they tend to work with and the context in which they practise (see Vos and van Rijn, 2021). Nevertheless, an understanding of the different variations in TA theory and methods, the history of their development and their suitability for different presenting problems and issues is a requirement for those seeking certification as a transactional analyst. The capability to move flexibly between different schools of TA and conceptualize and have a range of options available to work with client problems is also a requirement for certification.

One way of viewing the differences in schools/approaches to TA and how they view the person, their problems and indicated way of working is through taking Martha Stark's (2000) framework about the nature of therapeutic action. Although originally developed as a way of conceptualizing different approaches within psychoanalytic therapy, her model can be readily applied to TA where it can highlight the nature of a client's presenting problem, and how the therapist can best facilitate the process of change. Although some transactional analysts believe that it is important to choose a specific way of working and stick to it to ensure consistency in the therapy, I agree with Stark and believe that the effective therapist needs the capability to flexibly move between these types of working in response to the client, the type of issue that is being addressed in the moment and the emerging and unfolding therapeutic process.

STARK'S THREE MODES OF THERAPEUTIC ACTION

One-person psychology

This model emphasizes the 'importance of knowledge or insight ... its focus is on the patient and the internal workings of her mind' (ibid.: 3). From a TA perspective, a client generating greater knowledge or insight into their own process would develop the Adult ego state. The greater degree of executive control the Adult has over the personality, the less anxiety a person feels, and the greater the range of options the individual has in experiencing and relating. In this approach the stance of the therapist is as a neutral, objective observer. 'Her focus is on the patient's internal dynamics ... The therapist formulates interpretations with an eye to advancing the patient's knowledge of her internal dynamics. The ultimate goal is resolution of the patient's structural conflicts' (ibid.: 4).

One-and-a-half-person psychology

This model emphasizes the 'importance of experience, a corrective experience ... its focus is on the patient and her relationship with a therapist ... [for] whom it is not she that matters but rather what she provides' (ibid.: 3). Central to a one and a half person approach is either empathically validating the client's subjective reality and emotional experience and/or providing the client with a corrective emotional and/or relational experience. 'The ultimate goal is filling in the patient's structural deficits and consolidating the patient's self' (ibid.: 4). From a TA perspective, the empathic validation of a client's subjective experience may reduce felt levels of tension in different ego states (particularly Child ego states). The resultant reduction in tension may enable greater movement between ego states. The validation aspect may also strengthen Adult functioning. Perhaps most importantly, in this model the experience of sustained empathic understanding provides the client with an experience that may have been missing for them in their history, and which they have been seeking ever since in order to address, repair or make good the developmental deficit(s).

Two-person psychology

This model emphasizes the 'importance of relationship, the real relationship (between the therapist and client)' (ibid.: 3). The therapist pays keen attention to their emotional and countertransference reactions throughout the work, and uses their emotional reactions to deepen their understanding of the client and the client's way of relating to others, including the client's protocol. From a TA perspective this equates to social diagnosis and the analysis of transactions, games and enactments. Ego states manifest in the therapy room and transference is noted and tracked as part of the client's unique history and also in relation to how it colours the client's here-and-now experience of the therapist. The therapist seeks to promote the client's capacity for intimacy through this vibrant here-and-now engagement and new way of relating to another.

THE CLASSICAL SCHOOL: FOUNDATIONS

BACKGROUND

The classical school of transactional analysis is the original version of TA, as developed by Berne and the members of the San Francisco seminars. Almost all the core of TA theory springs from this group of people, which includes Claude Steiner, Steve Karpman, Jack Dusay, Muriel James, Fanita English and Franklin Ernst. This pioneering group of trans-actional analysts were particularly keen on developing con-cepts that were simple to grasp, and yet described complex human behaviours and internal processes and ideally could be represented with a diagram. The purpose of this was to 'facilitate Adult analysis of whatever problem the client brings, while stimulating the intuitive powers of the Child to aid in solving that problem' (Stewart, 1992: 132).

PHILOSOPHY AND APPROACH

The classical approach to TA stresses the importance of observation in psychotherapy. Berne repeatedly emphasized the importance of direct observation of the client as the basis for any theoretical and therapeutic formulations. The classical TA therapist also uses their intuition in making diagnoses, and in ascertaining the psychological level message in ulterior transactions. Observation and intuition were to be combined with theory and clear therapeutic rationale. To Berne, diag-nosis and much of therapy were 'a matter of acuteness and observation plus intuitive sensitivity' (Berne, 1972: 69). Berne was also interested in the therapeutic and appropriate use of

DOI: 10.4324/9781003375890-4   11

humour, particularly as a means of inviting the Adult ego state of the client to reappraise a situation, belief, or so on.

The therapy approach proceeds in sequence from structural analysis, transactional analysis, game analysis and finally to script analysis. Nowadays, most transactional analysts move between these different stages of analysis with a degree of fluidity. The initial aims of therapy are to decontaminate the Adult ego state, and identify the structural origin of the client's different thoughts, feelings and beliefs. Similar to the gestalt approach to therapy, the classical school of TA places emphasis on how the client's ego states, scripts, and so on are manifesting in the here-and-now (Barnes, 1977). Clients are discouraged from endlessly going over the past as this was seen to be a game of 'archaeology' (Berne, 1964).

The 'three Ps' of protection, permission (Crossman, 1966) and potency (Steiner, 1968) are a key feature of the approach of classical TA, and indeed all TA therapy (see Points 82 and 83). The therapist is expected to monitor their work to ensure that there is sufficient protection, permission and potency for the client to engage in the therapeutic work necessary to achieve script cure. Once the 'three Ps' are in place, therapy proceeds with establishing behavioural contracts which are seen as a central aspect of therapeutic change in classical TA (Stewart, 1992).

The classical school of TA is a one-person approach (Stark, 2000), as the emphasis is on resolution of structural conflict and generating increased Adult options. The conflict model (Lapworth et al., 1993) is the primary model of psycho-pathology in classical TA, which views psychopathology as being the result of conflict between and within different ego states and conflict between the individual's drive towards autonomy (*physis*) and the individual's script (Berne, 1972).

KEY THEORETICAL CONCEPTS

Much of the core TA theory forms the classical school of TA as developed by Berne. This includes: ego states, structural analysis, contamination, exclusion, functional analysis, transactional analysis, games and game analysis, scripts and script analysis. Other classical concepts developed by other TA authors include: script matrix (Steiner, 1966), contracting (Berne, 1966/1994; Steiner, 1974), OK corral (Ernst, 1971), options (Karpman, 1971), stroke economy (Steiner, 1971) and egograms (Dusay, 1972). Arguably, it is impossible to practise transactional analysis and not use classical TA concepts.

THE CLASSICAL SCHOOL: METHODS

METHODS

The eight therapeutic operations

The eight categories of interventions (interrogation, specification, confrontation, explanation, illustration, confirmation, interpretation and crystallization) (Berne, 1966/1994) form the nucleus of the method of TA therapy (see Müller and Tudor, 2001; Widdowson, 2016).

Decontamination

Decontamination (Berne, 1961/1986, 1966/1994) is a procedure designed to strengthen the Adult ego state and involves the challenging of distorted thinking and sometimes the provision of accurate information to facilitate reality testing.

Contractual method

Contracting is a central method used in all types of TA therapy (Berne, 1966/1994; James and Jongeward, 1971; Steiner, 1974), which was initially developed by classical TA writers. It involves collaborative agreement regarding both the goals of therapy and the therapeutic process.

Permission transaction

In permission transaction (Berne, 1966/1994, 1972), the therapist ascertains what key permission the client needs to promote their growth, and then seeks to give the client the key permission (directly and indirectly) throughout therapy.

    DOI: 10.4324/9781003375890-5

Script antithesis

The script antithesis is a decisive and focused intervention (Berne, 1972). The antithesis is like the 'spell-breaker' in a fairy tale. It is a bulls-eye transaction (Woollams and Brown, 1978) that aims to block the trajectory of the individual's script and challenge the major script theme of the individual.

Group therapy

Classical TA was developed extensively in group therapy settings (Berne, 1966/1994), and it is believed by some TA therapists that by virtue of these origins, TA is best done in group settings.

CRITIQUE

Although recognizing the admirable intention behind the use of colloquial language, some critics of this approach feel that TA has suffered from being considered superficial by people who look at the names of the concepts and dismiss them outright. Some of the terms used for concepts are now outdated and, as such, lack intuitive appeal to younger audiences.

The power of the therapist is emphasized in classical TA, in a way that can be considered incongruous with TA philosophy. The therapist is seen as a 'permission giver', and interpreter of the client's experience; analzing the client's life patterns using TA theory. This quasi-parental therapist stance of 'permission giver' is incongruous with a therapeutic approach that emphasizes the client's autonomy.

A classical TA approach can suggest that either knowledge about one's patterns (by gaining insight using TA theory) or direct behavioural change is sufficient for transformation and healing. Classical TA concepts can be used to gain understanding into one's process, patterns and ways of interacting with others, but as Berne (1971) cautioned, insight alone is insufficient to generate change. Although behavioural change can generate structural change, it is at its most effective when combined with insight and emotional experiencing.

THE REDECISION SCHOOL: FOUNDATIONS

BACKGROUND

The redecision school of TA was created by Bob and Mary Goulding. The Gouldings were original members of Berne's San Francisco seminars, who also trained with Fritz Perls, the originator of gestalt therapy. The Gouldings were interested in developing ways of working that were active and promoted rapid change. They integrated techniques from gestalt therapy, such as two-chair work, into a TA theoretical approach as they saw that these methods could be used to work directly with ego state conflicts. The Gouldings specialized in the therapy marathon format, and would hold extended group therapy marathons, sometimes for up to a month at a time.

Berne originally used the term 'redecision' to mean making a new (life) decision using the Adult ego state. In contrast, the Gouldings defined redecisions as involving the changing of a particular script decision within the Child ego state. Their view was that the original script decisions were made in the Child ego states, and therefore it is in these Child ego states that the change or redecision needs to occur. They developed their methods to work with a contractual regression and increased the affective intensity of the work to facilitate the redecision in the client's Child ego state(s). The process involved accessing this Child ego state and using the client's Adult ego state to provide support for the Child.

    DOI: 10.4324/9781003375890-6

PHILOSOPHY AND APPROACH

The Gouldings, located firmly in the humanistic and existential tradition and influenced by gestalt therapy, emphasized the client's personal responsibility. In their work, they invited a shift away from Berne's medical model, whereby the therapist cures their patients, to one whereby the therapist facilitates the process of the client curing themselves ('the power is in the patient' was the Gouldings' slogan) (Goulding and Goulding, 1978). The Gouldings developed a crisp and confrontational style in their work, for example, challenging the use of language which discounts personal power (see Point 5). Redecision therapists seek to create a nurturing and compassionate environment that supports and provides protection for the Child, and enables the client to access their Child ego state in order to make the necessary redecision.

In their work, the Gouldings often noticed the client holding on to magical or self-defeating thinking, for example, holding a position in Child that they wouldn't change until someone else changes (usually one of their parents). Such magical thinking was actively challenged. Vengeful Child beliefs, such as 'I'll stay sick until you're sorry', were also challenged and the client was invited to let go of these beliefs that were seen to be major blocks to the client's therapy.

The Gouldings would actively avoid, or 'side step', the transference. If the therapist becomes aware of the client transferring from their past onto the therapist, the therapist would invite the client into a two-chair dialogue. In this dialogue the client projects the transferential figure onto a chair, and engages the projection in a dialogue. The Gouldings believed that this approach was more effective than inviting transference onto the therapist and the owning of projections is congruent with the redecision philosophy of taking personal responsibility and owning one's feelings and projections (Goulding and Goulding, 1979).

With its emphasis on structural conflict and the therapist's role as facilitator, with an active confrontational approach and the avoidance of working with transference, the redecision school is a one-person approach (Stark, 2000) and is based on a conflict model of psychopathology (Lapworth et al., 1993). Impasse theory is perhaps one of the most obvious examples of a conflict model within TA psychotherapy.

KEY THEORETICAL CONCEPTS

- Injunctions (Goulding and Goulding, 1979) (see Points 79 and 80).
- Decisions (ibid.)
- Redecision (ibid.).
- Impasse theory, impasse clarification and impasse resolution (ibid.; Mellor, 1980) (see Point 84).

THE REDECISION SCHOOL: METHODS

METHODS

Redecision therapy begins with a clear and focused contracting approach, where the therapist facilitates the development of a clear contract for change. Passive language is confronted in the client's discussion of their problems/situation or contract goals, and the 'language of response-ability' is encouraged (such as changing 'can't' to 'won't') (Goulding and Goulding, 1979).

The client is then often invited to use a range of mental imagery and visualization techniques, such as two-chair work. This typically involves the visualizing of one or more of the client's Parents, or the client's Child as being in an empty chair. The therapist then facilitates a dialogue between the two different parts of the self to clarify and resolve ego state conflicts. Other imagery methods used include early scene work, where the client is invited to mentally go back in time, and recall the time they made the original script decision or to go back to a prototypical ('screen') memory of an event that in some way encapsulates the essence of the script decision or the environment in which the decision was made. In the event that the client cannot remember a specific scene, they are invited to invent one, as it is believed that the imagined scene, being a product of the client's psyche, will contain all the relevant aspects needed to facilitate a redecision. Passive language, or magical thinking, is confronted while the client verbalizes the dialogue in the visualized scene. The affective charge is developed through the use of heighteners (McNeel, 1976) or other gestalt methods. These are used to increase the discomfort in a

DOI: 10.4324/9781003375890-7

particular scene to emphasize the limiting nature of the decision. Further, this stimulates an organismic disgust reaction which mobilizes the client's *physis* and helps the client to throw off or reject the old limiting script decision. At this point, the client is invited to bring their Adult awareness and resources into the scene, or the therapist may provide new information to help the client make a new decision.

After a redecision piece, the therapist invites the client to generate a series of behavioural contracts regarding how they will maintain their redecision in their everyday life (McCormick and Pulleyblank, 1985). Although a redecision piece is a significant change event, redecision itself is considered to be an ongoing process and one which needs reinforcement to help the client maintain new healthy ways of living rather than slide back into familiar scripty ways of being (McNeel, 2010).

CRITIQUE

The Gouldings' model was developed primarily in a residential therapy marathon setting, whereby clients would attend for at least a week, and commonly as long as a month. The intense atmosphere of an extended residential marathon format and the protection this afforded participants provided a good setting for rapid and deep change work. This option is generally not open to the therapist working with individual clients in private practice. Most clients attending the marathons were therapy trainees, and all clients were in ongoing therapy and so were ostensibly 'couch broken' and well engaged with their own process of change. Therefore, to presume that the Gouldings' methods provide rapid change without substantial preparatory work is incorrect. The intense catharsis resulting from many of these methods could indeed trigger quite intense and unwanted reactions, which could be attended to in a residential setting in a way that they cannot in regular clinical practice.

The techniques of redecision therapy are often dramatic and engaging and can involve deep catharsis. This can be very seductive and a therapist can mistake catharsis for real change.

It is possible that some clients effectively 'go through the motions' and engage in redecision pieces as an overadaptation to the therapist without any change taking place. It may also be the case that with overadapted clients their script is inadvertently reinforced. The Gouldings were well aware of this potential problem in (mis)use of their techniques and advised against cathartic ventilation of feelings done for its own sake.

Redecision therapists actively seek to 'sidestep the transference', and deliberately avoid taking on a transferential role in the therapeutic relationship (Goulding and Goulding, 1979). This approach is not suitable for all clients and can be misused by therapists who are not comfortable with accepting or containing a client's strong transferential feelings. Similarly, this can be misused by therapists who struggle with accepting personal responsibility for making mistakes. This is not a critique of the redecision approach per se, but is a potential pitfall if used badly or by therapists who have not engaged with their own personal therapy.

The therapist needs to be mindful of the double message inherent in some methods of redecision therapy 'Assume responsibility the patient is told … and I'll tell you precisely how, when and why to do it' (Yalom, 1980: 250).

THE CATHEXIS SCHOOL: FOUNDATIONS

BACKGROUND

The cathexis approach was originally developed by Jacqui Schiff – one of the early transactional analysts in Berne's seminars. Shortly after taking into her home a young schizophrenic man and beginning residential therapy, she established a residential treatment centre for clients in psychosis. The centre was originally based in Fredericksburg, Virginia, USA, and then because of controversy, moved to Oakland, California, where in addition to the residential centre, they opened a day treatment facility. Following the success of the Oakland project, Schiff opened another centre in Hollywood. The theory and methods of the cathexis approach were developed by Jacqui and her colleagues who joined her at the Cathexis Institute. Within the relatively protected residential setting for therapy, the Schiffs experimented with 'allowing' the clients to regress, and 'redo' early developmental deficits and cathect new Parent ego states. The Cathexis Institute programme experienced huge problems (and Jacqui was expelled from the International Transactional Analysis Association [ITAA]) amid controversy relating to breaches of ethics including physical punishment of clients. Eventually a young man in treatment at the Cathexis Institute died following injuries sustained while at the institute and the Californian authorities closed down the programme. Despite this controversy and problems in methodology, many of the insights and methods developed at the Cathexis Institute have been successfully and ethically adapted by TA therapists and used with a wide range of clients. In a particularly interesting

DOI: 10.4324/9781003375890-8

development, a form of cognitive-behavioural therapy called schema-based therapy now uses procedures it refers to as 'limited reparenting' (Young et al., 2003).

PHILOSOPHY AND APPROACH

The Schiffs saw the nature of psychopathology as being twofold: the first being issues related to developmental deficit; and the second as being issues related to having 'defective' or pathological Parent ego states. Their methods were developed to both deal with the developmental deficits in the Child ego state through provision of a reparative experience and also to systematically decathect 'crazy' Parent ego states and then reintroject new, positive Parent ego states. Clients were not on medication while at the Cathexis Institute and treatment was purely psychotherapy (Schiff et al., 1975). The Schiffs created an environment which was reactive, and one which (in theory) invited clients to think about their problems (see critique below).

The cathexis approach is a one-and-a-half-person approach when the emphasis is on corrective experience, or one person if the focus is on discounting and redefining (Stark, 2000). Defective parenting is considered to be the primary cause of psychopathology and the cathexis approach uses a deficit model (Lapworth et al., 1993) for understanding and treating psychological problems.

KEY THEORETICAL CONCEPTS

The Schiffs developed a range of theoretical concepts that have been integrated into TA, particularly helpful concepts relating to how clients 'distort' reality, or make the world fit their script. The key concepts developed by the Schiffs include the following:

- Passivity and the four passive behaviours (Schiff and Schiff, 1971).
- Discounting and grandiosity (Mellor and Schiff, 1975; Schiff et al., 1975).

- Redefining (Schiff et al., 1975).
- Symbiosis (ibid.).
- Cycles of power and developmental affirmations (Levin-Landheer, 1982). Pamela Levin formulated her 'cycles of power' child development theory and associated developmental affirmations from her experiences at the Cathexis Institute and it is clearly based on a reparative–deficit model.

THE CATHEXIS SCHOOL: METHODS

A key method of the cathexis approach to TA therapy is the repeated confrontation of discounting, grandiosity and passivity. When well timed, not over-used, and in the context of a supportive and empathic therapeutic relationship, confrontation can be a highly effective intervention. It is possible that this emphasis accounts for some of the success of this model with clients with borderline personality disorder where consistent confrontation is recommended (see Point 89).

The cathexis approach relies also on the use of a reparenting/reparative model of psychotherapy (Clarkson, 2003). The principle behind this is that if the client is given a boundaried, reparative experience, then the original need and developmental deficit are repaired. The therapist can be deliberately used as a replacement 'parent' for the client. The practicalities and reality of this can be extremely draining for the therapist.

CRITIQUE

Despite the emphasis on clear thinking and the social-level message to 'get into Adult', the environment at Cathexis gave a clear psychological-level invitation to stay in Child ego states. Indeed, some participants in the Cathexis programme have stated that there was enormous pressure on individuals to regress. This apparent contradiction will no doubt have been confusing to a number of clients.

The approach of providing a reparative, corrective emotional experience (Alexander et al., 1946) is also particularly seductive to therapists who have rescuer fantasies or who have

DOI: 10.4324/9781003375890-9   25

not relinquished fantasies of having a new perfect childhood to make up for their own problematic childhood (Davies and Frawley, 1994). Furthermore, the provision of gratification of a client's 'needs' can keep the therapist in a permanent 'good object' position, and not provide scope for the development of a negative transference, and the dealing with optimal frustration that is necessary for full structural change. In practice, the provision of such a 'good experience' can also set up situations whereby the therapist becomes burnt out by ever-increasing and escalating client demands for more. Cornell and Bonds-White (2001) develop this critique further, and are particularly critical of how such reparative approaches can reinforce unhealthy merger fantasies. This reinforcement of such fantasies can also apply to the therapist who is susceptible to enacting their own needs in the therapeutic relationship. Despite this, creating corrective experiences (more generally, and not in a quasi-parenting role) is well known to be a key component of effective therapy (see Eubanks and Goldfried, 2019).

Jacobs (1994) has also extensively critiqued the Cathexis Institute's reparenting approach as being based on thought control with features of a psychotherapy 'cult' and therefore as inherently unethical and problematic. The Schiffs relied heavily on the concept of consensual reality, that is, a version of reality that was determined by popular consensus. Although such a definition can have a use in confronting crazy or distorted thinking, the concept of consensual reality is problematic in that general consensus, even wider social perspectives, can be 'wrong', and, as an approach, it does not account for multiple realities, or multiple construction of differing realities. This concept can also be problematic in working transculturally with unfamiliar and culturally embedded frames of reference (Hargaden and Sills, 2002).

Levin's cycles of power theory and the use of developmental affirmations is also problematic in that it does not relate to and is inconsistent with established and researched child development theory (Cornell, 1988; Matze, 1988) and is critiqued for being too prescriptive, oversimplified and deterministic

(Cornell, 1988). The use of giving developmental affirmations by the therapist is also problematic in that they implicitly infantilize the client (partly in their construction which emphasizes the 'giving of permission'), and also suggests an oversimplified approach to therapeutic change; if only therapy were as simple as giving clients a few key messages!

There is no doubt that many people were helped, either by the Schiffs, or by therapists who have used cathexis concepts or methodology. However, the use of reparenting strategies is not recommended, and the concepts and methods need to be used in the light of critique and with clear supervision. Concepts such as discounting and grandiosity, however, will continue to be potent tools for therapists working with clients with all levels of problems, and can be used effectively and ethically for the expansion of awareness and confrontation of contaminations and script beliefs.

8

RADICAL PSYCHIATRY

BACKGROUND

> Radical Psychiatry is a theory of human emotional disturbance
> and a method designed to deal with it.
>
> (Steiner, 1974)

Radical psychiatry was developed by Claude Steiner and
Hogie Wyckoff in Berkeley, California, in the late 1960s. It
was heavily influenced by the works of Karl Marx, Wilhelm
Reich and R. D. Laing (who wrote about the negative impact
of oppression on the psyche) which were combined with TA
theory, particularly its tools for analysing the transactional,
person-to-person mechanisms of oppression and liberation.

PHILOSOPHY AND APPROACH

The central principle of radical psychiatry is that psychiatric
problems are manifestations of alienation that results from
oppression that has been mystified in the isolated individual.
Mystification involves cultural discounting or justification of
oppression. Oppressive social structures and mystifying
myths promote emotional isolation of the individual. The
formula given for alienation is:

Alienation = Oppression + Mystification + Isolation

The radical psychiatry antidote to alienation is: contact to
undo isolation, awareness to demystify oppression and action
to combat it. The resulting formula is:

Power in the world = Contact + Awareness + Action

 DOI: 10.4324/9781003375890-10

Radical psychiatry opposes the medicalization of psycho-therapy and the use of psychiatric jargon and diagnostic labels and sees such usage as an example of oppression and aliena-tion of isolated individuals in emotional distress.

The accounting of the context of the person, and the impact of social and political factors on the individual and their way of relating to others locate radical psychiatry as what might be called a 'two-and-a-half'-person approach (Tudor, 2011a). As practitioners, we see the impact of oppression most clearly in our clients who are people of colour, those from the LGBTQ+ communities, women, neurodivergent people, and those with low socio-economic status, such as clients living in poverty and/ or poor social conditions. Taking account of the context these clients live in and of the impact of daily micro-aggressions and oppression, and of taking responsibility for our own unconscious bias and micro-aggressions are essen-tial for ensuring we do our jobs as therapists effectively and ethically.

KEY THEORETICAL CONCEPTS AND METHODS

Alienation

There are three principal forms of alienation, each one rep-resenting a script type. The script of lovelessness comes from the alienation from our loving capacities, leading to depression due to stroke starvation. The script of joylessness originates from alienation from our bodies and can lead to addiction. The script of mindlessness results from alienation from our minds, due to mystification and lies, and the alienation from work due to workers' exploitation.

Pig Parent

The Pig Parent, later renamed as the Critical Parent, refers to the Parent in the Child (P1) ego state. The Critical Parent is seen as the internalization of oppressive messages that per-petuate alienation. Radical psychiatry seeks to radically decommission the influence of the Critical Parent.

The stroke economy

The stroke economy (Steiner, 1971) is a set of restrictive internal rules about giving and taking strokes. The stroke economy rules, enforced by the Critical Parent, are considered to be the source of alienation from love. The antidote to the stroke economy is the free exchange of strokes.

Lies and discounts

These are seen as a principal source of alienation from the mind and rational thinking. The antidote to lies and discounts is radical truthfulness.

Power plays

Power plays are the transactions that people use to coerce and oppress each other. Power plays can be physical or psychological, crude or subtle: from murder, rape and threats, to lies, gaslighting, and propaganda.

Individual and group therapy

Group psychotherapy is the main therapeutic method in the radical psychiatry approach. Exploring oppression and the mystifications that support oppression through 'consciousness raising' (awareness) is a key method. Demystification of the oppressiveness of racism, sexism, homophobia, ageism, class prejudice and other oppressive systems involving developing awareness of discounting and power plays as they manifest in the activities of the group is also used.

The promotion of egalitarian and cooperative relationships between group participants is an important goal in radical psychiatry groups. Groups maintain cooperative contracts as 'rules of engagement'. The cooperative contract involves an agreement not to power play, especially not to use lies of omission or commission, and avoiding the roles (Rescuer, Persecutor and Victim) of the drama triangle (Karpman, 1968). Awareness of oppression and action against it are promoted inside and outside the group. Social action and active and vocal critique of oppression is considered essential since society requires improvement if people are to be empowered within it. In the mutually supportive environment of the group, participants are encouraged to confront and overthrow their Critical Parent and script.

In individual therapy, a radical psychiatry perspective would involve consciousness raising and accounting for internalized prejudice and unconscious bias, and the impact of living in an oppressive society which systematically promotes the discounting of oppression (Minikin, 2018).

CRITIQUE

Many of the concepts of radical psychiatry have now been adopted in wider society, partly as a result of the influence of feminism, an awareness of abuse of patients of medical and psychiatric practitioners, the formation of patient groups and wider social initiatives which promote equality and political awareness. As a result, some of the ideas of radical psychiatry can be seen to be somewhat outdated, and culturally and historically located within a radical, 1960s Californian frame of reference. Despite this, recent issues surrounding social justice (such as the Black Lives Matter and the 'Me Too' movements have highlighted deep inequality and privilege embedded in all aspects of society), and therefore in many respects, the need to identify and deconstruct power and oppression is just as important now as it was at the time radical psychiatry was first developed (ibid.). Although victim behaviour is discouraged and confronted in the radical psychiatry approach, critics suggest that it overly focuses on external and wider social circumstances and can result in users 'blaming the system' rather than taking personal responsibility for their situation. Considered as a whole, radical psychiatry has been criticized for being overly theoretical and not leading to easily accessible techniques in psychotherapy.

ECO-TA

BACKGROUND

Eco-TA was first developed by the British transactional analysts, Hayley Marshall (a psychotherapist who has been working outdoors with clients for over a decade) and Giles Barrow (an educational transactional analyst who has been working with holistic education and eco-pedagogy for many years) as both a response to their own views and ways of practice and of the concerns that their clients were increasingly bringing into their practices. Eco-TA has been heavily influenced by eco-psychology and eco-psychotherapy; both of which have been developed over the past 40 years (Roszak, 1992; Roszak and Gomes, 1995). Given its emphasis on ecology and on the relationship people have with their environment, and in light of the environmental crisis and climate change the world is currently facing, eco-TA is arguably the most important development within TA to have emerged over the last 20 years.

One of the basic assumptions of eco-TA is that Western psychology was developed with what Barrow and Marshall refer to as the 'indoor mind'; in other words, an intellectual pursuit which is cut off from nature and which sees humans as somehow apart from nature, instead of being a part of nature. Barrow and Marshall (2023) have taken care to emphasize that they do not consider eco-TA to be seen as another school or approach in TA and they state that eco-TA is not linked to any particular field of application within TA. This is a significant shift as almost all theory within TA to date has emerged from either the psychotherapy, counselling educational or organizational fields of TA.

In keeping with an ecological perspective on the Earth, Barrow and Marshall state that eco-TA 'belongs to everyone

  DOI: 10.4324/9781003375890-11

and is owned by no one'. This parallels a healthy relationship to the Earth; none of us truly own it and it belongs to us all.

KEY THEORETICAL CONCEPTS

Eco-TA is largely organized around a philosophical stance and a number of concepts which shift the emphasis on how TA is framed, and subsequently applied in practice.

Interconnectedness

In a manner reminiscent of Gaia theory (Lovelock, 1979), eco-TA holds the position that everything is interconnected. The planet and all organisms on it are seen as connected through complex, synergistic ecosystems that self-regulate. As humans, we are fundamentally (both practically and by nature) interconnected to others and a change in one part of a system can create ripple-effect changes in other parts of a system. Eco-TA would also hold that a lack of engagement with our intrinsic interconnectedness is a significant cause of reductions in physical and mental well-being.

Eco-TA also considers accounting for and examining exploitation (of the planet and of other persons), power, oppression, intersectionality, and the radical inclusion of those who are part of marginalized groups as being an essential component of working with interconnectedness.

Homonomy

TA was developed within the context of the 1960s American/ Californian culture and its emphasis on individualism. The prizing of individualism is most clear in what is seen as the central goal of TA – autonomy (personal freedom). The Hungarian psychologist, Andras Angyal (1939) proposed that in addition to the drive towards autonomy, individualism and uniqueness, that as social animals, humans have a parallel drive towards homonomy, or the desire, drive and compulsion to be with others and to seek connection (see also Point 17). Eco-TA seeks to help individuals find their own equilibrium between these two parallel innate tendencies and avoid the excesses of either; too much autonomy and individualism can leave the person disconnected, lonely, isolated and can drive consumerism and promote selfishness and lack of consideration to others, whereas too much homonomy can lead to loss of personal identity, psychological merger and enmeshment and at worst, the 'tyranny of the group'.

Eco-script

In addition to developing beliefs about self and others, eco-TA holds that as part of our script we develop beliefs about our relationship to nature and the planet. The development of a script which urges constant consumerism and excessive (and/ or mindless) use of the Earth's resources is one example of eco-script. Other aspects of eco-script might include the injunctions and permissions we internalize which influence our experience of the planet or nature, e.g., 'don't be outside', 'don't be in nature', being afraid of the dark, or of woodland, open water, and so on. Eco-TA practitioners actively engage their clients to critically examine their eco-script.

Embodiment and the environment

As humans, we are an embodied organism and we are constantly in an interplay with our environment. As soon as we step outside, the world makes an impact on our body. Eco-TA reminds us that the body has a long-standing propensity and capacity to be resourced by ecology and the outdoors. If we accept that we are only a part of nature, then it only stands to reason we can be psychologically nourished and refreshed by nature.

METHODS

Walk and talk therapy

Eco-TA is most strongly associated with working outdoors with clients. The practice of 'walk and talk therapy' became popular and hugely important for practitioners during the COVID-19 pandemic, when restrictions were placed on working indoors.

Although this transition was necessary at the time of the pandemic, many practitioners not only enjoyed working outdoors, but found that their clients experienced considerable benefits from this, and have continued to offer outdoor therapy.

Sufficiency

The concept of sustainability is woven into eco-TA by considering 'what is sufficient?'. This is done by helping a client to consider what is sufficient for them as a practice of social, emotional and ecological hygiene. One example of this is in eco-TA training, students are invited as part of the ubiquitous 'check-in' process to only discuss what is 'sufficient'; no more, no less.

CRITIQUE

Some within the TA community feel that eco-TA brings an unnecessary and unhelpful politicization of therapy and is simply following cultural fashions and is 'virtue signalling' by lentil-eating zealots who wish to impose mandatory recycling on everyone. However, it is clear that environmental destruction and climate change are perhaps the biggest existential threat to humanity in modern times. In this respect, the promotion of engagement with environmental issues (which may include examination of one's diet and the provenance of the food one eats, and may also include consideration of matters such as recycling) within therapy is perhaps essential for the survival of our planet.

Others critique eco-TA for its emphasis on being outdoors and highlight that this may marginalize those who do not live in or have access to the countryside. Eco-TA practitioners counter this by arguing that most of the eco-TA work that is conducted occurs within cities (Rebecca Elston, 2022, personal communication) and that promoting engagement with urban environments is a valid (and perhaps even more needed) way of practising eco-TA.

Eco-TA is still very much an emerging and developing way of thinking about and practising TA, however, time will inevitably tell as to its relevance and durability.

INTEGRATIVE TA: FOUNDATIONS

BACKGROUND

Integrative TA was developed primarily by Richard Erskine, in conjunction with his colleagues Rebecca Trautmann and Janet Moursund. Erksine, Moursund and Trautmann (1999) developed a synthesis of a range of theoretical concepts and methods, selecting concepts which were theoretically congruent and compatible with each other.

PHILOSOPHY AND APPROACH

The main external theoretical influences of integrative TA include self-psychology, gestalt and person-centred therapy. Integrative TA, like other TA approaches, considers the need for attachment and relationship to be a primary human need. Lack of contactful relationship, or disruption in relational contact or relational trauma, is seen as the main source of psychopathology. Just as relationships or problems in relationships are seen as the primary source of pain, relationships, and particularly the therapeutic relationship, are considered the primary vessel for change and recovery. The therapist seeks to provide a contactful relationship with the client that provides an environment which increases the client's awareness. 'Within this contactful relationship, each newly discovered piece can be integrated into the self, and the split-off parts reclaimed and re-owned' (ibid.: 13). In some of Berne's writings, he defines Child and Parent ego states as fixated ego states (although in others he appears to contradict this position). Erskine has taken this position, and views Child and Parent ego states as fixated and unintegrated ego states, and that in the process of change, the individual needs to deal

  DOI: 10.4324/9781003375890-12

with the trauma(s) that triggered the fixation and integrate the experience(s) into the Adult ego state (Erskine, 1988).

Integrative TA acknowledges that humans are fundamentally relationship-seeking and interdependent throughout life. Needs for relationship and contact are normalized and the integration of self-psychology concepts of selfobject transferences (Kohut, 1984) in the relational needs affirms this interdependence and the ongoing development of the self. Both internal and external contact are considered to be essential features of healthy human functioning.

With its emphasis on the provision of an empathic, corrective experience and addressing developmental and relational deficits, integrative TA is generally a one-and-a-half-person approach (Stark, 2000). However, when the emphasis is on fixation, it is a one-person approach. Psychopathology is understood as using a deficit model (Lapworth et al., 1993), whereby pathology arises from a deficit of internal and interpersonal contact.

KEY THEORETICAL CONCEPTS

Key transactional analysis concepts primarily used in integrative TA are: ego states, scripts and the racket system (referred to in the integrative TA literature and throughout this book as the script system). Integrative TA also draws upon a number of theories from other theoretical approaches.

Contact

The concept of contact is taken from gestalt therapy and also draws upon person-centred theory, particularly Rogers' (1957) six necessary and sufficient conditions. Integrative TA emphasizes the importance of both internal contact and interpersonal contact. Internal contact can be seen as a state of being whereby the individual is in relatively full awareness of their internal experience. In TA terms, it could be considered to be a state of minimal discounting of internal experience. Contact is seen as a dynamic state of continual flux. Interpersonal contact is seen as a primary motivating force, and is characterized by intimacy, an absence of defensiveness and is satisfying.

The individual who experiences repetitive lack of, or ruptures in interpersonal contact processes these experiences and the resulting cognitive dissonance by forming script decisions in order to make sense of the lack of contact.

Attunement

Drawing upon Stern's (1985) work on attunement, integrative TA considers lack of attunement to be experienced traumatically. Consistent and repeated lack of attunement and the resulting cumulative trauma are seen as a determining factor in the development of script beliefs. Attunement has similarities to empathy, in that close attention is paid to the client's subjective experience. However, in attunement, the therapist responds with a reciprocal appropriate affect (Erskine et al., 1999).

Relational needs

Erskine and Trautmann (1996) developed their eight relational needs. These needs are not considered pathological, but are seen as ongoing needs in relationships which occur throughout the life span. The relational needs can be seen as an elaboration on Heinz Kohut's selfobject transferences (Kohut, 1984) of mirroring, idealization and twinship self-object transferences which were considered also as ongoing needs. Of course, humans have a great many relational needs and are not limited to just eight. However, the eight relational needs presently described were identified by Erskine and Trautmann (1996) as recurring themes emerging in psychotherapy. The eight relational needs are:

1. security;
2. valuing;
3. acceptance;
4. mutuality;
5. self-definition;
6. making an impact;
7. having the other initiate;
8. to express love.

Erskine's position is that frustrated, or unmet relational needs not only result in script decisions, but also in games and other problematic processes as the individual is seeking a means of getting the needs met, albeit in a way which is scripty and painful. The diagnosis of, and attention to meeting of, these relational needs in turn reduce the need for engagement in games (Erskine et al., 1999).

The script system

The script (racket) system is used to understand the dynamic and mutually supporting nature of the individual's script (Erskine and Zalcman, 1979) (see Point 41).

Juxtaposition

Erskine and Trautmann (1996) identified the juxtaposition reaction. In juxtaposition, the experience of deeply empathic, attuned contact can be profoundly painful for clients as it contrasts with their experiences of misattunement and can activate different Child responses and reactions, which hitherto were buried. The therapist needs to watch for juxtaposition reactions, and to slow the pace of the therapy down if the client is experiencing a painful juxtaposition.

INTEGRATIVE TA: METHODS

METHODS

The principal methods of integrative TA are enquiry, attunement and involvement (Erskine et al., 1999). The combination of these in integrative TA creates a sensitive, empathic therapy.

Enquiry

Enquiry is subdivided into areas of enquiry: phenomenological enquiry, enquiry into the client's history and expectations, enquiry into coping strategies, choices and script decisions and also enquiry into the client's sense of vulnerability (see also Point 19) (Erskine et al., 1999). Enquiry is done from a position of respect for the client and their process and from a place of genuine interest in the client. The purpose of enquiry is to generate increasing awareness and to promote internal and interpersonal contact (ibid.).

Attunement

Attunement is a key therapeutic technique and begins with an empathic resonance with the client, but is added to in that the therapist remains open to responding accordingly to the client. The foci of attunement include attunement to the client's relational needs (an attuned response seeks to meet the relational needs in the therapeutic relationship), their developmental issues (related to developmental arrest or deficit; this may be addressed through setting up regressive work), cognitive processes (seeking to enter the client's frame of reference and understand how they think, as well as what they think), rhythms (this involves timing and pacing the work carefully) and affective

 DOI: 10.4324/9781003375890-13

attunement (which involves responding with a corresponding affect, such as compassion in response to sadness).

Involvement

Involvement is a less tangible and more attitudinal therapist activity. 'Inquiry is about what a therapist does; involvement is not about doing so much as about being' (Erskine et al., 1999: 83). Involvement requires the therapist to be willing to be impacted by their client, and the therapist's commitment to do their utmost to help each client. A commitment to continual professional development is another feature of involvement. The expression of involvement in practical terms is demonstrated primarily through the use of several therapeutic strategies: acknowledgement of the client, their experience and of who they are as a person; validation of the client and their emotional reality, normalization (e.g. 'that sounds like a very normal and understandable reaction to a very difficult situation'); and finally, through the therapist's presence. Presence is perhaps the least tangible quality, in that one can either feel someone's presence, or one cannot. Erskine et al. (ibid.) invite the therapist to remain curious about the client, to maintain internal and interpersonal contact, to be patient and consistent and to remain open and willing to be emotionally impacted by the client.

The integrative approach as described by Erskine et al. draws heavily upon gestalt two-chair methods, familiar to transactional analysts who use similar methods within a redecision therapy framework. Other methods used by some integrative transactional analysts include regressive techniques.

CRITIQUE

The use of regressive techniques in integrative TA is criticized by some, who see this as an infantilizing approach. The 'provision' of empathy can invite or perpetuate an idealizing transference, which would increase the potential for infantilization of clients. This is particularly the case with therapists who struggle with receiving negative transference or hostility from their clients, and who wish to remain in a 'good object' position (Cornell and Bonds-White, 2001).

Despite being based on TA theories of ego states and scripts (particularly the script system) and using Berne's human hungers as a motivational theory, some critics of integrative TA consider it to deviate too markedly from TA theory and practice.

PSYCHODYNAMIC TA 1

BACKGROUND

In his 'Minimal basic science curriculum for clinical member-ship in the ITAA', (ITAA Education Committee, 1969) Berne explicitly stated that TA psychotherapists must have a basic grounding in psychoanalytic theory. Indeed, most of Berne's writings assume the reader has a degree of familiarity with psychoanalytic theory, including the unconscious and defence mechanisms. In Berne's early writings, he referred to both deconfusion of Child ego states and script cure in psycho-analytic terms (Berne, 1961/1986). From psychoanalysis, Berne drew his understanding of intrapsychic forces acting upon the person. 'His major works … are only truly well understood given a sufficiently thorough grounding in psychoanalytic thinking … later readers, who may lack such background, may have missed some of this depth' (Clarkson, 1992a: 4).

The ideas that psychopathology and psychological conflicts have their origins in childhood experiences, that these conflicts are usually held at an unconscious level, unconscious material surfaces in therapy, usually indirectly through transference and symbolism are all psychodynamic in origin (McLeod, 1998), and also familiar to transactional analysts. The TA theories of ego states, life script and of analysis of repetitive unconscious interpersonal patterns (games) all clearly have psychodynamic roots. In much of the TA literature we see that concepts such as script are based on the assumption that the script was primarily formed in childhood and operates largely unconsciously and surfaces indirectly (Berne, 1966/1994; Woollams and Brown, 1978; Stewart and Joines, 1987). Other concepts such as con-fusion and subsequent deconfusion and the emphasis of the past

DOI: 10.4324/9781003375890-14

contained in Berne's analogy of the 'bent pennies' (Berne, 1961/1986) also clearly retain psychodynamic thinking around the importance of the past in the formation of the personality.

Berne was hugely influenced by his analysts, Paul Federn, Eduardo Weiss, and Erik Erikson, all psychoanalysts who were prominent ego psychologists. The ego psychology perspective of TA remains in the concept of ego states (a term originally used by Federn), as well as TA's interest in 'adaptation, reality testing, autonomy (and) self-responsibility' (Sills and Hargaden, 2003: xvi). TA is also in many respects an object relations therapy, in that the primary motivation for individuals is the need for connection and relationships (Berne, 1964, 1972; Novellino, 2003) and that people are by their very nature seeking relationship (stroke) from birth.

Psychodynamic TA is generally a one-person approach (Stark, 2000), although it may have elements of one-and-a-half-person or two-person approaches within it depending on the practitioner. Similarly, psychodynamic TA most commonly uses a conflict model for understanding psychopathology and conducting treatment, although the individual practitioner may also use deficit or confusion models in their work (Lapworth et al., 1993).

METHODS

Those who practise psychodynamic TA would use interpretation as a key therapeutic intervention:

> [An] interpretative intervention is to some extent a development of the empathic response: that response which tries to highlight half-expressed feelings and thoughts. There is, however, a difference in that an empathic response points to a conscious or semi-conscious feeling, of which the client is aware, although cannot verbalize to himself or the counsellor. An interpretative response is aimed more at elucidating unconscious feelings or ideas, of which the client is unaware. A skilful interpretation observes feelings which are close enough to the surface, and allows them into consciousness.
>
> (Jacobs, 1988: 35)

It is assumed that clients will unconsciously defend against certain feelings, particularly those evoked by the therapeutic relationship, and so will discuss them indirectly in the therapy by discussing problems in relationships with others. For example, following a break in therapy due to the therapist going on holiday, the client in the first session after the break discusses how they felt angry, hurt and excluded by some friends who went for a meal together without inviting the client. The therapist might wonder out loud if the client also has some of those same feelings about the therapist and their relationship (Gill, 1979; Novellino, 2003). While accurate interpretations which highlight themes or patterns in the client's behaviour and relationships can be hugely illuminating, there is considerable research which has shown that excessive use of, or inaccurate relational interpretations (where the therapist takes what the client is saying to indicate they are communicating something about their experience of the therapist) is actually damaging to the therapeutic relationship (Crits-Cristoph and Gibbons, 2002).

In line with more orthodox psychodynamic practice, restraint around self-disclosure is considered appropriate, and a firm (some would say rigid) holding of the boundaries of the therapeutic relationship is seen as essential for the maintenance of the 'therapeutic frame'. In contrast to other types of TA, whereby the therapist allies their position with that of the client's Child ego state (often in opposition to the client's Parent ego state), psychodynamic TA practitioners adopt a neutral stance in relation to both. This is considered to generate intrapsychic tension which allows the transference expression of unconscious process. Clients may reveal the hidden or repressed feelings they hold about the therapist but cannot express directly in an indirect, coded manner by discussing events with other people outside the therapy. The therapist invites the client into exploration of whether they hold the same feelings towards the therapist using transference interpretation (Gill, 1979; Hargaden and Sills, 2003; Novellino, 2003).

Psychodynamic TA, although sharing many commonalities with relational TA, is different. In psychodynamic TA, the transference is considered to be about the client's structure and pathology, and the therapist positions themselves as an observer and interpreter of this process (one-person approach). In relational TA, transference is considered to be co-created and although it does contain elements relating to the client's structure and pathology, it is also considered in part to be stimulated by the real, here-and-now interaction of client and therapist (two-person approach).

CRITIQUE

Some TA practitioners are deeply critical of developments in psychodynamic TA, as they consider TA to have been originally developed by Berne as a move away from psychoanalysis, and that any movement back to a more psychodynamic perspective is a regressive tendency. In response to this critique, psychodynamic TA practitioners see that psychodynamic concepts can add incredible richness and depth to TA and consider the wholesale rejection of psychoanalytic insights by many of the early transactional analysts as being a reactionary move, which at the time was important in forging a separate identity for TA, but is now outdated and inappropriate in a postmodern, pluralistic world.

PSYCHODYNAMIC TA 2: INTENSIVE TRANSACTIONAL ANALYSIS PSYCHOTHERAPY

BACKGROUND

Intensive Transactional Analysis Psychotherapy (ITAP) was developed by the Italian transactional analysts, Professor Marco Sambin and Francesco Scotta (Sambin and Scotta, 2018). It is an integration of short-term dynamic psycho-therapy (Abbass, 2015; Davanloo, 1980) and TA. The use of the word 'intensive' in ITAP refers to the level of therapist activity; there is no room for the psychoanalytic stance of 'abstention' where the therapist remains passive, reserved and quiet in ITAP.

METHODS

ITAP relies on the concept of Malan's triangles (Malan, 1979). The first, the triangle of conflict maps out on each corner of an inverted triangle the concepts of dynamic conflict. At the lower corner there is the Impulse. This may be an emotion, a desire or need which cannot be freely expressed. On the upper right corner is Anxiety. This anxiety is due to the emergence of the repressed impulse or emotion. From here we move to the upper left corner of the triangle where the Defence is represented. This is the defence mechanism the individual uses in order to manage or contain the anxiety arising from the expression or experience of the unacceptable feeling, impulse, desire or need. The therapist pays close attention to the client's transactions for any signs of potential emergence of impulses/feelings/desires, anxiety or the use of defences. The client is encouraged to express impulses or authentic emotions while the therapist monitors the client's expression of anxiety (generated by the expression of forbidden or dynamically repressed material) and the use of defence mechanisms. If the therapist determines that the client has sufficient Adult ego state available, then 'pressure' is applied to the defence in an attempt to release its repression of the emerging impulse. The therapist infers the presence of emerging anxiety by noticing changes in the client's posture or movements. Anxiety is seen as being discharged through striated (voluntary) musculature such as the client sitting in a very stiff, tense posture, or through fidgeting, tension in the hands and arms, chewing or pursing their lips, frowning or tension around their eyes. Such manifestations of anxiety indicate that the client has sufficient Adult to manage intensive confrontation of their defences.

Anxiety may also manifest through dry mouth, sweating, blushing, rumbling stomach, (Abbass, 2015) or through thought process becoming incoherent, accelerated or conversely, slowed down. In such situations, the therapist slows down and backs off from confrontation until the client shows sufficient Adult ego state.

The second triangle is Malan's triangle of insight. Again, an inverted triangle is used to represent the Past (lower corner of the triangle), the Transference relationship (upper right corner) and the client's Current life (upper left) or; back then-in here-out there (Jacobs, 1988). A psychodynamic approach explores the client's feelings and experiences that are related to the experience 'in here' in the therapeutic relationship, 'out there' in relation to other current relationships outside the therapy room, and 'back then' in historical relationships and experiences. Close attention is paid to what the client discusses regarding relationships or interactions with others, and the therapist makes interpretation to forge links between the three points on the triangle by looking for similarities or possible transference manifestations. The therapist will focus, generally in each session, on all three aspects of experience and linkage is made between different points on this triangle of insight (ibid.; Luborsky, 1984). Interpretations are made to link these points and the feelings evoked by two or three of these points repeatedly throughout therapy to generate insight and promote resolution of unresolved feelings. In TA terms, this linkage facilitates the exploration of rubberbands (Kupfer and Haimowitz, 1971) and promotes deconfusion.

PSYCHODYNAMIC TA 3: INTERPRETIVE DYNAMIC TRANSACTIONAL ANALYSIS PSYCHOTHERAPY

BACKGROUND

Interpretive Dynamic Transactional Analysis Psychotherapy (IDTAP) is an integration of Berne's TA and psychoanalytic object relations approaches, with the main influence from Kernberg's (1976, 1980, 1984) object relations theory and its manualized form of Transference-Focused Psychotherapy (TFP) (Clarkin et al., 2006; Yeomans et al., 2015).

It has been created by Ales Zivkovic with the specific purpose of attainment of the psychoanalytic cure (Berne, 1961/1986) through the deconfusion (ibid.) of the Child ego state, following also Berne's (ibid.; Berne, 1966/1994) notion that deconfusion is attained through the individual's coming to terms with unmet needs rather than through gratification and with having their needs met by the therapist. Its focus is on increasing the level of personality functioning and attainment of interpersonal functioning as well as symptomatic improvement through the consolidation of identity.

Because IDTAP is mainly interested in how dynamic intrapsychic dyads interplay between intrapsychic and interpersonal processes, IDTAP uses a so-called dynamic ego state model (Zivkovic, 2022) (a model that should not be confused with the one of Summers, 2011). This model deals with internal split-off object relations dyads. These dyads are represented by internal representations of self and other that are split into good (OK) and

 DOI: 10.4324/9781003375890-16

bad (not-OK) counterparts and linked by corresponding affects on each side of the dyad. They form a combination of good (C1+/P1+) and corresponding bad (C1-/P1-) dyadic counterparts. Both the good (OK) and bad (not-OK) internal representations are a residue of developmental violations, such as trauma, abuse, neglect, empathic failures, or the caregiver's own dependency on the child. The psychoanalytic cure is gained through deconfusion which involves their integration (Berne, 1961/1986, 1966/1994).

In Zivkovic's model, the representations of self and of other are simultaneously activated as is the emotional experience attached to these representations. For example, in the case where the individual had a developmental experience of a sadistic and punitive caregiver, the internal bad object representation (P1-) would be one of an abusive caregiver, alongside internalized anger, the bad self-representation (C1-) would be one of an impotent and worthless child with a corresponding affect of terror. Through the individual's defensive strategies these representations would then be pushed out of consciousness or projected into relationships. A corresponding idealized (OK) side of the dyad would also develop, whereby the internal object representation (P1+) could be one of an omnipotent gratifying saviour – a nurturing Parent. These dyads then characterize both the individual's subjective experience as well as, through projections and transference, the individual's relationships.

METHODS

The therapist uses transference and countertransference as the main concepts in analysis of the client's intrapsychic an interpersonal dynamic and in their guidance of interventions. The primary therapeutic stance is one of neutrality. This means that the therapist takes a neutral stance in relation to the client's internal conflict(s). This is very different to the position often taken by TA therapists who will typically take the 'healthy'side of the internal conflict as opposed to the 'destructive' or script one. Or the side of the Child ego state in conflict with the Parent ego state (such as one often sees in redecision therapy). IDTAP sees taking a side as helping the client remain in their script and hence inhibiting to the therapeutic process. Maintaining neutrality requires the therapist to pay close attention to their countertransference due to the intensity of emotion this can generate. Specifically, the therapist notices any internal pull they might feel towards taking a stance of Nurturing Parent (or Rescuer) or Critical Parent (or Persecutor) in response to their client. When using IDTAP, the therapists pays close attention to three distinct countertransference reactions: complementary, concordant, and what Berne referred to as the ego image (see Point 28).

The vehicles of change when using IDTAP are cognitive and affective insight, empathy, containing (Bion, 1962, 1970), and holding (Winnicott, 1960a/1965a, 1960b/1965b). As such, similar to relational TA, the use of empathy is a crucial aspect of IDTAP, however, Zivkovic draws an interesting distinction between expression of compassion and empathy and also between gratification of transference needs and empathic validation.

IDTAP begins with extensive use of clear contracting around the boundaries of the therapeutic relationship. The purpose here is to make it clear to the client, both on cognitive level (Adult), as well as on an affective level (Child) that there exist self-other boundaries between the therapist and the client. Cognitively, this means making it clear to the client that the therapeutic relationship is not a 'real' relationship in so far as it only exists for the purpose of the client's therapy. As part of the contracting process, the therapist explains that the maintenance of firm boundaries is essential to the effectiveness of the therapy. This may include being clear that between-session telephone contact will not take place as well as managing risk of harm. Throughout IDTAP, the therapist must be attentive to the boundaries, or 'therapeutic frame' as it is known, and addresses any pushing against or potential threat to it. Commonly, the client will struggle against this and express anger or regressive behaviour in response to the therapist's insistence on firm boundaries – especially, with clients at lower levels of personality functioning. This power struggle then becomes fertile ground for transference work, and, as such, becomes part of the client's reworking of their internal conflicts.

RELATIONAL TA: FOUNDATIONS

BACKGROUND

The relational approach to TA has developed over the last 30 years and is now a well-established approach within TA (Cornell and Hargaden, 2005; Fowlie and Sills, 2011). Hargaden and Sills (2002) describe their own journey to relational therapy as being driven out of recognizing a change in the typical presenting profile of clients and an increase in clients presenting with disorders of the self, such as borderline, narcissistic and schizoid structures (Masterson and Lieberman, 2004):

> When Berne first wrote, the common client was putatively an inhibited, rule-bound individual who needed the metaphorical 'solvent' of therapy to loosen the confines of his or her script. As we move into the twenty-first century, the 'typical' client is one who needs not solvent but 'glue'.
>
> (ibid.: 2)

In response to this need, they revisited psychoanalytic concepts and began a process of developing TA models that matched the experience of themselves and their clients and which integrated modern developments in psychoanalysis from the relational and intersubjective movements and from developments in child development theory, such as the work of Daniel Stern (Stern, 1985).

PHILOSOPHY AND APPROACH

The relational approach to TA emphasizes the emergence and analysis of unconscious processes in the therapy. As opposed to more goal-oriented, behavioural forms of TA, relational TA

DOI: 10.4324/9781003375890-17

therapists consider the deeper processes of change occur when the therapist and client pay attention to the emergence of these unconscious processes on a moment-to-moment basis in the dynamics between therapist and client. Relational TA is guided by eight principles (Fowlie and Sills, 2011) which were originally agreed upon by the founding members of the International Association for Relational TA (including the present author). These are:

1. *The centrality of relationship.* In keeping with Berne (1961/1986, 1964, 1972) and like all variations of transactional analysis, relational TA holds that humans are fundamentally relational in nature and relationship-seeking from birth. In line with a vast body of research on curative factors in psychotherapy, relational TA therapists champion the therapeutic relationship as being the primary agent for change (Norcross and Lambert, 2019a; Norcross and Wampold, 2019).

2. *The importance of engagement.* Relational TA emphasizes the need for the therapist to be an active participant in the therapy, instead of being 'a neutral observer on him/herself, the other, or his/her work' (Fowlie and Sills, 2011: xxx). They also state that the therapist needs to be authentic in the encounter and that their role is not to be a 'benign provider or what was once missing for the client – except perhaps in this quality of attention and engagement' (ibid.).

3. *The significance of conscious and non-conscious patterns of relating.* This principle is focused around the recognition that within relationships, humans are constantly engaged in a process of mutual influencing and shaping of both each other and of what happens between them. This happens at both a conscious and an unconscious level.

4. *The importance of experience.*

   The most profound change happens through here-and-now experience (as distinct from cognitive understanding) and, most powerfully, through relational experiences that both embody and enact different meanings from those that relationships once did for the client … this is a major way in which relational approaches are reparative.

(ibid.: xxxi)

5. *The significance of subjectivity and of self-subjectivity.* The relational approach to TA accounts for what both therapist and client bring to the therapeutic encounter, including the script issues and unconscious process of both. A relational TA therapist will be mindful of their own process and how this impacts the relationship and their client, and will remain receptive to learning more about their own unconscious process in an ongoing and unfolding way. This principle suggests that the therapist is also changed by the therapeutic encounter. This makes sense when we consider that our own scripts will invariably limit our own ways of relating, and the process of honest, intimate communication characterized by mutuality with our clients will repeatedly push us as therapists to move beyond and outside our own script into new patterns of relating.

6. *The importance of uncertainty.* There is a recognition within relational TA that certainty is 'not always possible nor necessarily desirable' (ibid.: xxxi), and that meanings can change and shift as a result of the client's context and the unfolding relationship between therapist and client. Hargaden (2007: 10) reminds us that 'it is important to learn to play with possibilities and not to get fixed on just one meaning'.

7. *The importance of curiosity, criticism and creativity.* Both therapist and client are encouraged to take a stance of curiosity towards their own process, the therapy and the process that emerges between them. Criticism and critique of the work, by the client and therapist are also encouraged as is the creative use of language, metaphor and symbolic imagery.

8. *The reality of functioning and changing adults.*

   Relational TA moves away from the 'parental paradigm' where the practitioner may be seen as a temporary provider for unmet

> relational needs and sees the client as an adult who is capable of a reciprocal and mutual (albeit asymmetrical) relationship with the practitioner. We privilege the activity of relating where both parties are willing to acknowledge the truth about themselves and each other.
>
> (Fowlie and Sills, 2011: xxxii)

So, with the emphasis on the therapeutic relationship, mutuality, here-and-now relating and co-construction of meaning, relational TA is a two-person approach (Stark, 2000).

Relational TA is interested not only in how the client replays their script both within and outside the therapy room, but in examining features of the therapeutic relationship that are unique and a product of the interaction of this unique client and this unique therapist. Enhancing the client's relationships in all areas of their life is a central concern in relational therapy.

KEY THEORETICAL CONCEPTS

Hargaden and Sills (2002) present an alternative model of the third-order structure of the Child ego state. One key difference is they diagram the C0 and P0 ego states as overlapping, with the intersection between the two as being the A0 ego state. Their inspiration for this amendment is the work of child development theorist Daniel Stern (Stern, 1985). In Stern's work, the 'self' emerges (Stern calls this the emergent self) from the interaction between the infant and the primary caregiver(s). The self does not develop independently or spontaneously but is entirely shaped by interactional processes. The overlapping of the circles is a play with the visual metaphor of the ego state model to illustrate this process. The primary caregiver provides an essential affect-regulating function (ibid.) for the infant. For the infant, the source of this affective regulation is not identified as being external to the self, and over time, the regulating function of the other becomes part of the self (as key brain structures, such as the orbito-frontal cortex mature). The mutually influencing processes of development, together with a relative lack of differentiation between self and other, mean that at these early stages the self-other boundary is not clear and the qualitative, affective nature of the interaction will become part of the individual's developing sense of self by internalization which is recorded in the early Parent ego states.

Both infant and primary caregiver(s) mutually influence each other, and it is the quality of the relationship which is internalized and recorded in the individual's protocol. The protocol forms the basis of our script and, in therapy, attention is paid to the interaction of transference and countertransference to shed light on and through here-and-now experience, rework the protocol and its unconscious processes.

RELATIONAL TA: METHODS

METHODS

The primary therapeutic interventions used in relational TA are empathic transactions (Clark, 1991; Hargaden and Sills, 2002). A revised version of Berne's eight therapeutic operations is offered that provides the basic empathic backdrop for the work. Interpretation is also used; however, empathic and interpretive interventions are primarily used to analyse, explain, highlight and work with the here-and-now processes occurring in the therapy. The relationally oriented therapist will regularly focus on the client's impact upon the therapist, the therapist's impact upon the client, and the here-and-now engagement between them (Stark, 2000). A relational TA therapist may also explore the significance in the therapeutic relationship of parallels in experiences the client reports in other relationships (see Points 12, 13 and 14).

All transactional analysts seek to detoxify the toxic introjects of their clients. With approaches such as redecision TA, the therapist joins the client in fighting back against these introjects, mobilizing Child and Adult energy to challenge these introjects, and possibly decathect significant aspects of the introjects. Relational TA takes a different approach. In relational TA, the therapist considers that it is not enough to simply provide a good, corrective experience, or to engage in analysis or seeking to mobilize forces against these introjects as, even if significant change takes place, the introjects are still there. A relational approach to working with such introjects is to metaphorically make space for them to emerge in the therapy via the transference/countertransference matrix. In this instance, the therapist takes on the client's transferential

 DOI: 10.4324/9781003375890-18

projection of the negative, bad object introjects and re-works them. In this process, relational therapists consider that the existing introject is detoxified and re-worked and the relational conflict that was bound up with the introject is resolved in the relational process (Little, 2013).

CRITIQUE

There are many within the TA community who are deeply critical of relational TA and who are of the view that is represents a regressive tendency back to the psychoanalytic theory that Berne sought to distance TA from. Some of the theory of relational TA can be difficult for beginning students to understand, and some of the articles published on the relational approach can be dense and heavy in their use of advanced and psychoanalytic concepts, and also light on clear links to TA theory and also light on practical recommendations, which those who are interested in developing their work in this way can use readily. Hargaden and Sills' (2002) book is, however, full of narrative to explain and illustrate the theory discussed.

Critics of the relational approach believe the often complex language of relational TA is contrary to the spirit of TA. However, relational TA therapists argue in response that some processes are not simple to understand or describe, and that the language used reflects the complexity of these phenomena and greater refinement in our understanding.

Furthermore, relational TA appears to primarily be an approach which is more suited to long-term psychotherapy. Long-term psychotherapy is rarely accessible to those who do not have the means to pay for it, which leaves relational TA open to the critique that it is largely the province of white, middle-class therapists conducting long-term therapy with white, middle-class clients. Although many relational TA proponents would argue otherwise, it remains a legitimate criticism of the approach.

CO-CREATIVE TA

BACKGROUND

Co-creative transactional analysis was developed by Graeme Summers and Keith Tudor (2000, 2005) and has had a significant impact on transactional analysis. In recognition of its impact, they were awarded the 2020 Eric Berne Memorial Award. Co-creative TA is seen as a meta-perspective, or lens through which to view TA, rather than a collection of techniques. It is also seen as a different approach to relational TA which is based on present-centred relating, as opposed to the more psychodynamically-oriented relational TA developed by Hargaden and Sills (2002). Co-creative TA also places emphasis on positive health and growthful forms of relating, as opposed to what Summers and Tudor see as the dominant emphasis within TA on psychopathology.

As its name might suggest, co-creative TA is particularly interested in what emerges – or is created – when two people interact:

> When two people converse or engage with one another in some way, something comes into existence which is a product of neither of them exclusively … There is a shared field, a common communicative home, which is mutually constructed.
>
> (Parlett, 1991: 75)

Co-creative TA is also interested in the narrative that individuals create in an ongoing and continuous manner which determines how they view and interact with reality, and how two (or more) interacting narratives create new, additional narratives. 'Meaning (constantly) evolves through dialogue.

DOI: 10.4324/9781003375890-19

Therapy is the co-creation, in dialogue, of new narratives that provide new possibilities. [And] The therapist is a participant-observer in this dialogue' (Summers and Tudor, 2000: 24).

GUIDING PRINCIPLES OF CO-CREATIVE TA

The principle of 'we-ness'

Co-creative TA places great emphasis on homonomy, and the importance of connection and connectedness. Similar to the gestalt notion of 'the whole is greater than the sum of the parts', co-creative TA identifies the therapeutic relationship as being greater than the sum of each individual person in the relationship.

The principle of shared responsibility

> Co-creative transactional analysis supports the practical manifestation of interdependence, co-operation, and mutuality within the therapeutic relationship by emphasizing the shared client-therapist responsibility for the therapeutic process. This is in contrast to traditional transactional analysis, which emphasizes the personal responsibility of the client. It also contrasts with more recent integrative transactional analysis approaches, which, in our opinion, tend to overemphasize the responsibility of the therapist. While the therapist must take a leading role in the creation of therapeutic safety, our emphasis on shared responsibility is intended to provide a conceptual frame for acknowledging and exploring co-created experience.

> (ibid.: 24)

The principle of present-centred development

Psychotherapy is conceptualized as an Adult-Adult relationship within co-creative TA, and although transference is recognized (as past transactional relating), the work of therapy is seen as being very much in the present. Ways of working which place the client in a Child position and/or the therapist in the Parent position (such as therapy where the therapist takes the role of a provider who fulfils the client's unmet needs) are rejected as inappropriate infantilization. Summers and Tudor also reject techniques of deconfusion and/or re-decision based on regression to childhood scenes. They argue:

> A person's emotional desire to complete an archaic scene through an exchange with, for example, a parental figure is not an attempt to resolve the transference; it is the transference. Our task as therapists is not to facilitate such completion and thereby to reinforce the transferential pattern; it is primarily to facilitate suspension of the transferential expectation and to invite co-creation of fresh experience/s.

> (ibid.: 30)

OTHER THEORETICAL CONCEPTS

Two types of relating

Summers and Tudor (ibid.) assert that there are two main types of relating: present-centred (Adult-Adult) or past-centred (where one or both parties is relating from a Child or Parent ego state). They also add in 'partial (co) transferential transactions' which are seen as stepping stones whereby the interaction between two individuals can be considered to have one foot in the past and one foot in the present. Each inter-action between two people is seen to have new, fresh possi-bility, whereby each can individually relate from the past, or can create a new, growthful way of relating in the present. Of course, the vista is seen as constantly changing, and new configurations of past and present, and both new and old meanings (or script) can emerge.

Reflections for practice

Summers and Tudor offer the following interesting questions for practitioners to reflect on about their work with a client in a self-supervision process, based on co-creative TA:

- What patterns emerge between us?
- How are we presently making sense of these patterns?
- What are we each contributing to these patterns?

- What happens if we create different meanings for the same patterns?
- What happens if we do something different?
- How do we make sense of different patterns that we co-create?
- What ego states are we evoking and co-creating in each other?
- Why are we creating these ego states at this point in time?
- What else may be possible?
- What version of reality might we be (have we been) confirming?

    How can we explore, acknowledge, and choose between different realities?

- What constructs are we using to define self and other?
- How do these constructs support or limit us?

Readers who are interested in learning more are advised to visit: www.co-creativity.com where they can read Summers and Tudor's original article from 2000, and also read the informative and accessible *Introducing Co-Creative TA* (Summers and Tudor, 2005).

Part 2

THE THERAPEUTIC
RELATIONSHIP

THE INITIAL SESSIONS

The initial sessions of therapy set the scene for the work that follows, acclimatize the client to therapy, and start the process of change. There is now overwhelming evidence that shows that a strong working alliance is the most reliable predictor of successful therapy (Flückiger, Del Re, Wampold and Horvath, 2018). It is during the initial sessions that the working alliance is formed and these sessions are therefore critical to the outcome of the therapy.

Cornell (1986) describes the tasks of the initial sessions as being engagement and collaboration, clarifying with the client how the therapy will work (what is involved in therapy) and assessment. One key aspect of the initial sessions is letting the client tell their story. The therapist's job is to listen carefully, incorporating sensitive use of questioning and clarifying questions to facilitate gaining the necessary information about the client, their situation and their process. The client will generally present with a great need to feel understood, and to feel emotionally safe. To this end, the therapist needs to offer regular empathic responses that communicate their understanding to the client. The emphasis is on establishing 'contact before contract' (Lee, 1997) and as such the therapist's interventions are likely to be simple and focused on clarification and conveying compassion, understanding and warmth. All through this stage, the therapist is building up a detailed picture of the client's process, and is noticing emerging patterns, both in the client's life, and in their manner of presenting in therapy. In allowing the client to tell their story, it is, however, important that the therapist does not encourage clients to tell them details of traumatic events at this stage in therapy, as this

DOI: 10.4324/9781003375890-21

may create an undesirable situation where the client is flooded with distressing emotion and destabilizing memories (see Points 31, 34, 58 and 87).

My own preferred opening invitation is: 'So tell me a little about what it is that brings you here', which is an open question that leaves the space clear for the client to discuss their concerns, reasons for coming for therapy and a little of their history. It is sometimes necessary to interrupt, seek clarification and guide the client towards maintaining focus, particularly with clients who give long, complicated stories with many tangents. The opening invitation can be followed with questioning that invites the client to discuss their therapy goals, which can then be used to establish an initial working contract. An example of such a question might be: 'Tell me a little about what you want to get out of therapy.' Responses here are often phrased in terms of what the client wants to stop, or get rid of ('to get rid of my depression', 'to stop feeling anxious'). Identifying a focus for the work and clear markers for ending therapy early in the work is desirable. Simply asking, 'How will you and I know that you have got what you want from therapy? How will you know when our work is finished?' will usually give a sufficient indicator. Asking the client for their thoughts on how they came to be in their current situation and what they think will best help them is a particularly useful strategy (Duncan and Miller, 2000). The working alliance can also be greatly enhanced by enquiring about the client's expectations of the therapist, therapy in general and what will happen in therapy. The therapy can get off to a rocky start if client and therapist have very different views about what the tasks of therapy are. An excellent way to clarify these expectations is to solicit the client's preferences for therapy. The most effective way to establish these is by using the Cooper-Norcross Inventory of Preferences (C-NIP). This is freely available online and can be used to spark a conversation about how these preferences can be accommodated in therapy, and to clarify how you do and do not work.

Nowadays, most therapists have an online presence via a website or profile with an online directory. Typically, clients will have read this and already identified that they feel you are a suitable match for their needs. Asking the client if there is anything they need to know about you will enable them to fill in any gaps in information (in my experience, most clients already have all the information they need from reading the therapist's website or profile).

The client needs to experience some of what therapy is about, and how the therapy will work during this opening stage. To this end, the therapist does need to introduce some interventions and find the right balance between challenge and support. If clients feel too challenged, they will get scared or feel offended and leave therapy; if there is not enough challenge, they will not experience the therapist as potent enough to help them change. Regular seeking of feedback by asking the client if they are happy with the levels of support and challenge you are providing in these initial sessions is recommended.

At the end of the first session, the client will need to leave with some sense of how the therapist works and what 'doing therapy' will involve. This is best done experientially as well as through explanation.

Highlighting that the therapeutic relationship may be used to promote change is also advisable. Yalom (2001) advocates contracting for this in the very first session by raising the following (or an adaptation thereof) with a client:

> It's clear that one of the areas we need to address is your relationship with others. It's difficult for me to know the precise nature of your difficulties in relationships because I, of course, know the other persons in your life only through your eyes. Sometimes your descriptions may be unintentionally biased, and I've found that I can be more helpful to you by focusing on the one relationship where I have the most accurate information – the relationship between you and me. It is for this reason I shall often ask you to examine what is happening between the two of us.
>
> (ibid.: 85–86)

In my experience, the overwhelming majority of clients are receptive to such an approach.

In terms of assessment, a holistic view of assessment is recommended, as opposed to one which focuses entirely on problems and the client's pathology (Cornell, 1986). It is very easy to focus on problem areas, and gaining some sense of the client's strengths is useful in orienting the therapy towards health and the promotion of strengths and in helping the client use their strengths to support their process of change.

I also engage the client in a discussion about what the first few sessions will focus on, which, if the client agrees, acts as an effective standard treatment plan for the first phase of therapy:

> I suggest that we spend the first few sessions focusing on getting to know each other better, so I can get a good sense of who you are as a person and how your problems are affecting your day-to-day life. At the same time, I think it would be useful if we explored how you came to be in this situation, which may involve exploring what has been going on in recent events as well as your past, and how these have all contributed to your current situation. We can also try out a range of strategies and techniques focused on helping you understand and manage difficult emotions so that you start to make changes in how you are feeling. How does this sound to you as a starting point for therapy?

THERAPEUTIC ENQUIRY

Use of enquiry is probably every therapist's third tool, after listening and empathy. Even if, as a therapist, all you do is use enquiry, you can have some degree of success (Erskine et al., 1999). The backdrop of therapeutic enquiry is a genuine interest in the client and their process and is done respectfully and sensitively (Hargaden and Sills, 2002). The intention behind the enquiry process is to deepen awareness – both for the client and the therapist. Sensitive, and carefully attended to, enquiry will often enable the client to see their own meanings and generate solutions to their problems with the minimum of therapist intervention. Elegant therapeutic enquiry leads to ever-increasing awareness and greater integration for the client. For the therapist, skilful enquiry helps to create a knowledge base of information about our client, and in terms of the overall process of therapy, it facilitates our clients talking about themselves and their deepest processes, and it enhances the owning of responsibility and implies the potential for problem solving.

Erskine et al. offer a 'menu' of areas for enquiry, including: physical sensations and reactions; emotions; memories; thoughts; conclusions and 'as if' script decisions; the meaning the client makes of experiences; hopes and fantasies. This list is not exhaustive, but is rather used as a prompt of suggestions for the therapist to consider. Erskine et al. also emphasize the importance in enquiry of promoting contact – both internal contact and interpersonal contact.

Another way enquiry can be used is to activate specific memories or experiential processes for a particular therapeutic intervention. Some examples include: by prompting a client to identify similarities between a current event and past events to generate insight. Through use of further questioning to activate the Adult ego state and call into question a particular implicit or explicit belief for the purposes of decontamination. By triggering emotional release and processing for the purposes of deconfusion. Or to bring together aspects of a past experience which is linked to a specific script decision, simultaneous with holding new or existing Adult information in mind to facilitate a redecision. As enquiry in these cases may include revisiting material previously discussed, I will usually tell a client early in therapy that 'I will probably sometimes ask questions about things we have talked about in previous sessions. It doesn't mean I wasn't listening, but is usually when I am trying to link up experiences to help you make a therapeutic shift of some kind.' In this way, I have made the therapeutic process explicit and engaged the client in contracting about the therapy process.

Enquiry plays a central role in many other interventions, for example, decontamination can be effectively done using the cognitive therapy method of the 'downward arrow' (Burns, 2000). Specification is one of Berne's eight therapeutic operations (Berne, 1966/1994) that can support and follow enquiry: 'The object is to fix certain information in his mind and in the patient's mind, so that it can be referred to later' (ibid.: 234–235). A specification can be highly effective at summarizing or highlighting key points emerging from the enquiry. It does not involve interpretation, and focuses solely on what the client has expressed and is a form of empathic enquiry (Hargaden and Sills, 2002).

THE CENTRALITY OF EMPATHY

Empathy has been firmly placed on the TA map since Barbara Clark's paper on empathy and its role in deconfusion (Clark, 1991). This has been subsequently developed by a number of other TA authors, including Erskine (1993), Erskine and Trautmann (1996), Hargaden and Sills (2002) and Tudor (2009). Second only to the working alliance, empathy has been identified as a crucial factor in effective therapy (Elliott, Bohart, Watson and Murphy, 2018).

Berne made little reference to emotions in his work, or how to work with emotions, yet Berne was firmly interested in the therapist working with the client's phenomenology – the client's construction of meanings and internal experience of themselves, others and the world. In approaching phenomenological enquiry, the therapist would need to account for and enquire into the client's emotional world in a process linked to empathy. It is now widely accepted that experiencing empathy is essential for the development of a cohesive sense of self (Hargaden and Sills, 2002). Stern (1985) has written extensively on the importance and centrality of affective attunement in the development of the self in child development. This emphasis has also been supported by developments in neuroscience (see Cozolino, 2017; Siegel, 2007, 2020).

So what is empathy? To be empathic means to temporarily move outside our judgement frameworks, our sense of what is right or wrong or how things 'should be'. Empathy is to enter our client's frame of reference and see and experience the world as they do. When we are empathic, we learn about the client's experience and their reality. Empathy is not about agreeing, or disagreeing with our clients, it is not about reassuring them, or

DOI: 10.4324/9781003375890-23

comforting them or providing them with support. Empathy might be gratifying, but the intention in an empathic response is not necessarily to be gratifying, it is simply to resonate with the client's experience. For example, in a situation where a client is directly seeking reassurance from their therapist, an empathic response would not be to provide the reassurance, but instead to empathize with the client's experience of need and the emotions which are fuelling the requests for reassurance.

Empathy is composed of two aspects: empathic understanding (listening and resonating) and empathic responding. In many respects, empathic understanding is useless unless it can be effectively communicated to the client (Clark, 1991; Rogers, 1957). Stern (2004: 241) refers to affect attunement as 'a way of imitating, from the inside, what an experience feels like, not how it was expressed in action' and includes attention to the temporal dynamics of the affect in terms of intensity, form or rhythm.

> [To be empathic] means entering the private perceptual world of the other and becoming thoroughly at home in it. It involves being sensitive, moment by moment, to the changing felt meanings which flow in this other person, to the fear or rage or tenderness or confusion or whatever that he or she is experiencing. It means temporarily living in the other's life, moving about in it delicately without making judgments.
>
> (Rogers, 1980: 142)

Empathy requires attending to, and resonating with the client's 'felt' experience. When we are empathic, we tune in to where the client is emotionally at. The emotions we resonate with will be within the client's sphere of awareness, or partially within their awareness, but nevertheless part of their experience. This is the key difference between empathy and interpretation: empathy addresses the client's affective experience – it is experience-near; interpretation draws the client's attention to where they are currently unaware and emotions that are not presently part of the client's experience – it is experience-distant (Jacobs, 1988; Stark, 2000).

Accurate empathy is not always the warm, pleasant experience we might expect it to be. To be truly empathic requires that the therapist be prepared to tolerate and contain intense and possibly confusing unpleasant emotions. If we are to have some real appreciation of what it is like to be in our client's skin, an empathic therapist will regularly feel high levels of fear, hatred, depression, despair, doubt, grief and shame, to name just some of the possibilities. Such attunement distinguishes empathy from compassion or sympathy (which can also be valid ways of responding therapeutically).

In terms of treatment planning, emphasizing empathy forms a crucial aspect of the formation and maintenance of the therapeutic relationship, and certainly helps cement the 'therapeutic bond' aspect of the relationship (Bordin, 1979). Clients generally present in therapy initially with an intense need to be understood, to unburden, to feel safe, knowing that their experience makes sense to someone. In many respects, interventions other than inquiry will have limited effectiveness until the client experiences the therapist's empathy:

> Nearer the beginning of treatment, it may well be that the patient will respond especially well to empathic interventions that validate the patient's experience and enable her to feel understood. In fact, the patient may not be receptive to interpretations that highlight recurring themes, patterns and repetitions in her life until she becomes more comfortable in the therapy.
>
> (Stark, 2000: 162)

In terms of later stages of therapy:

> The therapist must decide from moment to moment whether to be with the patient where she is or to direct the patient's attention elsewhere … There are times when the therapist senses that the patient is open to the possibility of acquiring insight. There are other times, however, when the therapist senses that what the patient wants is, simply, empathic recognition of who she is and what she is feeling.
>
> (ibid.: 16)

Although indicated in early stages of treatment, empathy is a vital ingredient throughout:

> The empathic bond is imperative when working toward deconfusion of the Child ego states. At this stage, the person has to believe that his or her most profound emotional states and needs can be understood by the therapist. In the empathic ambience, the patient and therapist will be able to access the early developmental levels of the Child ego states which is necessary for deconfusion to occur.
>
> (Clark, 1991: 93)

ACCOUNTING FOR THE IMPACT OF DIVERSITY IN THE THERAPEUTIC RELATIONSHIP

Our identity, who we are, is a socially embedded concept and one that plays a part in our unconscious process and our lived experience. Shivanath and Hiremath (2003: 117) highlight the therapist's commitment to self-awareness and personal exploration of issues associated with diversity and difference: 'as psychotherapists it is our responsibility to explore all our ego state responses to race and racism'. I agree, and would extend this to include other forms of diversity including gender, sexual orientation and class. It is also my view that not fully accounting for difference in the therapy room is unethical and borderline malpractice.

The concept of intersectionality (Crenshaw, 1989) is hugely important in helping us to understand the complex nature of our own identity, which includes (but is not limited to) our gender, race, cultural background, social class, and whether we are neurotypical or neurodivergent. Each of these identities impacts on who we are, how we experience the world and shapes our frame of reference. Baskerville (2022) has developed a detailed analysis of intersectionality mapped onto the ego state model in an article I fully recommend to all transactional analysts. In the modern world, and in light of the Black Lives Matter, Me Too and LGBTQ+ Pride movements, I believe it is imperative that we as a transactional analysts examine our own identity and attend to matters of social justice and systemic oppression, both within and beyond our consulting rooms.

DOI: 10.4324/9781003375890-24

Acknowledging and accounting for differences between the therapist and client are essential to develop empathic sensitivity and in beginning the process of understanding the frame of reference of the client, and how the therapist's frame of reference may be in accord with or discordant with the client's frame of reference. Oppression subtly but powerfully shapes the frame of reference of every single person, regardless of whether we are aware of it or not. People from a culturally dominant background can easily take for granted their privileges, and can discount the impact that growing up and living life as part of a culturally less powerful and oppressed group can have in the shaping of the frame of reference and script of an individual who has had, and continues to live with, such experiences on a day-to-day basis. Opening up the issue of difference in the room can be therapeutic and a relief to our clients. For example, I might ask a client who is a person of colour 'What is it like for you to be here with me, a white man?'. Equally, I might ask a heterosexual male client how they are experiencing being open and vulnerable with a gay man, or I might ask an LGBTQ+ client what it is like for them to be in therapy with someone from their community.

Awareness of cultural and social differences is a key feature in working across difference. Understanding and accepting cultural (and subcultural) differences avoid pathologizing behaviours and ways of living that are not part of the usual cultural frame of reference for the therapist and help the therapist to practise in anti-oppressive ways:

> It is sometimes more important, at least in the early phases of developing a therapeutic relationship, to consider the emotional implications of a person's age, race, ethnicity, class background, physical disability, political attitudes, or sexual orientation than it is to appreciate his or her appropriate diagnostic category.
>
> (McWilliams, 1994: 18)

Acknowledging the existence of power differentials and the potential for unconscious bias can be disturbing for therapists from the more culturally powerful background (white, heterosexual, cis-gender, educated, middle-class) and who experience themselves as liberally-minded and sensitive at some levels to issues of oppression. This disturbance and the associated guilt, shame or even denial can manifest subtly in the therapeutic relationship and significantly impair the therapist's capacity to be potent (Hargaden and Sills, 2002; Shivanath and Hiremath, 2003). Similarly, a refusal to acknowledge the role of difference or similarity between the therapist and client, and the potential impact it is having on the therapy is to discount entire areas of exploration of meaning and unconscious process and associated experiences and script decisions as well as large areas of the client's experience. Shadbolt (2004) describes the importance of accounting for our countertransference responses to our clients in relation to working with gay clients; however, her position is one which is very relevant when working with all clients and one which it is wise to pay special attention to when working with clients who are different from ourselves, or clients from minority cultures. Our countertransference feelings, particularly the more 'negative' ones, may contain vital information about the client's experience and may result in a 'detoxification' of the oppressive introjects, through processes of working with the projective or transformational transference. 'By owning and identifying such countertransference feelings, therapists understand, hold, manage and transform them for clients who have, as yet, been unable to do so intrapsychically' (ibid.: 121).

Another consideration for the therapist in accounting for how difference between therapist and client interacts and influences the therapeutic relationship is in the experience of empathy. Stark (2000) draws a distinction between 'easy' and 'difficult' empathy. In easy empathy, aspects of the client's experience are similar or close to the therapist's own experience, or how the therapist would experience the same situation. Difficult empathy 'involves understanding aspects of the patient's experience that are at variance with the therapist's worldview, aspects that are discrepant from the therapist's experience' (ibid.: 179). It can be very difficult to empathize with clients who have very different social, political and cultural experiences from us, and to account for the significance of, and respect culturally accepted etiquette, technicalities and characteristics (Drego, 1983) which are at variance with our own.

22

CONCEPTUALIZING THE THERAPEUTIC RELATIONSHIP

The therapeutic relationship is different from any other type of relationship. Repeated studies have demonstrated that the most curative factor in psychotherapy is not the techniques the therapist uses, or their theoretical orientation, but the strength of the therapeutic relationship (Elliott et al., 2018). The therapeutic relationship in many respects is a relationship of potentiality. It can be likened to a relationship laboratory, with client and therapist engaged in experimentation with different means of relating to each other and reflection upon these relational experiments. The potentiality includes the opportunity to relate to each other from a range of ego states, from scripted positions, and autonomous positions. The length of time needed to establish a strong therapeutic alliance can vary quite considerably and is substantially influenced by the client's level of organization and integration. Clients who have the discernible capacity for reflection and self-observation and also the capacity for and experience of secure attachment, are likely to form an alliance with the skilful therapist quickly, maybe even within the first session or within only a few sessions, whereas those with less or even no observing ego, low levels of self-reflection and/or a history of poor or limited attachment are likely to need extensive therapeutic input to get to the stage where such an alliance between the therapist and the observing ego is possible (Byrd, Patterson and Turchik, 2010; Daly and Mallinckrodt, 2009).

A particular feature of the therapeutic relationship is the therapist's willingness to be 'recruited' (Barr, 1987) by the client as a participant in the client's (transferential) drama. In

TA terms, this means the therapist being willing to be stimulated into partially entering the client's games, so that these games can be understood and analysed and so the underlying script issues can be healed within the context of a relationship. Therapists bring their own relational experiences (and associated script) to the therapeutic encounter, and these interact with our client's to generate the sum total of immediate relational potential at the outset. As the therapy proceeds, this potential increases. Berne (1961/1986) analysed relationships by their transactional possibilities, that is, the transactional vectors and ego states that are activated in the relationship, out of the nine types of transaction that are possible between two people. In TA psychotherapy, the transactional analyst takes time to consider the type and nature of the therapeutic relationship and transactions between them and their client(s), and will actually reflect upon and analyse transactions and transactional sequences that emerge in the therapeutic interaction. This analysis is done both to strengthen the quality of the therapeutic relationship, and also to help illuminate the client's internal dynamics and their manifestation and enhance their interactions with others (see also Point 100). The relationship is also analysed with reference to Berne's six categories of time structuring (Berne, 1961/1986): withdrawal, rituals, pastimes, activity, games and intimacy.

Many therapists believe that it is the intensity of the therapeutic relationship which creates the necessary conditions for therapeutic change. Indeed, there is evidence that the intensity of the relationship encourages the growth of new neural patterns and ways of relating (Cozolino, 2017). Some therapists who work with a deficit model (Lapworth et al., 1993) see that this intensity is needed to act as an 'antidote' to previous relational trauma:

> It is thought that part of what enables the therapist to be deeply effective is that she comes (by way of the patient's regression) to assume the importance of the original parent. When the therapist has been vested with such power, then and only then is the

therapy relationship able to serve as a corrective for damage sustained during the patient's formative years.

(Stark, 2000: 11)

Each therapist over time forms their own conceptualization of the nature and role of the therapeutic relationship and of the therapist's key tasks. This is part of creating a personalized approach to psychotherapy, and making personal meaning of theories and models. Erskine beautifully paraphrases Berne on the task of the therapist and the nature of the therapeutic relationship:

> The psychotherapist's task is to create a contactful therapeutic relationship that facilitates decoding of the client's transferential expression of past experiences, detoxifying introjections and rectifying fixated script beliefs and defensive structures, and helping the client identify relational needs and opportunities for need fulfilment through enhancing the client's capacity for internal and external contact.

(1998: 139–140)

23

STRENGTHENING THE WORKING ALLIANCE BY ATTENTION TO TASKS, GOALS AND BONDS

Bordin (1979) developed a formulation of the dimensions of the working alliance in psychotherapy, which he identified as comprising three main components: tasks, goals and bonds (Bordin, 1994). There has been considerable research on this formulation and it is now widely accepted that therapist-client agreement on the tasks, goals and bonds is a reliable predictor of strength of working alliance and as such can be seen as a reliable predictor of positive outcome and successful therapy (Flückiger et al., 2018; Horvath and Greenberg, 1994). Bordin's formulation can be used to establish, enhance and develop the working alliance.

TASKS

'What do we do here?' There needs to be agreement regarding the nature of the tasks of therapy. At the beginning, the client who is new to therapy is looking to the therapist for the therapist to provide structure and to indicate to the client what the tasks of therapy are, how the therapy will be done, what kind of things they can expect, and so on. This is true also for clients who have already experienced some previous therapy as they need to work out how this new therapist works. Agreement on tasks also provides a degree of emotional containment as a total lack of structure can be unsettling. Agreement on tasks can provide a sense of the boundaries of the therapy on an emotional level. Exploration of the client's expectations of therapy, and what they anticipate the therapist

DOI: 10.4324/9781003375890-26

will do, is often very helpful in establishing agreement on therapeutic tasks. Where the client has unspoken expectations of the therapy that conflict with the therapist's expectations of therapy and the different methods which will be used in the therapy, the alliance will be placed under enormous strain, and may not develop quickly enough unless the tasks are clarified.

Attending to the tasks of therapy also means explaining to the client how therapy works, and specifically, the therapist explaining to the client how they work and how they intend to approach the client's problems and promote change. This also has an ethical and contractual dimension, in that when a client has information regarding the nature of therapy and the 'nuts and bolts' of how it works and what is likely to happen, they are in a position to make an Adult informed choice, which meets Steiner's requirement of mutual consent (Steiner, 1974).

GOALS

'Where are we going?' In many respects, transactional analysts are incredibly thorough in seeking agreement regarding the goals aspect of the working alliance with their attention to contracting, and getting a clear agreement on the focus of the work. In the process of empathic enquiry during the first few sessions, the therapist will engage the client in a collaborative discussion around what the client's goals for therapy are. What do they want to get out of the process? How will they know when they've achieved their goals for therapy? It makes sense to also include a general 'exploration contract' to allow space to explore the client's problems of history in more detail. More clearly defined goals may well emerge out of this exploration process. Also, it is useful for the therapist to have a clear sense of what their view of some general goals of therapy is (e.g., personal autonomy, improvement in mood and emotions, more harmonious relationships, etc.), and to be explicit about these goals and bring them into the contracting process.

BONDS

'Do we have mutual warmth and respect for each other?', 'Have we established a rapport?' From the client's perspective, bonds require an Adult evaluation of the therapist's degree of perceived potency, credibility and a sense of confidence that the therapist can help them. The bonds also include a Child component: 'Will the therapist provide sufficient safety for me to do the work I need to?', 'Can I open up to them?' It is essential that the client experiences sufficient empathy from the therapist and also feels that the therapist is warm and genuinely interested in them. The client needs to feel understood, respected, valued, and so on. How the client attaches or does not attach to the therapist is also important. The therapist can gain useful significant (often at this stage, inferential and tentative) information regarding the client's attachment pattern, relational scripts, and script beliefs about self, others and the world. The client will likely be showing the therapist how they attach to others. Often there will be some element of distrust from the client towards the therapist. This is to be accepted and understood as being appropriate and having a protective function for the client. In many respects, the bond forms over time and attention to the goals and tasks – an empathic stance which is supportive and appropriately challenging – will help forge this bond.

24

CONSIDERING ADAPTED CHILD RESPONSES AS INDICATORS OF ALLIANCE RUPTURE

Relational approaches to TA psychotherapy pay particular attention to instances of therapeutic alliance rupture. A rupture is a moment where the therapeutic alliance comes under some sort of strain. The genesis of pathology is considered primarily as a result of repeated relational rupture, and the enactment of relational ruptures in the therapy is viewed as inevitable (Cook, 2012; Guistolise, 1996; Shadbolt, 2012). The subsequent consistent and repeated repair of these therapeutic alliance ruptures is considered to be a primary healing process in psychotherapy (see Points 25 and 76) and attention to rupture and repair has been demonstrated to have a significant impact on therapeutic outcome (Eubanks, Muran and Safran, 2018).

Safran and Muran (2003) explored various client behaviours as indicative of alliance rupture. Their observations can easily be translated into TA terms, giving the transactional analyst solid clues as to the potential presence of an alliance rupture and clear indicators for immediate treatment planning. Their framework presents two main categories of rupture markers: withdrawal and confrontation. In their framework, compliance/adaptation is linked to withdrawal. This classification of responses is consistent with a TA framework regarding Adapted Child (functional) responses of compliance and rebellion (Stewart and Joines, 2012), and also incorporates withdrawing as an additional type of Adapted Child response (Oller Vallejo, 1986). The rupture marker will likely be determined by the individual's protocol/script and

DOI: 10.4324/9781003375890-27

their stereotypical response of self, and the expected response of other. Below is a list of observable behaviours or ways of interacting that the therapist can use to identify a potential alliance rupture. This list is not exhaustive, and it is possible that each person will have their own set of rupture markers that are unique to that person. The therapist is advised to develop their sensitivity in noticing rupture markers, both observable and on the basis of their countertransference and subjective reaction to their client.

ADAPTATION/COMPLIANCE

Client begins describing what they think the therapist wants to hear; the client becomes overly accommodating or solicitous; the client offers many strokes to the therapist; accepting therapist interpretations or explanations too readily; submissive behaviour; 'Gee, you're wonderful'; client 'softens the blow' by qualifying or minimizing (discounting) negative feelings towards the therapist; client begins long over-detailed story.

WITHDRAWING

Minimal answers to open-ended questions; intellectualization, discussing problems or painful experiences in a non-emotional or dispassionate manner; getting quieter; silence; avoiding eye contact; client begins 'talking about' others.

REBELLIOUS/CONFRONTATIONAL

Client attacks the therapist as a person; the client criticizes the therapist's skills; the client expresses doubts about being in therapy; the client attempts to rearrange sessions; client expresses irritation about the therapist's questions or suggested tasks; client does not follow instructions for specific techniques (adapted from Safran and Muran, 2003).

DEFLECTION AND REDEFINING

Deflection is also a key indicator of alliance rupture. In TA terms this would involve the use of tangential redefining transactions (Schiff et al., 1975), such as the client changing the subject in response to a direct question. The cathexis approach would suggest that clients use redefining to preserve central aspects of their script-bound frame of reference. In this example, the relational context is relevant and the client can be seen to be defending or reinforcing their relational script beliefs, in terms of beliefs about both self and others. In terms of the above framework, deflection/redefining could be an indicator of either withdrawal or rebellion and is a potential rupture marker.

THE THERAPEUTIC ALLIANCE: RUPTURE AND REPAIR

An alliance rupture is a moment where the therapeutic relationship is under strain in some way. There is mounting agreement among therapists of all orientations that such ruptures are inevitable (Guistolise, 1996), and that learning how to identify and respond to such alliance ruptures are key skills for therapists (Eubanks, Muran and Safran, 2018; Safran and Muran, 2003). Transactional analysts pay attention to each transaction, and note both their own response to each transactional stimulus and the impact of their transactions upon their client and the therapeutic relationship. Analysis of transactions can suggest an alliance rupture, for example, an unexpected, jarring crossed transaction may suggest the presence of a rupture (although do bear in mind much therapy is done when a therapist deliberately crosses transactions). If the therapist suspects a rupture, or experiences some strain in the relationship, naming the tension and openly exploring it begins the process of rupture repair. Inviting the client into exploring how they have experienced a particular intervention can reveal rich information regarding their process and way of experiencing the world and others. The therapist here needs to adopt a stance of curiosity into their own experience, and also enquiry into the client's experience (by questions such as: 'What are you feeling right now?', 'What's going on for you?', 'What was it like for you to hear that?'). This may also provide historical or phenomenological diagnosis of recurring patterns ('I'm wondering if this is familiar to you in any way? Does it remind you of anyone or any situations from your past?', 'How old do you feel right now?'). In identifying and

DOI: 10.4324/9781003375890-28

deliberately seeking to repair an alliance rupture, the therapist is acting differently from the expected re-enactment of the client's relational protocol. In some respects, this is the equivalent of providing the therapeutically needed relationship and may act as an antidote to some of the more toxic introjects and relational script issues the client holds. The sensitive but frank manner in which the rupture is attended to, and the client's feelings empathized with, combined with the absence of defensive responses (minimize, blame, justify, defend, etc.) from the therapist may well be a deeply healing experience for the client. There are many ways ruptures can be attended to and repaired. I offer a few examples of the process of rupture repair below.

EXPLORING THE RELATIONAL AFFECTIVE SIGNIFICANCE OF RUPTURE

The current transactions that triggered the rupture need to be identified and explored. The nature and process of the rupture, together with the client's emotional experience of the rupture, need to be accounted for and explored. It is worth enquiring whether the relational and affective experience of the rupture is in any way familiar for the client. For example, a client who does not complete 'homework' assignments may have a sensitivity to feeling dominated, or may fear criticism (and, out of awareness, invite criticism) or a reluctant client may evoke an intrusive, 'digging' response from their therapist, which in turn provokes further withdrawal and resistance. A rupture around a misattuned response from the therapist may lead the client into an exploration of their experience of being repeatedly misunderstood, or a therapist feeling cautious around a client's anger and being willing to share and discuss their sense of cautiousness may result in the client exploring how others experience them as angry and avoid contact with them. Exploring the relational significance of the rupture can help the client gain insight into their relational patterns and how they are enacted in the therapy.

CHANGING DIRECTION TO PREVENT FURTHER RUPTURE

Sometimes as therapists we realize that a particular approach or line of conversation is 'off limits'. Perhaps the client has begun to get defensive or irritable with the therapist. At other times, certain topics or particular aspects of the client's history may contain so much emotional charge that the client does not want to open up that particular memory at that time. Sometimes the best thing to do in all of these situations is to leave the particular topic and change conversational direction. The direction can be explicitly changed through stating a change in the therapist's direction, recontracting and negotiating with the client to pursue a different topic of discussion or can be done discreetly and without raising the matter. The therapist will need to reflect after the session as to whether to reintroduce the 'off limits' discussion at a later date or not. By being sensitive to a client's receptivity to a particular line of conversation, the therapist demonstrates respect for the client.

RUPTURE DUE TO THERAPIST ATTITUDES

Sometimes when clients withdraw or change the direction of the session, it could be that the client is feeling reluctant to discuss something they believe the therapist will be judgmental about. 'I get a sense that you're holding back on something. I'm wondering if you are concerned I might judge you, or disapprove of something?' (Of course, this requires the therapist to pay very close attention to their reactions and notice any indicators of being judgmental, moralistic or disapproving.)

OWNING MISTAKES AND TAKING RESPONSIBILITY FOR MISCOMMUNICATIONS

It is part of the human condition that people misunderstand each other and also that people do not communicate as clearly as they like to think they do.

Sometimes, clients misinterpret our intention or rationale behind a particular transaction. Reactions can be quite intense at these times, for both therapist and client. It is absolutely crucial that at these times the therapist seeks to maintain as non-defensive a position as possible and has the humility to admit mistakes. Repair requires the therapist to own and acknowledge their part in any misunderstanding, by acknowledging that their communication was in this case probably not clear or effective or delivered clumsily. It is important that the client does not feel blamed or stupid for misunderstanding. Exploration of how the client came to their conclusions can also be productive in exploring their construal systems. Where a therapist has misinterpreted or misunderstood the client's meaning, it is wise for the therapist to simply apologize for misunderstanding. In the case where the misunderstanding is particularly significant and upsetting for the client, the therapist is advised to seek to empathically understand the feelings the client is experiencing in relation to feeling misunderstood. Often in relationships, individuals seek to blame each other for misunderstandings. By taking a non-defensive position, the therapist provides the client with a new, healing and healthy model for relating.

UNDERSTANDING TRANSFERENCE AND COUNTERTRANSFERENCE

Transference is an important concept in psychotherapy, as well as everyday life. It colours many of our interactions. It is how we relate to others in our present life as if they were figures from our past. In relating, we draw upon a vast internal repository of relational experiences and interactions with others. The quality of these interactions is recorded, together with an expected response of the other, a longed-for response of the other, and a particular outcome of how we end up feeling or experiencing ourselves in our interactions with others. This process has been explained in detail in the psychodynamic model of Core Conflictual Relational Themes (Luborsky and Crits-Cristoph, 1990). A summary of the main CCRT themes one sees in practice is given in Table 26.1. You may find this useful in identifying patterns in a client's relationships, and of course, in what might be happening (transferential) in the therapeutic relationship.

Transference is to some extent present in all relationships (we will inevitably view our relationships through the lens of our own experiences of relationships). In therapy, we can help our client to see transference patterns in their relationships with others, although it is in the therapy relationship that transference takes on extra significance. This is because as the past gets replayed in the relationship, it can be identified, explored and made available for healing. Unconscious aspects of how we relate to others are transferential phenomena. Below I describe how some basic TA concepts relate to transference.

 DOI: 10.4324/9781003375890-29

Table 26.1 Main Core Conflictual Relational themes standard category clusters

Wishes/Needs/ Intentions 'I am seeking ... .'	Response of others 'But the other person becomes ... '	Response of self 'And in response I become ... '
To be accepted and liked	Rejecting/abandoning/ withdrawing	Overly helpful/ accommodating
To be heard and undersood	Understanding	Passive and unassertive/passive-aggressive
To be respected	Humiliating/ contemptuous/ attacking/hostile	Self-reliant/self-controlled/withdrawn
To be cared for or loved	Untrustworthy/ unreliable	Helpless/dependent/ needy
To be independent, free and autonomous	Controlling/ domineering	Disappointed/jealous/ angry/depressed
To feel a sense of belonging/closeness	Upset/anxious/angry/ hurt/guilty/ashamed	Anxious/ashamed/ guilty/uncertain
To feel good and comfortable	Disrespectful/ dismissive	Helpful/ understanding
To achieve and help others	Unhelpful/obstructive/ oppositional	Comfortable/happy/ loved/accepted
To withdraw from or push people away or avoid conflicts	Helpless/dependent/ needy	Oppositional/defiant/ hurtful to others
To oppose or hurt/ control others	Disappointed/ disapproving	
	Accepting/welcoming/ loving/caring	

Abridged and adapted summary of common Core Conflictual Relational Themes standard category clusters (Luborksy and Crits-Cristoph, 1990).

SOCIAL DIAGNOSIS

The TA concept of social diagnosis (Berne, 1961/1986) provides the therapist with a rudimentary framework for beginning to think about transference and countertransference. The therapist needs to pay attention to their own internal flow and their own ego state shifts on a moment-to-moment basis in the room with their client. This is a complex task, and one which is being constantly refined through attention to ongoing personal development and ever-deepening analysis of one's own ego states. Attention to our phenomenological flow in the room may provide the therapist with useful indicators as to their client's internal process. In developing our use of social diagnosis as an accurate method of diagnosis, we need to spend time reflecting upon our client and checking for the significance of our shifts from the perspective of our own history. 'Who in my history does this client remind me of?' or 'What aspects of what is happening with this client remind of past events?' It is very likely that the client will indeed share features with significant people from our own past – in terms of how they look, how they speak, even their posture and gestures. This also includes personality traits and emotional presentation. We also may not be fully conscious of this information as we may be aware of resonance only through our implicit memory system. The therapist is advised to spend time thinking about this in relation to each client, and also exploring this further in supervision and personal therapy. Also, by paying attention to social diagnosis, we can start to gain insight into the responses our clients may elicit from others. For example, if we notice we often feel Parental around a client, we might check this against what the client reports in sessions, and we might invite our client into a conversation about the possibility of them being experienced by others as often being in a Child ego state.

TRANSACTIONS

Berne (1972) used analysis of transactions to understand transference reactions. Berne identified crossed transactions, whereby one person transacts Adult to Adult, and the response which comes back is, for example, a Child to Parent transaction or alternatively, a response which is a Parent to Child transaction, the former being the most common form of transferential response. In response to a transactional stimulus some internal event takes place, and some feature of the stimulus resonates unconsciously and a shift of ego states takes place. The process of resonance with the past and the accompanying shift of ego states is a form of transference. Transference may not be so apparent or obvious for basic analysis of transactions and is often better understood transactionally through analysis of ulterior transactions. In ulterior transactions, there are two levels of communication: the social-level transaction; and the psychological-level transaction. In practice, transference tends to operate at this psychological level. Reflection upon a therapy session and the types of ulterior transactions taking place can give the therapist a rich sense of the transference and its manifestations in the therapeutic relationship.

RUBBERBANDS

Rubberbanding (Kupfer and Haimowitz, 1971) is another evocative phrase to describe how certain situations lead us to 'respond at times as though we had been catapulted back to early childhood scenes' (Stewart and Joines, 1987: 111). This rubberbanding is a transferential response. Learning about our ego state shifts gives us information about our own patterns of rubberbanding, and we may be able to identify triggers and features over time. TA therapy involves the recognition of rubberbanding, the identification of the triggers and the gradual healing of the original scenes we rubberband back to.

SWEATSHIRTS

Berne (1972), in his ever creative manner, encouraged therapists to imagine that their clients had imaginary sweatshirts on, each bearing a slogan relating to the client's unconscious presentation to the world (the slogan on the front of the sweatshirt) and the client's script pay-off, or required outcome (the slogan on the back of the sweatshirt). Berne believed that these operate out of awareness, possibly at an unconscious level, and that our unconscious will intuitively identify and respond to the slogans on both the front and back of the sweatshirts the people we meet are 'wearing'. How we react to these depends, of course, on our own script.

GAMES

Games are transferential phenomena. Individuals issue game invitations to repeat the past in some way. The 'gimmicks', or vulnerabilities (Berne, 1972), that trigger the response to the game invitation are also based on an individual's script. The interaction of these two transactions and the various moves of the game are all connected with transference and represent some unconscious desire to repeat the past. Games also include elements of projective identification (a form of transferential phenomenon) as the projector will behave and relate to the recipient of their projections in ways which provoke, or invite the recipient to act out the sought-out response (Woods, 1996). This in turn reinforces the script and does not 'heal' the original issue, which will come back to haunt the client again and again. Understanding games provides the transactional analyst with a useful way of understanding transference interactions and enactments.

THE DRAMA TRIANGLE AS A TOOL TO EXPLORE COUNTERTRANSFERENCE

The drama triangle (Karpman, 1968) is a widely used piece of TA theory that is easily grasped and readily applied in understanding and analysing games. The drama triangle describes three psychological roles that people adopt in the course of their games. The roles are: Persecutor, Rescuer and Victim (see Figure 27.1). The words are capitalized to draw a distinction between a 'real-life' rescuer, persecutor and victim, for example, in the case of a person who has slipped into the river and is drowning and who gets pulled from the water; the person who was drowning would be a 'real-life victim' and their saviour would be a 'real-life rescuer'. Similarly, a mugger would be a real-life persecutor (although they would probably also be a psychological Persecutor!).

Berne (1964) understood and described games as unconscious processes which place them in the realm of transference phenomena. As the drama triangle is a method of game analysis, it can be used in identification and analysis of the transference and countertransference dynamics aspects of the therapeutic relationship. Using the drama triangle to analyse the transference/countertransference provides the therapist with a simple but rapid method of exploring the subtle relationship dynamics unfolding in the therapy. At the simplest level, the therapist pays attention to their urges, or impulses with regard to which of the drama triangle positions they want to take up with their client at any given point. Noticing which position we want to take up in relation to the client is useful in beginning to explore our countertransference.

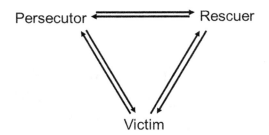

Figure 27.1 The drama triangle
Source: Karpman (1968).

Countertransference rarely exists in isolation, and is usually woven up with the client's transference. Analysis of the therapist's drama triangle countertransference may well shed some light on the position the client is taking. It may be that this is characteristic of the client's way of relating; however, it will also have features which are unique, and which are being co-created by the therapist and client at this particular time. They may also relate to the therapist proactively projecting some aspect of their own script into the relationship, or of inviting some kind of response from a client. For example, negative transference (such as the client believing the therapist does not like them) can have its basis in the therapist's behaviour or demeanour. Many therapists have been trained to maintain a 'neutral face' during sessions. This is problematic because a number of research studies have shown that people with depression and anxiety are more likely to perceive neutral faces as hostile (Leppännen et al., 2004; Yoon and Zinbarg, 2008). No amount of attentive listening is going to overcome this intrinsic bias, and therefore the negative transference this elicits may well generate an obstacle in the therapy that is easily remedied by the therapist consciously relaxing their facial muscles and conveying warmth instead.

One means of analysing the therapist's reactions is to explore whether we are adopting a complementary role to the client, for example, a desire to Rescue in response to the client adopting a Victim stance, or they may be concordant and represent the therapist identifying with and resonating at some level with some aspect of the client's psyche, for example, by feeling like a victim in the same way the client did as a child (Clarkson, 1992a; Racker, 1968). Generally, positions on the drama triangle are not static, and at some point in the process of a game, a switch of roles occurs. It is important that the therapist notices their own internal shift in relation to the drama triangle positions.

This, of course, presupposes that the therapist has a great deal of awareness of their own particular configuration of experiences, feelings, impulses and behaviours in relation to each of the drama triangle positions. The overwhelming majority of therapists are drawn to the profession by their tendency to Rescue, therefore identification of being drawn into a Rescuer position is not difficult for most therapists, but still needs careful attention to be paid to the textural differences between its different manifestations. Many therapists are also familiar with the Victim position, and can offer a great deal of understanding to the plight of others in this position. What is not so comfortable is exploring our tendencies towards Persecuting, and the many guises, variations and subtle differences between our differing Persecutory behaviours. These often manifest as feeling some sort of disapproval about some aspect(s) of a client's life, or from using confrontation perhaps a little too often or too heavily. It is prudent for the therapist to spend a great deal of time systematically gaining more information on their own particular brand of drama triangle manifestations, from each of the positions, and particularly to explore these in therapy. Group therapy is especially powerful at generating situations where we can explore our own tendencies. As we develop and change in terms of our sophistication, so do our games, and our manifestations of our games, and the therapist is therefore advised to periodically review and update their understanding of their drama triangle manifestations, as well as be attentive to how others experience them (and ideally, seek feedback from others about this). This greater self-awareness is likely to increase the therapist's sensitivity and responsiveness to their clients.

TRANSFERENCE AND COUNTERTRANSFERENCE: AN AIDE-MÉMOIRE OF TA MODELS

There are essentially two aspects to transference: (1) the needed relationship; and (2) the repeated relationship (Little, 2013). All taxonomies of transference are ultimately differing ways of conceptualizing these two dimensions. The needed relationship relates to the client's (unconscious) desire to meet historical needs, and can be viewed from a humanistic perspective as being driven by the client's striving towards health; the client's urge to obtain the needed relationship experience which will 'heal' their script. The repeated relationship refers to the client's (unconscious) urge to repeat the original scenario, which is usually one that mirrors the client's early experiences with their caregivers/parents. One perspective on this is that this repetition seeks to 'do it right' at last, and gain mastery over the original traumatic scenario.

Clarkson (1992a), developing the material of Racker (1968), discusses two types of countertransference: (1) complementary; and (2) concordant countertransference. Complementary countertransference involves the therapist being 'recruited' to take a complementary role in the client's script, usually by taking on the projected experience of the client's Parent. The therapist experiencing complementary countertransference may find they feel subtly critical of their client or that they are distracted in sessions and not paying attention to their client or taking them seriously.

With concordant countertransference, the client is somehow communicating to the therapist some aspect of their Child

 DOI: 10.4324/9781003375890-31

experience that the therapist resonates with in some way. The therapist experiences first-hand the feelings the client felt as a child. This can be a deeply unsettling and disturbing experience. For example, in working with a client who was abused in childhood, the therapist may find in sessions they are left feeling powerless and despairing and filled with desires to make it all OK for their client. They may be left questioning themself, and feeling inadequate. If understood as concordant counter-transference, the therapist can be seen in this situation as taking on board, and understanding at a profound level, some important aspects of the client's internal experience.

Clarkson also discusses two additional types of counter-transference: (1) reactive countertransference; and (2) proactive countertransference. Reactive countertransference is where the therapist reacts to the client's transferential material. Proactive countertransference is considered to originate in the therapist, and the therapist's transference towards the client. The relational approach to therapy considers that understanding countertransference includes examining both proactive (related to the therapist's own vulnerabilities and script) and reactive (reacting to the client's material) countertransference, and how the two interact. Countertransference is considered to be an interactive, co-constructed story that inevitably includes both proactive and reactive elements.

Moiso (1985) also developed TA thinking around transference by linking types of transference to the structural model of ego states. He categorized transference into P2 transferences, which are a relatively straightforward projection of the Parent onto the other, and P1 transferences, which involve the projection of earlier, more primitive, split (all good or all bad) Parent ego states onto the other. Hargaden and Sills (2002) developed Moiso's thinking and identified three types of transference: (1) introjective; (2) projective; and (3) transformational. Introjective transferences are deep relational longings, held and originating in the C0 ego state. They integrate Kohut's (1984) selfobject transferences of mirroring, idealizing and twinship as the varieties of introjective transference needs. Introjective transference is a variety of the therapeutically needed relationship. Introjective transference is considered to be always present, although it may be hidden by projective or transformational transferences as it relates to the emotional nourishment the client takes from therapy throughout (C. Sills, 2 May 2008, relational TA forum).

Projective transferences originate in the P1 ego state. They are defensive and splitting transferences. The projective transferences are aspects of the repeated relationship, whereby the client recapitulates aspects of the primary relational experience in the therapy in order to gain mastery over their unconscious process. For example, experiencing the therapist as either hated or hateful or, conversely, as an object of idealization. The projection reduces their internal tension and can be seen as an attempt to re-work their early introjects.

Transformational transferences may originate from either the C1 or P0 ego states. They involve the projection of primitive affect onto the therapist for the therapist to metabolize, process, detoxify and, eventually, to re-present the experience back to the client in a form the client can assimilate. This is usually discussed as projective identification.

The approach to working with the transference varies, and is dependent upon careful diagnosis of the client's level of internal organization (McWilliams, 1994). More disturbed clients may need greater levels of disclosure and transparency from the therapist, to contrast with their projections. As clients with more severe problems often experience projections in global terms, it is important that these projections and distortions be corrected. Clients with higher levels of functioning may need the therapist to be more opaque so that their projective distortions emerge and become apparent and thus are able to be worked with in the therapy.

ENDING TA THERAPY

Effective and therapeutic endings are a central part of the therapeutic journey, and need to be given due acknowledgement as an important part of the therapy process. The psychotherapy relationship is peculiar among relationships in that the ending of the relationship is at the very least implicit from the start; clients come expecting that the therapy will be effective and they will move beyond it and eventually have no need for therapy or the therapist. The contracting and goal-setting process at the beginning generates an initial idea of what the criteria for ending the relationship will be and the estimated length of therapy. Generally, people do not enter relationships that are as intense or important in their lives as the psychotherapy relationship with the expectation that they will end, and yet as therapists this is exactly what we do with every new client we meet. Berne (1966/1994) identified three types of endings in therapy:

1. *Accidental.* Sometimes changes in a client's work patterns or circumstances mean that they are no longer able to attend therapy. Such changes are commonplace, and a feature of modern life that often cannot be avoided. However, there is also always the possibility that the changes enable a client to satisfy some kind of unconscious process such as them seeking to avoid or withdraw from therapy because it is generating a lot of unconscious turbulence for the client. Obviously the therapist has no way of knowing that this is the case, and regardless of the cause of the accidental ending, the therapist needs to be attentive to ending as satisfactorily as possible under the circumstances.

2. *Resistant.* A resistant ending would be seen in a client who suddenly and inexplicably withdraws from therapy. Sometimes excuses or 'reasons' (as in the acting-out process described above) are given for this that mean that a formal ending process cannot take place.

3. *Therapeutic.* Obviously the most desirable type of ending is the therapeutic ending which 'occurs when the therapist and patient agree that the planned therapeutic goals have been attained, and that either an interruption or a final termination is in order' (Berne, 1966/1994: 13).

4. *Enforced.* Tudor (1995) adds a fourth type of ending: enforced. An example of an enforced ending might be where a therapist closes their practice, for instance, when relocating to another city. Enforced endings can be very difficult to manage and must be done sensitively, and with due regard to the client's issues (e.g., 'abandonment wounds'). To some extent, enforced endings are likely to be difficult for therapists to manage in a maximally therapeutic way. The ethical therapist is wise to do all they can to conduct the ending in a way that minimizes reinforcement of the client's script wherever possible, although even with the best will in the world, a script-reinforcing ending may occur.

The ending process can also facilitate the surfacing of a range of issues that have not previously emerged in the therapy. Such issues need to be recognized and dealt with to enhance the ending as a significant part of the whole therapy. Clarkson (2003) offers some common client reactions to the ending of therapy. In summary, these themes that may require working through include: satisfaction and achievement; guilt and re-grets; anger and disappointments; sadness and nostalgia; fear and trepidation; envy and gratitude; relief and release; anticipation; past losses; existential themes. Working through these, or similar issues as they present in the final stages of the therapy will add to the value of the therapy, and provide for a more complete therapy process, providing that in the ending process script issues are not inadvertently reinforced.

Longer-term therapy may require a period of reflection on the process and mourning, so both client and therapist can end the relationship in a mutually satisfying, growthful way (Maroda, 1994/2004).

The planned, therapeutic ending of relatively short-term therapy is usually a positive experience; the client has got what they wanted out of therapy and is leaving, feeling satisfied with the outcome. There are certain procedures I include in therapy endings. The first is to engage the client in a conversation about what might be signs for them that things are not going well. These early warning signs (or 'prodromes', as they are called) can be noted, so that the client can identify that they need support should problems arise in the future. I also engage the client in identifying an action plan about what they would do in those circumstances. One option is usually to return to therapy. The other procedure I use as part of ending therapy is to ask the client for feedback regarding what has been the most helpful, useful or important thing that I have done as a therapist. The responses to this can be quite surprising. They seldom relate to some stunning intervention the therapist made, and usually refer to a supportive relationship with an authentic, caring human being who offered them compassion, acceptance and understanding.

Part 3

ASSESSMENT, DIAGNOSIS AND CASE FORMULATION IN TA

THE IMPORTANCE OF
OBSERVATION

Observation is the basis of all good clinical work, and takes precedence even over technique.

(Berne, 1966/1994: 65–66)

All assessment or diagnosis begins with observation.[1] Without observation, the therapist cannot make any kind of assessment or diagnosis. Indeed, observation forms the backdrop for all interventions and treatment planning. Observation is more complex than simply noticing facets of the client's behaviour. It involves detailed observation of both self and the client and the maintenance of a curious, enquiring stance in relation to what we observe.

'The therapist should be aware of the probable physiological state of every one of his patients during every moment of the session' (ibid.: 66). Although this is a rather unrealistic expectation of the therapist, the essence of what Berne appears to be saying here is that the therapist needs to develop their observational skills, going beyond the purely obvious, and to maintain this throughout therapy. Observation includes being sensitive to the client's facial expressions and fluctuations in facial muscular tone, facial colouring, gestures (even absent gestures), and wondering about the significance of these. The therapist needs to observe even minute changes on a moment-to-moment basis and maintain an attitude of curiosity about what these changes might indicate about each client's internal state. Listening forms a central part of the observational process in psychotherapy. The therapist is not just listening to the content of what the client is saying, but also to the words used, vocabulary, metaphors, sentence structure, breathing sounds, pitch, tone and rhythm (Berne, ibid.; 1972). Beyond this, the therapist is also listening to the client's process behind the words and the way they speak; is the client's language, for example, descriptive, evocative, brief, flat, precise, disjointed, or over-detailed? Observing and checking for inconsistency or incongruity between a client's words and their body language, or even how they say what they say is an important skill for TA therapists (Stewart, 2007) and can suggest the presence of areas of conflict which can then be sensitively brought into the therapy for discussion. Berne, however, cautioned against a 'navel-gazing' approach to observation, and gave transactional analysts a clear instruction not to be complacent about the complex nature of communication when he said: 'The therapist should not be beguiled by the currently fashionable talk about nonverbal communication into forgetting the fact that it will take years of study for him to master the subtleties of verbal communication' (Berne, 1966/1994: 71).

It can be very fruitful for a therapist to sensitively share their observations, and their 'wonderings' about their observations. This is done in a spirit of curiosity and collaborative dialogue, to engage the client in the process of learning about their own mental states. Such an actively curious enquiring approach enhances both the therapist's and the client's capacity for mentalization (Bateman and Fonagy, 2006). To a transactional analyst, everything is important. Even seemingly insignificant details and ways the client presents or expresses their self are important (Erskine et al., 1999). The same authors also highlight the importance of the therapist avoiding the temptation of making presuppositions about the client's experience, and suggest the therapist adopts a tentative stance in their inferences.

Berne invited transactional analysts to sensitively and unobtrusively find opportunities to observe people of all ages engaging in natural social interaction. Berne did not advise making inferences on the basis of these observations, but to simply note which behaviours the individuals engaged in, and what happened next. Such observation can reveal information about age-appropriate behaviours, which can be helpful in making behavioural diagnosis about an individual's ego states.

Observation should not be just of the client though – the therapist should pay close attention to observing themselves, their own internal state, their feelings, memories and thoughts that are evoked in the therapy and by the client when thinking about their client outside therapy sessions. Observation of one's own internal state is particularly useful in developing social diagnosis of the client, and in monitoring one's countertransference and analysing its significance (Hargaden and Sills, 2002; Lammers, 1992; Novellino, 1984; Widdowson, 2008).

Transactional analysts in the UK seeking certification as a transactional analyst and registration with the UK Council for Psychotherapy (UKCP) are required to undergo a mental health familiarization placement. An important part of this placement involves having an opportunity to sensitively observe people with a range of mental health problems. The placement can help the therapist develop skills in noticing what mental health professionals are looking for in determining the severity of the client's problems. The placement can also help the therapist gain insight into what it is like having a range of mental disorders, including the cognitive and affective symptoms of various disorders. Taking time to find out what being a service user within mental health services is really like can be an eye-opening, and sometimes distressing, experience. It is one that nevertheless is important for a therapist, who can then use this learning to increase their empathy towards clients who use such services. The insights from the placement can be especially important for lay people with no previous background in mental health.

From their observations, the therapist begins to form tentative inferences about the client. The therapist then uses these tentative inferences to inform their next stage of assessment or diagnosis.

NOTE

1 The word diagnosis is one which many therapists find problematic, due to its pathologizing associations and links to 'the medical model' of therapy. As such, I will use the words assessment and diagnosis interchangeably throughout this book – the reader can settle on which word they prefer.

CONDUCTING A STRUCTURED INTAKE ASSESSMENT

Developing a clear and thorough picture of the client through assessment is an essential part of the initial stages of any psychotherapy. Ideally, this is best done in a structured intake assessment process. This can be done by asking the client to complete an intake form and a brief initial consultation, or by inviting the client for a longer assessment session (personally, I use the former method). It is important to strike a good balance between letting the client discuss their presenting problems and how they affect them, letting the client 'offload' to some extent (for a number of clients, this will be the first time they have discussed many of their issues) and obtaining information that is useful in identifying the client's central concerns/problems, selecting a focus for therapy (or several areas of focus), and establishing the client's goals for therapy. These then inform the overall assessment/diagnosis and treatment plan for the client. I offer here areas of consideration that may help in this process. Another important aspect of assessment is identifying if you are a 'good match' for the client, not only in terms of whether you and the client experience a sense of rapport, but also if you feel you have the right set of skills and experience to work with them effectively.

1. *Demographics.* Client age, gender, current living situation/relationship, type of job (if relevant). Accounting for the client's intersectional identity here is important in contextualizing the client and identifying whether any potential adjustments need to be made to the therapy (e.g., with neurodiverse clients), or if the impact of minority

stress needs to be accounted for (Meyer, 1995; Mirowsky and Ross, 1989). Note: when presenting in supervision, it is advisable to hide some details to preserve the client's anonymity.

2. *Presenting problems and client's theory of problems and theory of change.* What are the client's main concerns and problems they are seeking therapy for? How do these problems manifest in their everyday life? How severe does the client feel they are? What is the client's view on the origin of these problems? What do they think will help? If there is more than one problem, which does the client feel is most important to address? Which problems cause them the most difficulty? What, in your view, would be the most rational area of focus for the therapy?

3. *Symptoms.* What symptoms does the client experience? How severe are they? How do they affect the client's functioning? Do the symptoms seem to indicate a particular psychological disorder or fit the symptom pattern for a particular diagnostic category from ICD-11 (WHO, 2019) or the DSM-5 (APA, 2013)? I strongly recommend that all therapists routinely use screening tools and outcome measures as part of their assessment process. I personally use CORE-10 (which measures overall levels of functioning and distress), PHQ-9 (which measures depressive symptoms), GAD-7 (which measures anxiety symptoms) and ACE's form (which identifies a number of Adverse Childhood Experiences). All of these measures are freely available online (see also Point 90).

4. *Medical and mental health history/previous therapy.* Does the client have any diagnosed physical or mental health problems? Are they taking any medication? When did they last have a general health check-up? Have they had any previous counselling or therapy? What was their experience of previous therapy? What was helpful and what wasn't? Have they used any self-help methods?

5. *Goals.* What are the client's goals for therapy? (I suggest the client identifies between three and five goals.) Are these goals realistic? How motivated is the client to make

changes in their life? How will they know when they have achieved their goals?

6. *Lifestyle and psychosocial factors:* What is the client's sleeping pattern? What is the client's diet? Do they engage in regular exercise? What is their typical weekly alcohol/recreational drug consumption? What does a typical day look like for the client? Do they have a support network? Do they have long-term friendships or relationships? Are they experiencing any relationship conflict either in their family, with friends, or at work or school?

7. *Life history:* How does the client describe their childhood and adolescence? What was school like for them? What are the major life events or significant events or periods of time in their life? Have they ever experienced anything traumatic? Did anything happen in childhood or adolescence which might be considered abuse? Where clients disclose trauma, I also use the PCL-5 measure to identify trauma symptoms and as part of a trauma-informed approach (see Point 58).

8. *Mental state.* How did the client tell their story? Over-detailed? Impressionistic? Vague? What were the client's gestures? Was the client smartly dressed? Did the client appear not to be taking care over their appearance? Did the client seem focused or were they easily distracted and confused? Was there any agitation? Is there a slowness or a flight of thought? Is there a flatness of mood, or extreme emotional lability?

9. *Attachment style.* What is your impression of the client's attachment style? Secure, avoidant, ambivalent or disorganized? What do you provide as evidence of this? What do you imagine the impact of this will be on the development of the working alliance? How does this impact upon your treatment planning and approach to therapy with this client?

10. *Obstacles to therapy.* Ask the client how they might potentially sabotage their therapy. What do you anticipate problems in therapy to be? Are there features of the client's presentation or perspective that may pose problems in the

therapy process? Are there external factors that may interfere with the therapy?

11. *Expectations and preferences.* What are the client's expectations of therapy and the role of the therapist? What is the client's expectation regarding the length of therapy, and their engagement in the process? Does the client have any specific preferences regarding the type of therapy they want, what they want from the therapist and what they think they need?

12. *Strengths and resources.* What strengths does the client have? What resources do they have that will be useful in the change process? This can include friends and family relationships, personal qualities, level of insight, and may also include additional factors, such as a client's economic situation (which can mean greater opportunities for change potentially available to the client). What personal qualities or perspectives does the client have that will be useful in therapy or in effecting change in their life?

13. *Motivation for therapy.* Does the client appear to be well motivated for therapy? Is the client being encouraged, coerced or pushed into therapy by someone else?

14. *Prognosis.* Taking into account the nature, severity and duration of the client's problems, and the resources they have, their level of motivation, and the level of rapport between the client and the therapist, what conclusion can be drawn regarding the expected length and frequency of therapy? Does this match the client's expectations? What will the client's problem severity be at the end of therapy, as an educated guess?

ASSESSING SUITABILITY
FOR TA THERAPY

LIMITATIONS OF THE PRACTITIONER

Recognition of the limitations of one's training and experience is important in determining whether we should take on a particular client. It goes without saying that we should not work with clients when we do not have the skills or knowledge to work with these clients effectively. The issue is, where do we draw the line? We have to gain experience at some point, and sometimes it may not be apparent at the outset that we do not have the required skills or knowledge to work with someone. In this instance, the primary determining factor has to be the principle of protection; is there sufficient safety to work with this client, at this time? If we cannot provide sufficient safety, we must refer the client on appropriately.

If in the course of working with someone the therapist discovers issues or problems that are unfamiliar to them, it is important that the therapist seeks supervisory advice and makes serious attempts to extend their knowledge in the particular area, through reading and attending relevant workshops. To some extent, therapists who regularly engage in a wide range of reading on different presenting issues will be in a better position to judge than those who do not.

RESOURCES

Do you have the resources to work with this client at this time? It is not advisable to take on new clients who present in intense distress if you have a lot of holiday time coming up, or if you do not have the space in your diary to see them at least

DOI: 10.4324/9781003375890-36

once a week. If the client is presenting with risk of harm to self or others, or clients who have more severe levels of distress and impaired functioning, do you have the resources to support them? Explaining in detail during intake what your limitations are (such as no out-of-hours calls unless in an emergency) is advisable. Unless you have specialist training, and immediate access to necessary medical back-up, generally therapists will not have the resources to work with someone presenting with drug or alcohol addiction until the client has completed a medically supervised withdrawal and detoxification programme.

LIMITATIONS OF AVAILABLE SERVICE

Are there limitations in terms of the service the client can access? Therapists who work for agencies sometimes have to work with the constraints of maximum numbers of sessions, which can range from 6 to 20 sessions. In this case, it is important that the therapist be realistic regarding what change is possible for the client in such limited circumstances. Sometimes clients presenting in private practice also have limitations to their resources, and so may not be able to afford to come for weekly therapy. In general, if a client is not able to afford to come weekly for at least three months, then it is perhaps better to refer the client on to a low-cost or free counselling service.

PSYCHOLOGICAL MINDEDNESS

Psychological mindedness refers to the individual's capacity for self-observation, self-reflection and a capacity to consider psychological factors as being significant in one's problems and present situation, as well as the possibility that unconscious psychological forces impact upon our motivation. This includes a capacity to consider one's past as being significant in relation to how one is in the present. In order to engage in therapy a degree of psychological mindedness needs to be present from the outset. Does the client have some self-awareness and insight into their problems? How strong is their capacity for self-reflection? Do they have any understanding as to how they impact on others or on how others experience them?

AVAILABLE ADULT EGO STATE

In the initial sessions the therapist needs to make an assessment of the client's available Adult ego state. This assessment is by nature subjective and needs to take account of the client's presenting problem and whether the client appears to have the Adult resources needed to engage in therapy at the level required. Clients who appear to have little Adult ego state to the extent that functioning is seriously impaired may need referral for psychiatric evaluation and possibly medication before therapy can proceed safely. With clients with little Adult ego state available, the therapist needs to determine, in consultation with their supervisor, whether they have the skills and resources to help the client develop and strengthen their Adult ego state.

ABILITY TO ENTER A CONTRACT

Can the client reasonably consent to therapy? Is the client being coerced or otherwise being persuaded to enter into therapy? Is the client in a position to make a reasonably informed choice about whether to enter therapy or not? Is the stated contract goal realistic? This includes attending to the client's level of motivation for change (Woollams and Brown, 1978).

USING BERNE'S FOUR METHODS
OF DIAGNOSIS

Berne identified four methods of diagnosis needed for an accurate diagnosis of ego states (Berne, 1961/1986): (1) behavioural diagnosis; (2) social diagnosis; (3) historical diagnosis; and (4) phenomenological diagnosis. Although in practice behavioural diagnosis is the most commonly used for initial diagnostic purposes, to form or verify an accurate diagnosis, all four methods must be used. These methods were originally developed for diagnosis of ego states, but can be adapted for a range of diagnostic purposes.

BEHAVIOURAL DIAGNOSIS

Often, the initial behavioural diagnosis is based on the therapist's first impression of their client, which can begin from the client's first contact with the therapist, as well as the client's behaviour in the initial session. In forming a behavioural diagnosis, the therapist needs to maintain an open-minded position and keep any diagnostic hypotheses as tentative. By nature, behavioural diagnosis is often generalized in that we make an inference about the ego state someone is 'in' based on generalized assumptions on how children or parents behave. Due to the relatively universal way that both children and parents behave, and the experience we all have with children and parents in general, behavioural diagnosis can be somewhat reliable. Behavioural diagnosis may also include the therapist referring to child development theory in considering the developmental stage of the presenting Child ego states in terms of how the displayed behaviour would be age-appropriate for a

    DOI: 10.4324/9781003375890-37

particular age group. It is important, however, that behavioural diagnosis is not based simply on one behavioural clue, but is made up from detailed observation and behaviour clusters which together show a consistent pattern. Once an initial behavioural diagnosis is made, the therapist should ask themselves: 'What is my evidence for my conclusion? Would this diagnosis or hypothesis sound plausible to others?'

SOCIAL DIAGNOSIS

Social diagnosis is used when we draw upon our own reactions to a person, and notice our own ego state response to the individual to inform our diagnosis of the individual's ego state. Social diagnosis in therapy involves use of the therapist's countertransference. The use of the therapist's countertransference can add a degree of potency to the social diagnosis; however, the degree of self-awareness of the therapist making the diagnosis is absolutely critical. To effectively use one's own responses, one has to have a good degree of understanding about the meaning of one's own responses and own shifts in ego states as well as having the ability to pay attention to one's own internal experience on a moment-to-moment basis. These responses must be acknowledged and reflected upon, rather than being immediately acted out. Some questions the practitioner can reflect upon include: 'What is my internal reaction to this person? What ego state do I go into? How do I want to respond to them? Would others likely have a similar reaction to the same stimulus?'

HISTORICAL DIAGNOSIS

In historical diagnosis we find out the historical significance of the behaviour, thought patterns or feeling(s). The therapist builds a picture of the historical diagnosis through the usual conversational flow of psychotherapy, but can establish or verify a historical diagnosis by asking, 'Did you or anyone else do this in the past? Does this remind you of anyone or anything?' Such questioning can reveal sometimes surprising data, in that behaviour we had considered to be Child, is in fact Parent, which is established by a client, for example, describing how one of their parents, who was often in a Child ego state used the same behaviour. Similarly, behaviour we think of as Parent can in actual fact be Child, as in the case of people who were overly responsible, or even 'parentified' as children. Historical diagnosis also needs to be tentative, as it is possible that the client may not have certain information, or not be able to remember certain things in order to verify the historical diagnosis.

PHENOMENOLOGICAL DIAGNOSIS

Phenomenological diagnosis is the subjective experience of an individual as being in a particular ego state as if it were happening now. This is most easily recognized with Child ego state, as we can all remember to some extent how we were and how we felt as children. Asking 'How old do you feel right now?' is often useful. Getting a subjective sense of what it felt like for one of our parents is more difficult, in that we have no way of knowing exactly how the individual was feeling at any one time, although we can have an intuitive sense that how we are feeling is probably how a particular parent felt in a particular situation. Phenomenological diagnosis also includes the transferential domain (Hargaden and Sills, 2002). In transference, the client is experiencing the therapist as if the therapist were in actual fact the transferential figure, although because of the unconscious nature of transference, the client may not be aware of the transference. Analysis of the transference can suggest the phenomenological diagnosis of a particular experience in that the client may be transferentially responding as they did as a child (complementary transference – seeking a complementary Parental response), or they may be responding as one of their parents did (concordant transference – seeking to replicate their parents or induce their child response in the other) (Clarkson, 1992a). Clearly, social diagnosis of the therapist's countertransference needs to be accounted for if diagnosis is made in this way.

Subjective, phenomenological diagnosis of the Adult ego state is also difficult in that most people would assume that most of the time they are in Adult ego state. This is complicated by the fact that when we are coming from a contaminated Adult ego state, by definition, we are mistaking some Parent or Child content for the Adult ego state. It is unfortunate, and perhaps a weakness in TA theory, that we form a diagnosis of the Adult by a process of elimination.

Diagnosis can also require the analysis and interpretation of vague, amorphous feeling, particularly when diagnosing early Child ego states (C1 or earlier structures). With such early Child ego states, the client is unlikely to have a specific memory to verify historical diagnosis. At this level, diagnosis may be done using the therapist's knowledge of child development theory (behavioural diagnosis), the therapist's countertransference (responses to the client's use of primitive defences), and the client's affective, phenomenological experience that will probably be overwhelming, oceanic and unexplainable or 'irrational'. A question which can be helpful in identifying pre-verbal issues is: 'Based on what you know, and what you feel in your body, what would you say your first three years of life were like for you?' (Sandra Paulsen, workshop presentation, 2021). It is the nature of such experiencing which provides the phenomenological diagnosis, rather than being able to link it to a specific incident or period of life.

DEVELOPING A CONVERSATIONAL INTERVIEWING TECHNIQUE

A number of TA authors have presented detailed script analysis questionnaires that they recommend therapists use with their clients in a structured way. The reality is that the overwhelming majority of TA therapists do not do script analysis in such a structured format. I advise therapists not to follow formal, structured methods of script analysis, but rather encourage therapists to draw the information out in a more conversational and informal manner (Cornell, 1986). I am not advocating the total abolition of script questionnaires, but rather that the therapist takes a different approach to the information gathering needed for script analysis. Despite this, I do advocate using a structured approach to assessment (see Point 31), although I recommend this is done using a semi-structured format. What I mean by this is that the therapist has a series of open-ended questions, and that they encourage the client to freely respond to these, prompting them to say a little more as seems appropriate. Striking a balance between being professional and having a level of informality the client is comfortable with is essential to this. Essentially the conversational flow within the session should be relaxed. Some ways therapists can improve their ability in this is by taking steps to improve their own verbal fluency, increase their vocabulary (especially around emotions), and match their language use to that of the client. For example, many clients from working-class backgrounds appreciate a more informal and relaxed approach. Telling the client that you don't mind if they use swear words can help people

DOI: 10.4324/9781003375890-38

feel more comfortable (and if it feels right, the therapist can swear too).

As clients tell their story, they often reveal aspects of their process. This becomes apparent in the consistencies, inconsistencies, jumping around from one area to another, aspects they focus on and aspects they minimize or discount, fractured or incoherent narrative which are parts of how the client presents in therapy (Allen and Allen, 1995; Holmes, 2001). These all provide information about the client's attachment style (Holmes, 2001), the client's level of developmental organization (McWilliams, 1994), their internal process and way of experiencing that world.

As the therapeutic 'conversation' unfolds, it is useful for the therapist to keep in mind what information they are seeking to obtain. What does the therapist need to know about their client in order to build up the case formulation and get a clearer idea as to how they might best help them? TA therapists are generally interested in developing some hypotheses about a client's injunctions, the kind of counterscript slogans they have internalized, their script themes in relationships, their overall script themes regarding their life course, their life position, the modelling and attributions they picked up from their environment while they were growing up.

Take some time to think about which aspects of the script apparatus you are most interested in exploring with your client, and think about what such information will tell you. What questions could you ask to find out this information? What information could the client volunteer for you to begin to formulate tentative hypotheses about these aspects of their script? What might you observe or experience in response to your client that might potentially shed some light on aspects of the client's script? Developing your own list of questions you might ask in therapy to elicit information can be a useful exercise. You can then embed these questions into your work with your clients, and ask them as and when the therapeutic conversation naturally turns to that topic. For instance, a client discussing how they struggle with receiving praise might be asked how both their parents praised them, and for what reason. What is their internal process when they do get praised? Do they avoid praise? If so, how? The process of enquiry and of expansion, clarification and obtaining detail of the emotional and cognitive content in situations provides you with adequate information to develop your script analysis and diagnosis for each client.

USING PRO-FORMAS FOR RAPID SCRIPT DIAGNOSIS

One surprisingly effective method for rapid script diagnosis is to use pro-formas at appropriate points in therapy (preferably in the first few sessions as you are building up your assessment picture of the client). The two I prefer are Adrienne Lee's (1998) drowning person diagram (see Figure 35.1) and a negative script beliefs list, which I adapted from a number of sources including a list of negative cognitions developed by Francine Shapiro (see Table 35.1).

I have printed, laminated versions of these two pro-formas to hand in my therapy room. When it feels the right time to do so, I will give my clients one of them. I ask the client to read through each of the statements on the page, and notice which ones resonate with them, and which out of the statements they feel they might be carrying. I ask them to pay close attention to their physical reactions as they read each statement, telling them that they will likely experience a 'gut reaction' to the ones that 'fit for them'. I ask them to tell me when that happens and what the statement says and I make a note of that. At the end of the process I may or may not repeat using the second pro-forma, if that feels appropriate. Sometimes clients want to process their experience first, in which case, it is best to follow the client's lead.

As injunctions and script beliefs are held at the unconscious, or edge of consciousness level of awareness, and are part of our implicit memory systems, it can be difficult to articulate them. Offering the clients a set of established common themes to

DOI: 10.4324/9781003375890-39

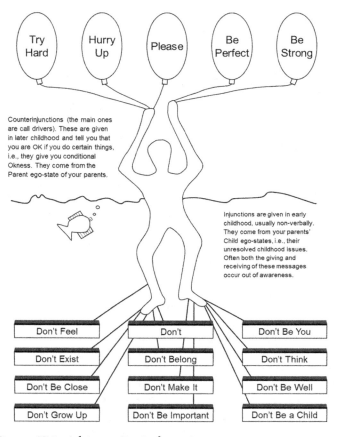

Try Hard

Hurry Up

Please

Be Perfect

Be Strong

Counterinjunctions (the main ones are call drivers). These are given in later childhood and tell you that you are OK if you do certain things, i.e., they give you conditional Okness. They come from the Parent ego-state of your parents.

Injunctions are given in early childhood, usually non-verbally. They come from your parents' Child ego-states, i.e., their unresolved childhood issues. Often both the giving and receiving of these messages occur out of awareness.

Don't Feel

Don't

Don't Be You

Don't Exist

Don't Belong

Don't Think

Don't Be Close

Don't Make It

Don't Be Well

Don't Grow Up

Don't Be Important

Don't Be a Child

Figure 35.1 Adrienne Lee's drowning person

choose from can help them identify which ones fit their own personal experience. By using the physical, 'gut reaction' means of confirmation, we allow the client's implicit memory system to 'recognize' what implicit belief or learning they have developed, based on past experiences, and that are relevant in making sense of their current problems (Ecker, Ticic and Hulley, 2012).

Table 35.1 Negative script beliefs list

Self-beliefs, worth, and value as a person	Beliefs about self in relation to others	Beliefs about other people	Beliefs about life, and the world in general
I am not good enough	I am too much for other people/too needy	Others are unreliable and untrustworthy	Life is painful
I am inferior/weak	I can't let other people in	Others will reject or abandon me	The world is a dangerous and unsafe place
I am inadequate	I never fit in or belong anywhere	Other people intentionally do bad things to hurt me	The world is a cruel and unfair place
I am insignificant	I must always worry about what other people think of me	Other people will criticize and mock me	Life has no meaning
I am a bad/terrible person	I must always take care of others	Other people don't want me around	There is no point to anything
There is something wrong with me/I am defective	I don't get on well with other people	Others are more powerful and smarter than me	Everyone is destined to be unhappy
I don't deserve anything good/to be happy	I am not a people person	Others are selfish	The world is confusing and nothing makes sense
I am unlovable/unlikeable	I am better off on my own	Other people's needs and wishes are more important than mine	

(Continued)

Table 35.1 (Cont.)

Self-beliefs, worth, and value as a person	Beliefs about self in relation to others	Beliefs about other people	Beliefs about life, and the world in general
I am stupid	I am a relationship disaster	Other people only hang out with me because they feel sorry for me	
I am a failure	I must keep the peace at all costs	Other people manipulate and take advantage of others	
I always things up	I need someone to take care of me	Other people don't understand how special I am	
I cannot cope with life	I must be compliant and do what others want	Other people are stupid and deserve to be taken advantage of	
I am dull and boring	I must be approved of by others	Other people deserve all the bad things that happen to them	
I am unsuccessful and can never achieve anything	I cannot trust other people	Other people are worthless and insignificant	
I deserve special treatment	I don't have to follow the same rules as everyone else		
I am better than most other people			
I am a disappointment			

USING FUNCTIONAL AND STRUCTURAL ANALYSIS OF EGO STATES

A transactional analysis diagnosis begins with functional analysis and structural analysis of the client's ego states (Berne, 1961/1986). In formulating a TA diagnosis of their client, the therapist makes observations and starts to make inferences about the content and process of the client's ego state structure. These inferences are checked using the four methods of ego state diagnosis for verification (see Point 33).

You may find it helpful to make some notes about the relative and apparent strength or predominance of each ego state, including different Child ego states with their different ages and also including different Parent introjects in your structural analysis. Which ego states are used most? How are these ego states used? Which are underused? Which Parental introjects seem most powerful or most virulent and toxic? What is notable by its absence? What is your subjective sense of the most commonly presenting Child ego state that manifests in the therapy room? And in using the functional model (see Figure 36.1), what are your impressions of the client's internal Critical/ Structuring Parent, their internal Nurturing Parent, how these manifest in the client's day-to-day life and in their interactions with others? How do these contribute to the client's internal dialogue? Similarly, what is your impression of the client's level of Adapted Child responses (both compliant, rebellious and withdrawing), and also the client's capacity to access their Free Child ego state? Do they have sufficient Adult ego state for functioning and to engage

DOI: 10.4324/9781003375890-40

133

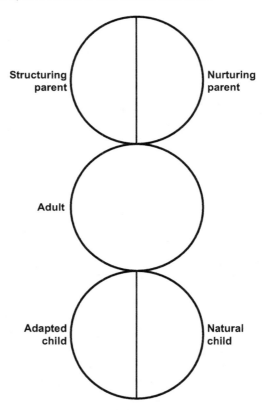

Figure 36.1 Functional model of ego states

in therapy? Can they use their Adult for reality testing and problem solving? Under what circumstances do they struggle to remain in Adult ego state (for instance, when feeling distressed, or during arguments with their partner, etc.)?

The content, affect and disturbances of each ego state category need to be accounted for. In TA, we use a second and third level of abstraction in sub-dividing ego states. Second-order and third-order structural models allow refinement in developing a comprehensive structural analysis of each client (see Figure 36.2). It can be hard to understand these various

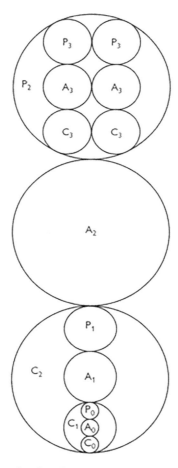

Figure 36.2 The third-order structural model
Source: Based on Berne (1961/1986).

sub-divisions of ego states. Perhaps the best explanation I have heard came from the organizational transactional analyst, Sari van Poelje (2022) in a workshop presentation. She likened the three circles, first-order model of ego states as being like filing cabinet drawers. When we access something, we open the relevant drawer and retrieve the relevant 'records'. Sometimes, she explained, we need a little more detail, so we might imagine three stacked archive cupboards, each containing three drawers, which represent the 'ego states within ego states' of the second-order structural model. We can sub-divide even further using the same archive cupboard and drawers metaphor to understand the third-order model. The purpose of these sub-divisions is to create more accuracy in identifying *where* a particular thing is located within a person's structure. However, it is important to note that structure is inferred – we cannot know it for certain. Also, remember: the circles used in ego state diagrams are only a schematic representation of the ego state model. They are not 'truth', but simply a way to understand levels of development and where a person might be 'holding' a specific issue or experience. Having the capacity to draw incredibly detailed and intricately complex diagrams of circles within circles has no bearing on anyone's ability as a therapist.

When engaging in structural analysis, apply Occam's razor, or the principle of parsimony, as Berne (1966/1994) recommended. In other words, use the simplest explanation that sufficiently explains the matter at hand and avoid unnecessarily complicating matters. In practice and when applied to structural analysis, this means starting using the first-order structural model (whereby there are three circles, to represent the Parent, Adult and Child ego states). Use this as an explanatory framework to make as much sense as possible of the client's experience. Once you have explained in as much detail as the model allows and if you think it is necessary, go to the next level of second-order structure, and so on with the third-order level of structure. As you proceed, it can be useful to ask yourself, 'How will this level of analysis help me in the room with my client?' If it is likely to be of little or no benefit or does not help you to construct or refine your interventions, then there is no point in engaging in this level of analysis; only use what will help you in the room.

The content, affect and disturbances of each ego state category need to be accounted for. Second-order and third-order structural models allow refinement in developing a detailed structural analysis of each client (see Figure 36.2). For example, accounting for the different Parental introjects a client has can be useful (e.g., mother, father, older sister, aunt, grandmother, grandfather, school teacher(s), religious leader, etc.), as can identifying which Parental introject(s) seem to be most problematic for the client, or which introject seems to be driving an internal ego state conflict. Similarly, identifying which introjects seem to carry transgenerational trauma can help with case formulation and intervention planning. We also need to remember that the client's introjects are not necessarily historically accurate representations of the client's actual parents, but are introjections of how the client experienced them at a particular point in time.

Structural analysis can include consideration of the client's different Child ego states according to age. The client will experience and present qualitatively different Child ego states according to the age and developmental stage of the ego state cathected. Social diagnosis and phenomenological diagnosis are most useful here. At its simplest, this involves checking with the client, 'How old do you feel, right now, as you think about this?' However, the therapist is advised to use a combination of their knowledge of their client, their understanding of typical child developmental trajectories, and their own clinical judgement and intuition in guiding their structural analysis of their client.

ACCOUNTING FOR INTERNAL EGO STATE DIALOGUE

When seeking to understand our client's internal world, it is helpful to consider what might be the content and process of the client's internal dialogue. Adding such dialogue in your analysis will add a dynamic element that accounts for the interactions and conflicts between the client's ego states and illustrates the script in action. Berne invited transactional analysts to account for this dialogue, which he described as 'voices in the head'.

> This dialogue between Parent, Adult and Child is not 'unconscious', but preconscious, which means that it can be easily brought into consciousness ... Once he understands what is going on, his next task is to give the patient permission to listen, and to teach her how to hear the voices which are still there in their pristine force from childhood. Here he may have to overcome several kinds of resistance. She may be forbidden to listen by Parental directives, such as: 'If you hear voices, you're crazy.' Her Child may be afraid of what she will hear. Or her Adult may prefer not to listen to the people governing her behaviour in order to maintain her illusion of autonomy ... As a general rule, phrases in the second person ('You should have', etc.) come from the Parent, while those in the first person ('I must', 'Why did I?' etc.) come from the Adult or Child. With some sort of encouragement, the patient soon becomes aware of his most important script directives as spoken in his head, and can report them to the therapist.

> (Berne, 1972: 369–370)

In practice, most of our clients experience a strong self-critical internal dialogue, which in TA we would consider as an internal

DOI: 10.4324/9781003375890-41

Critical Parent to Child dialogue (which then stimulates feelings of shame, inadequacy, and so on in the Child ego state), and a distinct lack of internal Nurturing Parent dialogue.

To facilitate awareness of the internal dialogue, invite clients to notice their internal dialogue, over a period of a week or more, and to simply note it. This can be done by inviting clients to jot down in a note-pad examples of the mental dialogue they 'hear'. At this point, the client is not being asked to consciously change or challenge the nature of the dialogue, but simply to become aware of it. From the therapist's point of view, obtaining a fuller picture of the dialogue is helpful for assessment/diagnosis purposes. Many subtle aspects of the dialogue from a variety of situations, at different times and in interaction with a range of people, or when experiencing different moods, can be lost if not captured at the time. Inviting clients to keep a writing pad handy (or to make use of the notes app on their phone) and make a note of the nature of the dialogue over a period of a few weeks will assist with increasing awareness of the dialogue in a range of situations. Analysis of the dialogue in terms of its historical origin ('Did anyone actually say this to you? If so, who?', or 'Does this remind you of anyone?', or 'How did you come to such conclusions about yourself?') can also suggest possible sites within the client's ego structure where the particular part of the dialogue may be coming from. For example, is the critical dialogue coming from the Parent ego state (P2), or a more primitive, earlier Parent, such as the Parent in the Child (P1)? Becoming aware of such dialogue will allow the client's process to open up, move into awareness, and as such, become amenable to later intervention.

The therapist has several choices of how to intervene, largely dependent upon their own interests and approach. Cognitive-behavioural methods can be used, by directly challenging or questioning the dialogue, similar to the way cognitive therapists challenge negative automatic thoughts (NATS) (Beck and Beck, 1995). A more psychodynamic approach is to direct the client's attention to the nature of the dialogue and to experience the conflict consciously. The dialogue can be explored in terms of its historical origins and the relational wishes, responses of self and expected responses of others encoded within it. This dialogue can also be brought into the relationship by repeatedly inviting the client to become aware of the internal dialogue they experience in sessions and in relation to the therapist. Redecision-based techniques where the client is invited to engage in a dialogue between ego states (using their Adult ego state to mediate between and respond to each ego state) during a session can also be fruitful.

An additional refinement that can be useful is to make a note of the nature and quality of interactions and means of interacting of each of the client's parents used in relation to the client. These can then be included in the dialogue in the structural analysis diagram. For example, perhaps one parent ignored the client, whereas the other was often angry with them and blaming. This interaction will probably be repeated either intrapsychically or interpersonally in the client's current life, and the client may also anticipate such responses from the therapist in therapy (Benjamin, 2003). Awareness of such interactions and inclusion of them in the diagnosis facilitates using any enactments therapeutically. Bary and Hufford (1990) highlight indicators for a client's readiness for ending psychotherapy. One indicator relevant here is that the client is ready for ending psychotherapy when 'She has an internal dialogue that nurtures and guides versus one that excuses or condemns' (ibid.: 220).

38

ACCOUNTING FOR CULTURAL AND RELIGIOUS PARENT

All development and all behaviour is culturally embedded and needs to be considered in relation to the culture in which the individual grows and lives.

(Tudor and Widdowson, 2008: 222)

Pearl Drego's (1983) concept of the Cultural Parent has been a significant contribution to transactional analysis theory, and consideration of the client's – and the therapist's – Cultural Parent and the potential interaction between the two is, in my view, recommended as standard routine practice with all clients. In doing structural analysis of the Parent ego state and script analysis, it is easy to focus exclusively on the client's parents, and the influence they had in the formation of the client's script, and to ignore the impact of cultural and religious Parent ego states. It is even easier to overlook these influences when they are identical to our own. Yet our environmental, social and cultural context plays a significant role in our script. Our cultural (and religious) introjects play an important part in our internal experience, and are mostly reinforced daily (certainly for those who are of the majority culture) in an implicit manner by dint of our being within a society and through our interactions with others. 'The dominant culture's wishes, demands, behaviour, and love are introjected through parental, family and community relationships and become part of the client's sense of self and personality' (Shadbolt, 2004: 120–121). All therapists can appreciate the powerful impact that having a quietly disapproving, or even an outright condemnatory parent would

DOI: 10.4324/9781003375890-42

have on the self-esteem of a developing person, and yet it is all too easy to overlook the experiential fact that similar processes take place intrapsychically on an implicit and unconscious level. These processes are influenced by an introjected cultural Parent, and the interaction between this cultural Parent and our sense of self, our Child ego state. The feminist movement first drew our attention to gender scripting and the related gender-stereotyped cultural Parent, and the powerful but hidden impact that patriarchy and misogyny have in shaping the self-esteem, the way of thinking and the expectations and behaviour of both women and men. The intrapsychic interaction between our cultural Parent and our own sense of self undoubtedly shapes our behaviour, our expectations, our way of thinking and our self-esteem. The components that interact include and go beyond our gender into our culture, our race, our sexuality and other factors which shape who we are.

Shivanath and Hiremath (2003) extend the concept of cultural scripting and develop a script matrix that accounts for cultural scripting factors. In their model they develop three layers of scripting: (1) the scripting that occurs within the family; (2) the individual's religious and cultural script; and (3) the wider (predominantly white and heterosexual) cultural scripting. Cultural scripting is indirect, and insidious. It is the implicit messages and values all around us, that are constantly present and which inform the workings and values of institutions, such as society, government, religious institutions, the media and, more recently, the influence of social media. For example, many people are rightfully very concerned about the impact social media is having on young women and their body image.

The socialization of the child also takes place in a wider social context, and in thinking about the individual we need to account for the powerful impact of peers, schooling, socialization, and the media. Peer relationships are enormously important to children and it is important to consider their contribution to the shaping of an individual's sense of self and self-esteem.

Religious aspects of a person's life also form part of an individual's Parent ego state, as religious figures, such as priests and ministers, as well as the religious institution, together with its own rules, code of conduct and beliefs, all become powerful introjects. Even people who have rejected religion are not exempt from its forces, and it is not unusual for people who had religious upbringings to be heavily influenced by them in adult life. Our sense of morality, our internal valuing processes, our ways of judging ourselves and our sense of personal ethics may all be deeply impacted by our own religious upbringing. This also has a powerful impact on an individual's Child ego state, and especially on their sense of being worthy of love and acceptance, and on the development of persistent shame and guilt. Religion and spirituality can be profoundly comforting and health-promoting for some people, however, for others, they can be limiting, punishing and at worst, destructive. Taking into account and working with a client's sense of spirituality and religion is recommended by many authors both within and outside of the TA community (e.g., Evans and Koenig Nelson, 2021; Mellacqua, 2016; Tudor, 2019).

The Dutch transactional analyst, Jennine Rook identifies how many religious clients experience the tension between homonomy (belonging) to the religious group and autonomy (self-determination) (Rook, in press). She goes on to explain:

> The Religious Parent can provide a positive loving and supportive culture where people can belong. A culture of forgiveness and a promising future in heaven. On the other hand the Religious Parent can cause problems relating to conditional belonging, adherence to strict rules and prejudices against people outside the group. This always results in the fear of not being forgiven, the fear (and felt sense) of not being good enough to belong and – in the end – not being good enough to go to heaven.
>
> (ibid.)

> As psychotherapists working with different cultures and communities, we need to work on both an intrapsychic level and at a level which addresses their [co-existing, multiple] cultural scripts. To ignore a person's cultural script, and the scripting from the wider white society, would be to deny the impact of culture, race and racism on their everyday lives.
>
> (Shivanath and Hiremath, 2003: 173)

Our cultural Parent also plays a part in how we feel about and experience our sexuality. As part of our socialization, we internalize messages about our gender, sexuality in general, and our own sexual orientation. Non-heterosexual people have to deal with the impact of carrying a cultural Parent which is not affirming of their very being, and will need to deal with the oppressive introjects as part of their own movement towards greater self-acceptance. For people who are not part of the dominant culture (white, heterosexual, able-bodied, etc.), then it is highly probable that the person has in effect two cultural Parents: one of the dominant culture; and one from their own (sub)culture. Inevitably, the sub-cultural Parent will be hugely influenced by, and shaped in relation to the dominant one, but will nevertheless be different. Individuals who do not conform to either cultural Parent's expectation are likely to feel disaffected and alienated; an experience which needs to be attended to in the diagnostic process and not misdiagnosed as being an indicator of psychopathology. One example of this is how many women who choose not to have children are often made to feel that they are somehow strange, or worse, that there is something 'wrong' with them for their choice not to have children. There is a dominant cultural expectation that one should want to have children. Anyone who varies from this cultural expectation lives with the spectre of non-acceptance on a day-to-day level.

39

ACCOUNTING FOR INTERSECTIONALITY AND OPPRESSION

As part of the process of understanding our client's internal world, the social and relational context of their development (and, as such, of the development of their script) and of their day-to-day lived experience, the therapist needs to account for the client's intersectional identity. Furthermore, as therapists, we need to also account for our own intersectional identity and of how our intersectional identity interacts with our client's intersectional identity (Baskerville, 2022).

Intersectionality is the term developed by Crenshaw (1989; 2019), which encompasses our different identities and lived experiences. In considering intersectionality, we take into account aspects of identity categorization, such as gender, race, cultural/ethnic background/heritage, sexual orientation, social class (which can include past and present social class, where these differ), economic status, physical (dis)ability, age, and whether one is neurotypical or neurodivergent. Each of these aspects of identity either holds power and privilege or has a lack of power, lack of privilege and an experience of systemic and lived oppression (Baskerville, 2022).

In accounting for our own and our client's intersectional identities, and the interaction of conscious and unconscious dimensions of power, privilege (and lack thereof) and oppression within the therapy room, we enhance the potential for therapy to be not only a source of personal liberation, but also a powerful agent of social justice and social change. The co-created dialogue in the therapy room which acknowledges the reality of intersectional identity and the experience of power, privilege and oppression can be a powerful force for transformation and healing (see also Point 21 for examples of discussing difference in therapy).

Society is full of deep inequality, which shapes not only an individual's sense of self, but also their day-to-day existence and options. For example, the experience of poverty or having a low socio-economic status has a direct effect upon the way of life, sense of self-esteem and self-worth and the resources available for change for a large number of people. Socially responsible therapy needs to take account of this inequality. It is very difficult to think about deep personality change if you are hungry and/or have no heating or hot water at home.

Language patterns and cultural/literary references can also be symbols of exclusion or oppression, which can be very relevant to clients from non-educated backgrounds who may be particularly sensitive to the therapist's (perceived) higher status and educated position. The use of overly complicated, wordy or formal language can be a subtle seduction for therapists who are keen to emphasize their credibility with the client or in the interests of presenting a professional persona, or for therapists who feel the need to 'prove' themselves, perhaps driven by script issues related to not being taken seriously. A therapist who accounts for oppression will be mindful of the powerful impact their words can have on the client, and will sensitively, but not patronizingly, adapt their language to suit the client's own language style. Indeed, verbal fluency (which includes the ability to adapt and change one's language style) has been identified as a facilitative interpersonal skill, which is predictive of positive therapy outcomes (Anderson et al., 2009; Anderson et al., 2016).

Sexual orientation and gender identity are another arena where oppression operates. There is an implicit assumption in society that the 'normal' way of being is cis-gender and het-erosexual, and that to be anything other than cis-gender and heterosexual is at best unfortunate, and at worst, sinful and profoundly evil. Shadbolt (2004) describes the toxic effects of introjected homophobia on gay people:

> It is not hard to understand how a core sense of self, however confident, will be conflicted and possibly eroded as it dawns on the individual that he or she is not a member of the majority heterosexual culture, not conventional and outside the norm intrapsychically. The person may have introjected … the sense that homosexuality is wrong, abnormal and culturally unacceptable.
>
> (ibid.: 116)

Although the past 30 years have seen significant social change in acceptance of non-heterosexual/non-cis-gender people, LGBTQ+ people have to live with the reality of daily prejudice and very real threats to their physical safety. Some feel that this threat can only be dealt with by living in a way that hides their true nature and so remain closeted, or hide aspects of their life which, while acceptable and perhaps even normative within the LGBTQ+ community, are disapproved of or not accepted in heteronormative society. In this context, any acceptance or strokes can only ever be conditional, and conditional on the basis of a continued collusion with this falsely portrayed image. Even what is presented as acceptance from heterosexual people who are aware of the individual's sexual orientation/gender identity is often only tolerance, and again, is sadly also often conditional. The pervasive messages the LGBTQ+ person internalizes from the wider society include: 'Don't exist', 'Don't be you', and 'Don't belong'.

In *What Do You Say After You Say Hello?*, Berne (1972) expanded on the concept of life positions to include 'three-handed positions'. (In this lamentably short piece, he described how life positions move beyond the 'I'm OK (or not)' and 'you're OK (or not)' to include the extra position of 'they're OK (or not)'). Analysis of three-handed life positions can be useful in exploring an individual's experience and response to oppression, and can be used for wider social analysis of oppressive systems, and the different responses of oppressed groups of people to the oppression. Many marginalized groups, for example, develop an 'I'm OK – you're OK (because you're "in") and they're not OK' position as a way of legitimizing their struggle and developing a sense of community and belonging in response to hostility from the outside world. This can also be true for members of the dominant majority, and is a position often seen in tabloid newspapers who take the political position of the newspaper and its readers as being 'OK', but whoever is considered to be the threat (immigrants, European government, gay people, etc.) as 'not OK'.

ACCOUNTING FOR NEURODIVERSITY

Neurodivergence and neurodiversity are non-pathologizing concepts which recognize that there is enormous variation in human brains and that there is no clear agreement on what 'normal' brain functioning actually is. While people who are neurodivergent experience significant challenges, each neurodivergent condition also has features which could be considered strengths, and sometimes even 'superpowers'.

Over recent years, the field of psychotherapy has started to recognize the sheer number of people who are not neurotypical, and to consider the impact neurodivergence has on a person's development and lived experience. There have also been developments in identifying ways we can adapt psychotherapy practice to accommodate the different needs of neurodivergent clients and provide them with an affirmative, inclusive experience of therapy.

People who are neurodivergent have brains which operate and develop differently to those who are neurotypical. These differences may occur in cognition, perception, information processing, attention, memory, sequencing, emotion, mood, sociability and other mental functions. The term 'neurodivergent' was coined by sociologist Judy Singer (1998; 1999), and refers to a community of people who have variant neurological conditions including: attention deficit and hyperactivity disorder (ADHD), autism/autistic spectrum disorders, dyscalculia, dyslexia and dyspraxia.

Society, our educational systems and the world of work are set up to privilege those who are neurotypical. There are widespread cultural expectations regarding social and relational

DOI: 10.4324/9781003375890-44

functioning and what is considered desirable which many neurodiverse people struggle to live up to. Moreover, psychotherapy models were developed with neurotypical brains in mind, and as such, are not intrinsically adapted to work with the specific challenges or meet the needs of neurodivergent clients. The experience of neurodivergent people living in (and trying to adapt to) a neurotypical world is frequently a cause of distress and neurodivergent people have a substantially higher incidence of psychological disorders than the neurotypical population. Furthermore, there is an increased prevalence of trauma among neurodivergent people, both developmentally, and in adult life. Therapy which is not adapted to the needs of neurodivergent clients can at best have limited effectiveness, and at worst, can be harmful.

The TA literature relating to neurodivergence is rather sparse, although the reader is strongly encouraged to read Baker and Widdowson (2016) for a discussion of the impact of dyslexia on training as a TA therapist, Oates (2021) for reflections on the historical neurotypical bias in TA, and Bowers and Widdowson (2023) for an examination of the lived experience of psychotherapy from the point of view of neurodivergent clients, and detailed neurodivergence-affirmative practice recommendations.

Growing up different in a neurotypical world can result in many unhelpful script beliefs, which unfortunately often get reinforced throughout the lives of neurodiverse people. For example, script beliefs about being 'not OK', not being good enough, being weird or a misfit, being inadequate, being stupid, being difficult or problematic in some way are all common among this population. Injunctions one might expect to see include: don't exist, don't be you, don't belong, don't be close, don't feel, don't think and don't succeed. Psychoeducation and helping a client recognize that these script beliefs are an understandable response to a world which has not recognized their difference, has not valued or given them what they need, and has not prized their gifts and special abilities (Bowers and Widdowson, 2023).

Neurodivergent clients require a high level of acceptance, understanding and patience in therapy. Experiences of rejection, judgement, shaming and lack of understanding are universal among neurodivergent people. Therapy should not repeat these experiences. Therapists are advised to learn about neurodivergent conditions, their features, and the typical challenges experienced by people with these conditions. However, it is important to see the uniqueness of each person and not to make assumptions, and instead to empathically enquire into each neurodivergent client's experience, and to responsively find out what each client finds helpful. This can include adjustments to pacing and drawing on active techniques (such as visualization or the two-chair technique), and creative methods (ibid.).

BUILDING UP THE SCRIPT SYSTEM

The script system (formerly called 'the racket system', Erskine and Zalcman, 1979) is a useful table which captures the central aspects of a client's life script, how it manifests, and links these to the client's symptoms and life history. As such, the script system maps out the client's internal landscape and provides the therapist with a clear set of targets for therapeutic work and treatment planning. I encourage therapists to start to compile a script system at the start of their work with a client, adding to it over a period of a few weeks as more details about a client's script and the memories associated with their script decisions (implicit conclusions) come to light.

I have included a simplified version of the original table (Table 41.1). Here, we see the script system representing in three columns script beliefs, manifestations of script and reinforcing memories respectively.

SCRIPT BELIEFS

To start to build up a client's script system, think about your client's script beliefs, and write them down in a list. You can use Table 35.1 of script beliefs as a starting point. I suggest using the four types of script beliefs listed in Point 35: beliefs about self, beliefs about self in relation to others, beliefs about others, and beliefs about life in general or the world.

Questions to elicit script beliefs include: 'So when you feel really terrible, what are you saying inside your head about yourself? When you feel at your worst, what kind of things do you think about yourself? What kind of person are you?'; 'What do you think your current problems say about you as a person?'; 'What kind of thoughts do you have about yourself

 DOI: 10.4324/9781003375890-45

Table 41.1 The script system

Script beliefs	*Scripty displays*	*Reinforcing memories*
1. Beliefs about self	1. Internal experience	1. Memories where script beliefs were learned
2. Beliefs about others	2. Observable behaviours	2. Memories when script beliefs were reinforced
3. Beliefs about the world/quality of life	3. Fantasies	
Repressed emotion		

in relation to other people?'; 'Are there any particular "rules" that you have about how you should be around other people?'; 'When you feel like that, what are your views about other people?'; 'What beliefs do you have about how other people generally treat you?'; 'When you're feeling bad, how do you view life in general?'; 'When you're in a bad place, what thoughts do you have about the future?'; 'What kind of world do you think we live in?'

Erskine and Zalcman (1979) consider these beliefs as being contaminations, usually mutually reinforcing ones. It is my view that, while some script beliefs are contaminations, some of the 'deeper' ones (such as 'I am inherently bad') are more properly script decisions, which will be reinforced by contaminations.

SCRIPTY DISPLAYS

The scripty displays include the client's reporting of their subjective internal experience and externally observable behaviours in times of distress, in other words, their symptoms. A client's fantasies or imagined negative outcomes also come under the classification of scripts displays. Questions you might ask include: 'When you are feeling bad, what do you feel internally in your body?'; 'Could you describe to me exactly how it feels for you when you are feeling at your worst?'; 'When you are feeling bad, how does it show itself to others? What might they notice?'; 'If I were a fly on the wall, what would I notice about you when you're feeling bad? What would I actually see?'; 'What are your worst-case scenario fantasies?'; 'When you're not in a good way, what terrible outcome do you imagine will end up happening?'; 'If nothing changes for you, how will things end up?' Or 'If you don't change, what will things be like for you in ten years' time?'

From enquiry into the client's internal experiences when they 'feel bad', the therapist facilitates greater awareness of the experience of the emotional state and the subtle physiological changes which accompany the identified feeling state. This process of awareness is often useful to clients who may be relatively unaware of the physical cues that accompany their flow of feelings. The process of enhancing awareness of the physical aspects of feeling states frequently has the result of clients feeling more empowered in relation to their feelings. In the case of feelings, such as anger or fear, which can often feel overwhelming, this can sensitize the client to their onset, development and possibly even associated cognitive processes and, as such, give the client some opportunity to tackle the problematic emotion directly as it emerges, or to prevent escalation of feelings to problematic levels by use of various behavioural strategies to shift mood state or by deliberately changing internal dialogue. Internal experience can also include psychosomatic symptoms and disorders or disorders exacerbated by stress, such as migraine, irritable bowel syndrome, and so on.

Information regarding observable displays can enhance the client's awareness regarding how their emotions operate, particularly on a behavioural, observable level, and can also lead the client into exploration regarding how others experience them and how the client's emotional behaviour impacts upon others (this may in turn provide further reinforcement of the script beliefs, depending on the response of others). The client may, if you think it would be helpful, ask people such as family and friends for specific feedback on what they notice to gain more information on observable scripty displays.

In analysis of the scripty fantasies, the therapist will usually discover what the client's fantasy of their script pay-off will be. These fantasies are often doom-laden and contain themes of abandonment, rejection or annihilation. Alternatively, these fantasies may be idealized, and contain elements of some unidentified rescuer coming along and dramatically changing the client's situation, or magically providing the client with the idealized childhood they never had.

REINFORCING MEMORIES

Reinforcing memories or memories of occasions that provided 'evidence' of the client's script beliefs are often remarkably easy for the client to access. One way of eliciting memories is by guiding the client:

> Just allow those negative thoughts and feelings to run through you for a moment right now. Just allow yourself to think (repeat one or two of the client's script beliefs). As you think that, what memories come to mind? What times can you remember when you felt the same way? What was the first time you felt like that? Can you recall what was happening when you came to the conclusion that (name the script belief)?

It is probable that these memories are accessible through the process of state-dependent memory. State-dependent memory means that when we are in one 'state' we can access memories more readily that match that state. If you have ever spent time with an old friend recalling ever-increasingly hilarious events and situations for hours on end, you have experienced state-dependent memory. Similarly, people who feel depressed or hurt can at the time access what can seem like an unending stream of emotional memories that are linked. It is important to note that reinforcing memories will not include ones from very early childhood due to the 'childhood amnesia' relating to specific, episodic and verbal memories that exists around events roughly prior to the age of 3. This is due to lack of neurological development in areas of the brain associated with memory (although the events will still be encoded and represented unconsciously, and held in the implicit memory systems). Despite this childhood amnesia, it is possible to get a sense of potential pre-verbal memories by asking, 'Based on what you know, and what you feel in your body, what do you imagine the first three years of life were like for you?'

Contained within the model of the script system is the notion that there will be some kind of underlying or repressed emotion and that the script system, or racket is a substitute or permitted feeling (English, 1971). It seems problematic and unhelpful to take the stance that a client's felt sense is somehow not authentic, although it is possible that the client's presenting emotions are in fact secondary emotions, covering a dynamically repressed emotion which the client (usually unconsciously) believes is unacceptable or forbidden in some way (see Widdowson, 2016, for more discussion of primary and secondary feelings). In this instance, the therapist's job is to help the client to identify and express the previously unexpressed emotion, through the process of deconfusion.

EXPLORING DRIVERS

In transactional analysis, we identify five drivers, which are processes clients use in order to maintain a sense of 'OKness'. While their drivers may work well for them in many situations, in therapy, we often find that getting caught in intense, compulsive and/or rigid patterns of their driver(s) can contribute to our client's problems and keep them stuck in their script. Drivers are seen as a manifestation of a client's counterscript (Stewart and Joines, 2012).

The five driver patterns are:

Be Perfect! Please Others! Try Hard! Be Strong! Hurry Up!

So a client may believe and feel that they are only OK if, for example, they are perfect and please others. In this example, any time a client shows signs of imperfection, or completes a task in an imperfect way, or any time they disappoint others or put their own needs before others, the client will end up feeling Not-OK, and is therefore likely to experience the full force of their most negative script beliefs about their self. This tension is most vividly depicted in Adrienne Lee's drowning person diagram (see Figure 35.1 in Point 35). In my experience, people have an accurate intuitive sense of their own drivers, and will readily identify them if presented with them (again, see Point 35), or will confirm or reject them if asked directly by the therapist. For example 'It strikes me that you are a bit of a perfectionist, and give yourself a real hard time if you are anything other than perfect. Does that seem true to you?'

Drivers are also culturally embedded in that they are all behaviours which are present, valued, and stroked to some degree in most (western) cultures, and, as such, each driver

DOI: 10.4324/9781003375890-46

will be more or less present for everyone. It is not the presence of the driver that is necessarily problematic, it is the extent to which is dominates a client's experience and limits their options which becomes problematic.

Through their role in ensuring 'conditional OKness', each driver acts as a defence against experiencing 'heavier', more destructive aspects of a person's life script. Because of this, TA therapists tend to be cautious in dismantling them, instead, focusing more on increasing the client's awareness of their own drivers, and encouraging them to think about whether they need the driver in order to feel OK about themselves. If we consider that our job as therapists is to help clients feel OK about themselves, to find more flexible ways of being in the world and relating to others, and to help a client develop increased options for living, then helping them to notice and question their own driver-related internal process and/or behaviours is part of the therapeutic process.

Petruska Clarkson (1992b) reframed drivers as strengths, and socially desirable qualities. By discussing these positive strengths and aspirations with our clients, we help them to draw on the advantageous aspects of their drivers, but also help them to see their limitations. So, using Clarkson's model, we would help our clients strive towards *Excellence*, instead of perfection, *Agreeableness*, instead of pleasing others, *Experimentation*, in place of trying hard, *Endurance* instead of being strong, and *Speed* instead of hurrying up. Also, by helping our clients recognize that they are fundamentally OK as a person by helping them build an unconditional sense of self-worth, they can relax their drivers and respond with self-compassion and acceptance on the occasions where they do not fulfil the demands of their drivers.

The concept of drivers was developed by Taibi Kahler (1975). In Kahler's original model, drivers were shown in brief clusters of behaviours which a person displayed immediately before a person moved into 'script' behaviour or feelings. While there is a certain appeal to this position, unfortunately it leads to reductive and restrictive thinking around the manifestation of life script (Tudor and Widdowson, 2008). It is unrealistic and inaccurate to assume that all intrapsychic processes have observable behavioural cues associated with them. Life script is subtle, and, arguably, always present to a greater or lesser extent, and shifts in a person's internal state and/or unconscious process are not always observable. For example, a person can at any time be experiencing intense emotions due to the activation of some aspect of their life script, without showing any signs of emotional experiencing. Furthermore, given the cultural and social desirability of driver patterns, and the influence of these on how individuals engage with others and the world, it is perhaps more useful to consider these as processes a person uses to maintain a sense of OKness than of an indication that a person is about to 'move into script'.

ANALYSING GAMES

First, in discussing game analysis with clients, it is generally unhelpful to use the term 'games'. The word 'game' has a pejorative connotation (Woods, 2000), and tends to be received by clients as the therapist implying they are being manipulative, or are on the receiving end of conscious manipulation. I find using the phrase 'unhelpful relationship patterns' to be generally acceptable, as well as more accurate in conveying the nature of games as an unconscious interpersonal enactment which reinforces the script.

Game analysis has changed dramatically over the years within TA. It seems that during the 1970s and 1980s, TA therapists watched for and confronted 'the opening con' in a game (Berne, 1964). Following Berne's formula G (Berne, 1972), a number of methods of game analysis were regularly used, such as the James Game Plan (James, 1973). These methods assume games to be relatively predictable sequences that can be brought into conscious awareness. Although this is often the case, my clinical experience suggests that some games are so unconscious that analysis using such methods yields poor results. Furthermore, as games are so inextricably linked with an individual's script, unless the underlying script issues are dealt with, the game will manifest again in another, possibly even more covert form if confronted without first fully accounting for the significance of the game.

When exploring the client's relationship patterns, the therapist is listening for the patterns of the games (or, unhelpful relationship patterns) the client gets caught up in, together with indicators that might suggest the underlying script issues which the game reinforces:

DOI: 10.4324/9781003375890-47

Full game analysis therefore requires an appreciation of the underlying motivations for the game, and a sense of the original scenario the game symbolically represents. To understand the deep motivations of a game, it is necessary to identify the unconscious conflict from which the game develops ... the switch in a game is designed to manage an unconscious conflict.

(Terlato, 2001: 106)

If considered as a symbolic re-enactment of the past, or of some troubling interaction (often between the client and their parents), the game can be understood as a form of communication: '[I]n the context of therapy, externalizing or playing out one's internal scenario with others may serve as an unconscious attempt by the patient to communicate to the therapist the exact nature of the patient's internal conflict' (Woods, 2000: 96). 'The game is the externalization or projection of this internal scenario onto the external world in the form of an interpersonal interaction' (ibid.: 94). A thorough game analysis therefore requires consideration of the nature of the unconscious communications the game contains.

Game enactments allow an individual to externalize their internal conflicts, and thus may temporarily stop the internal attack and conflict between Child and Parent ego states. This reduction in internal attack and externalizing of the conflict make the original game scenario more receptive to deconfusion or, equally, reinforcement. When operating in the therapy room, the client's games therefore should be partially allowed, but contained (Bateman and Fonagy, 2006). This is consistent with Berne's concept of 'game dosage' (Berne, 1972). Because games are so woven into the fabric of relationships and have their origins in our preverbal relational experiences, many transactional analysts (myself included) believe that we can never truly stop playing games, we just get better at them. In other words, they become less destructive, problematic or distressing and are either more easily recognized and stepped out of, or just much more subtle and barely noticeable.

In the ongoing and unfolding analysis of a client's games, here are some questions for the therapist to reflect upon:

- What is the basic repetitive relationship pattern my client keeps getting caught up in?
- What do they keep on doing, and end up feeling in their interactions with others?
- What are their (potentially implicit) expectations about how others will treat them, how situations will end and what they will have to do?
- What do they report others keep doing to them?
- What might they be doing to elicit that response from others?
- How might they be keeping themselves susceptible to getting caught in these patterns?
- What 'early warning signs' might my client usefully look out for as a sign that they are back in a game?
- What was the original early life scenario that the game is seeking to replicate?
- What beliefs about the self does the game reinforce?
- What beliefs about the client, or expectations about how others relate to the client, does the game reinforce?
- What were the original relational needs that were not met? What would be the intrapsychic and interpersonal impact of meeting these needs?
- What is the nature of the central conflicts that the game seeks to manage?
- What is the client trying to communicate to me through this game?
- What is my part in this? What is my vulnerability to this game? What aspects of my script does this game reinforce?
- How can I best manage my feelings so I remain therapeutically available for my client?
- What can be healed, both for my client and for myself, in understanding this game?
- Which behaviours and ways of responding might my clients use to either step out of or minimize the impact of the game and move into healthier ways of relating?

ESCAPE HATCHES AS
A FRAMEWORK FOR
UNDERSTANDING CLIENT SAFETY

Escape-hatch closure is a controversial piece of TA theory. It was developed by Drye et al. (1973), Holloway (1973), Boyd and Cowles-Boyd (1980), and Stewart (2007). The central premise of escape-hatch closure is that individuals, as part of a tragic script, may incorporate an 'escape hatch'. The escape hatch is not the positive thing we might ordinarily assume it to be, but is one whereby the individual escapes from their dire situation into something better. The three traditional escape hatches referred to within TA are: 'kill or harm self, kill or harm others and go crazy'. Some TA therapists add a fourth escape hatch of 'run away'. According to the theory, if an individual has an escape hatch 'open' within their script, the idea is that the individual believes at some level that 'if things get really bad around here, I will kill or harm myself or others, or go crazy, or run away'. These are seen to be manifestations of a tragic script, and may be the culmination of a third-degree game. In reality, this is unlikely to be the case. First, the idea that individuals have an open escape hatch as part of their script is contrary to the humanistic drive towards growth that is encapsulated in the fundamental TA concept of *physis* (Berne, 1972). Second, it does not account for the impact of stressful (possibly even traumatic) life events which can contribute to crises. Third, a considerable amount of research has shown that what drives suicidality or risk of harm to self is a sense of despair and a feeling of being trapped (O'Connor and Kirtley, 2018) (see Point 81).

DOI: 10.4324/9781003375890-48

Nevertheless, the concept of escape hatches is useful in conceptualizing types of risk and client safety. Certainly transactional analysis places great emphasis on client protection (Crossman, 1966). However, protection goes much further than inviting a client to close escape hatches. To consider whether a particular client, at any particular point in time, may be potentially moving along a trajectory of kill/harm self, kill/harm others, go crazy, or run away is a helpful shorthand framework as part of a comprehensive risk assessment process.

Drye (2006) invites therapists to use 'no-harm contracts' as an assessment tool:

> Whenever I believe suicidal risk may exist – other than an actual attempt or thought and including self-destructive behavior, high risk-taking, gallows humor, and so on – I ask the patient to take a test to clarify the situation. I say, 'Please say out loud, "No matter what happens ... I won't kill myself ... accidentally or on purpose" and tell me how you feel about what you just said.' If the patient states, 'It's true', the risk evaluation is complete and treatment planning can continue.
>
> (ibid.: 1)

Drye goes on to invite therapists to pay particular attention to any qualifying statements or clauses clients may give for reasons why they wouldn't feel able to maintain the contract. He then suggests that the client be invited to repeat the statement with increasing time-spans included to get a sense over what period of time the client is prepared to keep themselves safe. Interestingly Drye states that this tool is only effective in monitoring suicidal risk and has not been effective at monitoring or containing clients who self-harm.

'In closing escape hatches, the client makes a commitment from Adult to renounce all three tragic options. Thus she accepts she is responsible for her own situation. She acknowledges she has power to alter that situation' (Stewart, 2007: 102). Stewart also emphasizes that escape-hatch closure is a procedure undertaken by the client from their Adult ego state that invites the client to make a decision that they will not under any circumstances kill or harm themselves, anyone else or go crazy. 'The escape-hatch procedure is not intended to address any Child issues she may still have around the tragic options' (ibid.: 102). Escape-hatch closure, and, in particular, 'no harm contracts', must not be viewed as a replacement for ongoing and thorough risk assessment of your clients. Indeed, a client closing escape hatches, no matter how congruent that appears to be, is no guarantee that they will not subsequently engage in harmful or third-degree behaviour.

Stewart (ibid.: 110) argues that there is a distinction between the decisional nature of escape-hatch closure and a no-harm contract. 'A contract can be reviewed, renegotiated and changed if client and counsellor so agree. By contrast, the essence of closing escape hatches is that the client's decision is irrevocable and non-negotiable.' In reality, this position is unworkable and does not account for changing circumstances and the loss of hope, increase in despair and sense of entrapment that a client will experience before entering a suicidal crisis.

Boliston-Mardula (2001) discusses escape hatches in relation to the human hungers (Berne, 1970), and how harmful behaviours often represent script-driven ways of meeting these hungers. Boliston-Mardula invites therapists to account for these hungers in their work with clients who present with harmful behaviours and to promote healthier replacements for the destructive paths. Many transactional analysts view a range of behaviours which are self-harmful, such as smoking, excessive drinking, over-eating leading to obesity, and so forth as being symptomatic of a strong 'don't exist' injunction and the presence of an open 'kill/harm self' escape hatch. There are indeed a wide range of behaviours that many people engage in that are to a greater or lesser extent harmful. However, to claim that they are all indicative of open escape hatches and a don't exist injunction oversimplifies matters, and does not fully or accurately account for the complexity and significance of the behaviour(s). Furthermore, such ways of thinking are potentially laden with moral judgement, and as such can be non-therapeutic. It is certainly the case that a don't exist injunction is, from a TA perspective, an important factor in thinking about harmful behaviours and can be useful short-hand for describing part of the internal process that surrounds such issues. There are many reasons why people act in ways which appear to be self-destructive or harmful and a thorough analysis of the components of the harmful behaviour and the motivating factors driving it is essential to effective and thorough therapy. Therapists are advised to avoid such reductionistic, simplistic and potentially pathologizing ways of thinking about client behaviours.

SUICIDAL IDEATION: A BRIEF INTRODUCTION

Transactional analysts have for many years worked with clients with suicidal ideation, and have tended to understand their client's urges as indicative of the presence of a don't exist injunction (Goulding and Goulding, 1979; Stewart, 2007) and related to their script pay-off (Berne, 1972). Understanding suicidal ideation only as a manifestation of a don't exist injunction and an indication of a third-degree script pay-off (Berne, 1964) is insufficient in understanding what is a complex phenomenon.

For the therapist, being with a client who is in such profound pain that they seriously wish to end their life is a disturbing experience, and some therapists, out of fear (and possibly also ignorance), unwisely react to such expressions of intent by rapidly introducing time-limited 'no harm contracts', or escape-hatch closure procedures. Instead, the therapist's first task is to understand the nature of the client's thoughts and feelings on the matter by identifying whether the client's suicidal thoughts are occasional, passing and transitory thoughts or more persistent. If the client's thoughts are severe and persistent, the therapist then needs to ascertain if the client had made a plan as to how they will end their life, and, if so, (1) do they have the means to act on their plan?; and (2) do they intend to act on these plans? Where clients have persistent suicidal thoughts, and have a plan to end their life and the means and intention to do so, then the client needs to be immediately referred for emergency medical treatment (see Point 81).

Suicidal ideation needs to be understood for what it is, and what it represents to the individual. Invariably any suicidal ideation will include as a central feature a wish for the individual's profound pain to stop. Effective therapy with clients who experience suicidal ideation needs to account for this wish, and the therapist needs to repeatedly and empathically communicate their understanding of the extent and depth of the client's pain, and the desire expressed in the suicidal ideation for the pain to stop. When considered in this light, suicidal ideation can also be viewed as a contextually adaptive (albeit distorted) expression of the client's *physis* (Berne, 1972; Goulding and Goulding, 1979). The 'final solution' to one's pain is ultimately what is sought in suicidal ideation, this is only part of the picture, and each client's experience needs to be explored and accounted for fully. The urges to destroy the self can generally be structurally modelled to originate in the P1 (Parent in the Child) ego state, although deep emotional pain or 'psycheache' (McLaughlin, 2007) and internal conflict are generally central contributing factors in suicidal ideation. The most effective and therapeutically useful approach for the therapist to take is to enquire sensitively, directly, and without euphemism or ambiguity, into the client's experience of suicidal thoughts and feelings and to provide the client with unwavering acceptance. Each aspect of the client's experience needs to be carefully and empathically attended to (ibid.). Many people who harbour suicidal thoughts feel shame and guilt about these feelings, and often feel profoundly isolated. Such an empathic and accepting stance on the part of the therapist is therapeutic in itself as it reduces the client's shame and guilt, and the sense of isolation associated with their suicidality.

Suicidal ideation also often includes an aspect of wishing to destroy some aspect of the self. Commonly the parts to be destroyed are aspects of either the Child (C1 or even third-order Child), or the Parent in the Child – P1, and possibly even both. Occasionally the part the client would like to destroy is some aspect of themselves that they recognize as an aspect of one of their parents (and so represents destroying an identification with a P2 introject). In my experience, directly asking the client to describe which parts of their self they would like to destroy is effective, as clients will have some sense of this that they will be able to articulate fairly readily. You may need to return to this question, as the parts can be 'layered' and the aspects of self which are most disturbing to the client at any one time may change (see Goulding and Goulding, 1979: 181–204, for examples of working therapeutically with such 'layering').

Sometimes one purpose of suicidal ideation can be the desire to punish, particularly punishing the self. This desire to punish the self is particularly prevalent in clients who hold deep guilt and shame. The desire to punish may also extend to others, whom the client is wishing to punish for how they have treated the client (ibid.). In considering the communicative aspects of the suicidal urge, the therapist is invited to explore with their client what the ideation represents in terms of a communication, and what acting upon the urges would communicate to others. Injunctions, as aspects of an individual's script that was formed relationally by the infant in response to their environment, also may be useful to consider in helping to understand the client's process. When considered from the perspective of injunctions, suicidal ideation can be perhaps considered as an 'obeying' of a don't exist injunction that the individual took from their environment – either directly, or indirectly and inferentially.

In working with suicidal thoughts and urges, the therapist is advised to account for the existential aspects that these thoughts represent. Paradoxically, suicidal ideation can be a manifestation of death anxiety (Yalom, 1980), or can be considered as an alternative to 'taking responsibility' for the client who feels desperately anxious and overwhelmed at the prospect of taking full responsibility for their life, with all the implications therein. Suicide can also seem to some people to be a means of taking charge of their own lives or pain and for reinstating some control over a life that can seem to be spiralling out of control, with hopelessness around regaining control. For further exploration of these themes, see Yalom's (1980) *Existential Psychotherapy*. As TA is an existential therapy, transactional analysts will find much rich material in his book.

Returning to a 'pure' TA perspective, although script theory offers some explanations of suicidal wishes, reducing suicidal urges only to a manifestation of a single script issue or seeing it as a client's script pay-off will almost certainly be an over-simplification. It is important to account for the complexity of the associated dynamics and issues connected with, and fuelling, the suicidal ideation. Therapists working with clients who experience suicidal ideation, in any degree, are advised to take considerable time thinking about and discussing in supervision their client's ideation, and the different components of it and how they structurally and dynamically interact within their client's internal world and experience. Certainly, understanding any identified script outcome is a key task for transactional analysts. However, there may be multiple outcomes, or even none specified in an individual's script. Where specified outcomes are present, the complex interaction of script issues associated with them needs to be accounted for and understood in their context and in relation to what circumstances would call for each potential outcome.

Finally, this point is not designed to provide the therapist with a full account or methodology for working with suicidal clients. There is no substitute for undertaking full training, including reading on risk assessment, treatment approaches and referral procedures. This material is to be viewed rather as an adjunct, or perhaps even a preparation to such training, and a beginning approach for therapists to consider suicidal ideation.

DIAGNOSIS CHECKLIST

The simplest way to proceed with diagnosis in TA is to systematically go through the basic concepts of TA and determine how your client may experience their particular pathology. It can be useful to print out a list of TA concepts and, when writing your notes for each client, go through your diagnosis checklist, making relevant notes along the way for each client. Your notes will gradually build up over a number of sessions into a comprehensive diagnosis using TA. You may choose to use the sample list below or devise your own according to your own way of working.

---

1. EGO STATES

Remember Berne's four methods of ego state diagnosis: behavioural, social, historical, and phenomenological.

- Parent ego state: general comments and strength
    - Strength of the client's Internal Nurturing Parent
    - Strength of the client's Internal Critical Parent
- Adult ego state: general comments and strength
- Child ego state: general comments and strength
- Contaminations
- Other structural pathology
- Main introjected significant caregivers/siblings
- Nature of the client's Internal ego state dialogue

2. TRANSACTIONAL STYLE

Common transactions

DOI: 10.4324/9781003375890-50

- Which ego state does this client most frequently transact from?
- Which ego state responses do they commonly elicit from others?
- What is their predominant functional style?
- Which transactional patterns do they report?

3. RELATIONAL PATTERNS

- What is the client's expected response to self and others? (See Point 35.)

4. STROKE ECONOMY

- Which stroke economy rules does the client exhibit?

5. GAMES

- Which games does this client frequently get into?
- What game do I think the client and I might get into?
- What is this client's familiar drama triangle pattern?
- What drama triangle pattern do they report that they elicit from others?
- What is my countertransference drama triangle urge with this client?

6. RACKET/SCRIPT SYSTEM ANALYSIS

- What are the secondary (racket) feelings this client reports? (Widdowson, 2016)
- What script beliefs does this client appear to have or report that they have about:
  - themselves?
  - others?
  - the world and nature of life?
- What physical reactions do they experience when they feel bad?
- What observable behaviours do they get into when feeling bad?

- What is the scary fantasy that they envisage as the outcome?
- What are the feelings that are repressed under the racket/ or what feelings does the client experience as 'not being allowed' or unacceptable?
- What are the missing pieces of emotional literacy work this client needs?

7. PERSONALITY TRAITS

Contemporary views on personality have moved away from outdated categorical approaches (where personality is categorized into 'types', or 'adaptations') and instead have moved to a dimensional approach which focuses on the presence of specific personality traits (APA, 2013). The dimensional model is not only evidence-based (whereas there is little evidence for the existence of many of the old diagnostic categories/ types) and allows for greater accuracy and specificity in personality diagnosis and treatment planning. The dimensional model is based on what are known as 'The Big Five' personality traits and pathological traits. These are:

- Openness to experience
- Conscientiousness
- Extraversion
- Agreeableness
- Neuroticism

In your diagnosis, comment on which traits appear to be most predominant. You might also indicate as to whether the client scores high or low on each trait dimension using a standardized Big Five inventory or measure. There are many good articles and resources available online which explain these personality traits. Therapists who are new to this model are strongly advised to undertake some background reading to familiarize themselves with the Big Five personality traits.

The DSM-5 has developed an evidence-based model of maladaptive personality traits which was derived from the Big Five model. The pathological personality traits are:

- Negative affectivity
- Detachment
- Antagonism
- Disinhibition
- Psychoticism

When assessing for these traits in clients whom one suspects may have a personality disorder, it is worth using the Personality Inventory for the DSM-5 Brief Form (PID-5-BF), which is freely available online (www.psychiatry.org/File Library/Psychiatrists ....). Therapists are advised to also read Widiger and McGabe (2020) to develop their familiarity with and understanding of this model.

8. PERSONALITY FUNCTIONING

The level of personality functioning is used to identify the type of impaired self-functioning and interpersonal functioning that is characteristic of all personality disorders. Therapists are advised to familiarize themselves with this model in DSM-5 (APA, 2013), or by reading online resources.

- Self:
    - Identity (includes experience of self as unique, stability of self-esteem, capacity to regulate a range of emotions)
    - Self-directedness (includes capacity for pursuit of coherent and meaningful goals, prosocial standards of behaviour and capacity for self-reflection).
- Interpersonal:
    - Empathy (includes comprehension and appreciation of others' experiences and motivations,

tolerance of differing perspectives and under-standing the effects of one's own behaviour on others)

- Intimacy (depth and duration of connection with others, desire and capacity for closeness and mutuality of regard).

To enhance the accuracy of assessment you may wish to use the Levels of Personality Functioning Scale Brief Form 2.0 (LPFS-BF 2.0) with clients who present with more serious impairment and who may have a personality disorder (Weekers, Hutsebaut and Kamphuis, 2018).

9. INJUNCTIONS

Tick those that apply and make brief notes about what evidence you are basing your diagnosis on.

- Don't exist
- Don't be you
- Don't be close
- Don't belong
- Don't be important
- Don't succeed
- Don't be a child
- Don't grow up
- Don't be well
- Don't think
- Don't feel
- Don't do anything

10. PASSIVITY

Tick those that apply and make brief notes about what evidence you are basing your diagnosis on. Usual reported or observed passive behaviour (include general comments about manifestations of passivity) is:

- Doing nothing
- Overadaptation
- Agitation
- Incapacitation/violence

11. IMPASSES

- Type one (include key dialogue forming the conflict).
- Type two (include key dialogue forming the conflict).
- Type three (include key dialogue or central theme of conflict).

12. LIFE POSITION

- I'm OK – you're OK.
- I'm OK – you're not OK.
- I'm not OK – you're OK.
- I'm not OK – you're not OK.

13. MAIN SCRIPT BELIEFS

_____

14. NOTES ON DECONFUSION NEEDED

_____

Part 4

CONTRACTING

CONTRACTING FOR THE TASKS AND GOALS OF THERAPY

There is now considerable research evidence which shows that clarity and consensus in collaborative goal setting enhance the outcomes in psychotherapy (Tryon, Birch and Verkuilen, 2019). Specifically, early agreement (within the first few sessions) between therapist and client on the tasks and goals of therapy is known to facilitate the development of the working alliance, and as such contribute towards a positive outcome of the therapy. Clients presenting for psychotherapy generally have an idea of their overall goals for therapy, which commonly relate to symptomatic relief. Many of these clients are also aware that considerable intrapsychic and interpersonal restructuring work may well be required for the resolution of their presenting problems. The problem for transactional analysts in contracting is how to negotiate a clear contract that leaves room for flexibility and for potentials to emerge in the work. One difficulty we have is that if we assume that the client is entering therapy in a relatively script-bound position, then any articulated goals are potentially constrained by the client's capacity to envisage an autonomous state. The client's stated goals may also be script-driven and may relate to a furthering of the individual's script. The humanistic value base of TA assumes that, at some level, clients do indeed have this knowledge, although it may well be rather hidden at the outset. Hargaden and Sills (2002) suggest that a good therapeutic contract should ideally relate to increased options, rather than committing oneself to a set outcome or course of action from the start of therapy. This more relational approach to contracting is in contrast with TA approaches that value specificity in contracting (Stewart, 1996; 2007).

DOI: 10.4324/9781003375890-52

CONTRACTING FOR THE TASKS OF THERAPY

As part of the process of engaging in therapy, it is good practice to provide the client with information regarding how therapy works and what kind of activities they will be involved in both in the therapy room and also outside as part of the therapy (such as behavioural 'homework' contracts). It is also helpful to provide clients with some guidance on how to engage with self-reflective processes. This may also involve exploring expectations and preconceptions the client may have regarding the nature of the goals and tasks of therapy, as these may differ quite considerably from the therapist's. The use of tools such as the Cooper- Norcross Inventory of Preferences (Cooper and Norcross, 2016) (which is freely available online) can be valuable not only to identify client expectations and preferences, but also to trigger a conversation about the process of therapy, how the therapist works and which techniques and approach they might use. Contracting for tasks also includes the specific and ongoing seeking of the client's consent to work on a particular issue in the therapy. 'It sounds like this is important. Do you want to discuss this now?' or 'OK, I've heard that you feel X, can we come back to that later?' which marks issues that arise naturally as points for further exploration at another time.

CONTRACTING FOR TASKS RELATED TO THE THERAPEUTIC BOND

It is wise to specifically contract with the client that they will discuss feelings related to therapy and the therapist in sessions. This creates a contract that accounts for the tasks of using the therapeutic relationship and working with transference. A suggested wording for such a contract would be:

> The feelings people have about therapy and their therapist are often of vital importance. I have found that by paying attention to these feelings, and exploring them together, we can learn a great deal about people's problems, their ways of viewing things, their thinking patterns and, of course, how they relate to people.

Therapy provides a unique environment to do precisely this. For example, sometimes people feel a little anxious, or inexplicably ashamed, or sometimes they even start worrying that I might be judging them. All of these feelings are important. Even though it will feel a little strange at first, I'd encourage you to share whatever is on your mind, particularly relating to coming here, or to me, no matter how strange or irrational it might seem. Would you be willing to do that?

CONTRACTING FOR THE GOALS OF THERAPY

Clients presenting for therapy often have some idea about what they want to get out of therapy. There are many TA sources the therapist can draw upon in helping their client form clear contracts related to their goals. As Berne (1966/1994). pointed out, a contract is 'bilateral' and requires the agreement of both client and therapist. The therapist will also have their own set of implicit goals, their concept of the 'ideal' or 'cure'. These goals will subtly influence the therapy and inform the therapist's interventions. It is important that the therapist has a clear construction of their 'goals of therapy' and is open with clients about these goals from the start. This reduces the potential for the therapy being influenced by covert intentions and operating on a non-contractual basis. In determining the therapist's own implicit ideal goals, the therapist can reflect upon several questions: What is important to them about being a therapist? What do they consider to be the most important changes a client can make as a result of psychotherapy? For example, it may be increased options and resources for living, or it may be increasing capacity for relationship. The therapist who is aware of their own overall goals of therapy can then engage the client in a discussion about these goals, and therefore the client can enter therapy (or decide not to) from a greater position of informed consent.

DOING GOAL-ORIENTED AND PROCESS-ORIENTED TA THERAPY

As stated in Point 47, ethical and effective psychotherapy requires identifying clear goals for the therapy in a collaborative process. Although contracting is indeed a crucial part of the initial phases of TA therapy, it is important that we do not sacrifice the importance of forming a working alliance and of psychologically 'meeting' the client first. This is summed up elegantly by Adrienne Lee who reminds us 'contact precedes contract' (Lee, 1997: 101). Lee suggests the therapist use what she refers to as process contracts (ibid.), which invite the client into a here-and-now process of engagement, exploration and experimentation. Process contracting begins with therapeutic enquiry and then uses the response of the enquiry to determine the next movement. It is important to note though that one can use both process contracting and goal-oriented contracting. Indeed, contracting for the tasks and goals of therapy (see Point 47) usually requires both. As part of contracting for tasks of therapy, I recommend the use of an open contract which invites the client to give the therapist feedback on their experience of therapy which helps the therapist to adjust their way of working accordingly. This is in line with current thinking on the importance of therapist responsiveness in facilitating positive outcomes. A suggested wording for such an open contract is:

> Let's meet for a few weeks, and keep checking in with each other in each session how we're doing and how we're working together. How does that sound to you? And, of course, if at any point you

DOI: 10.4324/9781003375890-53

decide that you want me to do more or less of something, please
do tell me and we can discuss it.

Attention to the formation of the working alliance and
process contracting does not, however, preclude attending to
a client's goals and establishing a clear 'direction of travel'
for the therapy. I find it helpful to ask clients in the first
contact we have to think about their goals for therapy. On
my intake form, I ask clients to identify between three and
five goals for therapy or between three and five things they
want to achieve from therapy. In the several years I have
been doing this, every single client has been able to identify
at least one, and usually several clear goals of their own,
without any additional prompting. We have then discussed
these goals in the initial sessions, and clarified and refined
them where necessary. It is also useful to break down goals
into a series of smaller goals which are more easily achieved.
Achieving a smaller sub-goal can significantly enhance a
client's motivation and can give them encouragement that
they can achieve their larger goals. This is particularly
helpful for clients who feel discouraged, disheartened and
despairing. Gaining a sense of momentum and forward
direction gives the client hope, which in turn has beneficial
effects on the overall therapy outcome. Also, achievement of
goals is known to stimulate the release of dopamine. As
dopamine is intrinsically related to motivation and learning
(in addition to giving a sense of reward and pleasure), this
helps to further catalyze change, supporting the client's
process of change.

Woollams and Brown's treatment plan (Woollams and
Brown, 1978) has developing the treatment contract as a
specific stage of therapy; however, there are two preliminary
stages prior to the contracting stage: motivation and
awareness. Their approach suggests the therapist take a
'lightness of touch' approach to contracting in these first two
preliminary stages of the therapy. Of course, the client will
generally present with some wants or goals for the therapy,
which the therapist can accept, and rework at a later stage in

the therapy. Although the Woollams and Brown model is presented as a series of linear stages that one progresses through, in reality, motivation, awareness and contracting usually occur simultaneously during the initial phase of therapy. The attuned therapist will adjust their way of working and move back and forth between these different therapeutic tasks.

USING A STANDARD WRITTEN BUSINESS CONTRACT

Using a standard written business contract (Berne, 1966/1994; Steiner, 1971) that you can give to all clients in their initial meeting ensures clarity around arrangements, administrative matters and the terms and conditions of the therapy. A written contract is useful in that many clients are often highly tense or emotional during their initial meeting with their new therapist, and may well forget important information relating to the business contract. Providing a written contract not only minimizes the potential for confusion, but it is also good ethical practice. All of the professional organizations governing the practice of psychotherapy, and the transactional analysis organizations advise members to be as clear in their contracting as possible. Ethical contracting requires the practitioner to attend to a range of areas where lack of clarity could cause potential problems in the therapy. Contracting usually takes place at the very outset of the therapy process, and so some details such as length of the work may not yet be determined. However, the practitioner can give an indication as to the expected format of the work, such as short term or long term. In relation to some of the above issues, as well as some additional points, I recommend making the following items explicit in a written business contract.

THE DOCUMENT TITLE OR NAME

It is common for clients to feel a little apprehensive about the use of the word 'contract' which can give the impression that they are signing a formal legal document. I explain to clients

DOI: 10.4324/9781003375890-54

that the word contract is not used in the legal sense but instead is a technical term relating to the working agreement that we have together. I also explain that its purpose is for clarity and also so that the client can enter into therapy from a position of informed consent (in fact, I have a longer informed consent document, as well as a brief contract, which provides more information about how I work, my expectations of clients, what they can expect from me, and so on).

The following issues are important in a contract:

- fees
- cancellation policy
- confidentiality
- recording of sessions
- GDPR compliance privacy statement.

FEES

What are the fees per session and the arrangements around payment of fees?

CANCELLATION POLICY

What is your policy regarding the notice period for cancellation of sessions and payment of fees for missed sessions?

CONFIDENTIALITY

What are the boundaries and limitations of confidentiality? An acceptable clause is: 'I will not maintain confidentiality if I think that you or someone else is at risk of harm. In this instance, I will discuss my reasons and plans for disclosure with you before proceeding.' This clause covers a range of possibilities and does not tie the therapist down to specifics, but is clear about the boundary of confidentiality with regard to the management of risk. Special clauses regarding confidentiality and protection for clients on medication or where there is psychiatric history might include:

If you are on medication, it will be useful for me to have some contact with your medical practitioner. Generally I do this in letter form, and would discuss the contents of that letter with you, and would not divulge the content of our sessions, but make general comments.

This allows for professional discussion with medical practitioners around the management of clients on medication.

It is important to be clear around case discussion in clinical supervision. A suggested clause is:

In accordance with codes of ethics and professional practice I regularly discuss my case load with my clinical supervisor. Any discussion about you would be anonymized in such a way that you could not be identified from the material discussed.

Trainees also need to provide a clear statement regarding using client material in essays and case studies. A suggested wording might be:

From time to time I may refer to our work in assignments connected with my ongoing professional training. All case material will be anonymized and presented in such a way that you could not be identified from the material presented.

It is not ethical to include client material in assignments without prior consent from the client. If this clause is included in the general business contract, the therapist is advised to request that the client sign a copy of the document for the therapist to retain. Trainees are also advised to seek specific consent from clients about whom they intend to write extended case studies.

Trainers and supervisors also need to account for disclosure of client material in teaching. The clause I use in my contract is: 'I may refer to our work in teaching psychotherapists and counsellors, or for the purposes of publication in professional journals and textbooks. Again, any identifying details will be obscured to ensure you could not be identified from any material.'

RECORDING OF SESSIONS

If you make audio or video recordings of your work, you will need to include a clear statement regarding how the recordings are used ('five-minute segments selected for the purposes of supervision, monitoring and evaluation of my work'), how they will be kept and procedure for destroying recordings. Therapists in the UK are advised that the keeping of digital voice recordings constitutes an electronic record of the work, and therefore will require the therapist to register with the Information Commissioner's Office.

Supervisors are also advised to put together a written business contract that covers the above as adapted to suit the supervisory situation but also addresses details, such as emergency telephone supervision arrangements, approval of supervisees, advertising materials, provision of supervisor's reports, contact with training establishment/trainer, arrangements for frequency of supervision, ethics codes which impact upon the work and any special arrangements for group supervision.

GDPR COMPLIANCE PRIVACY STATEMENT

It is a legal requirement for therapists based in Europe to provide clients with a General Data Protection Regulation (GDPR) compliance statement. The wording below is recommended:

Privacy statement

Keeping your personal information private is very important to me. I do have to take some details from you, such as contact details and name and address, and also sensitive data regarding your personal history and the problems you are experiencing. This information is used to provide you with a psychotherapy/counselling service, and for quality assurance and statistical purposes. These are legitimate interests under the law.

All records are kept for as long as needed to provide a service for you, and as required for insurance purposes. You have the right to have access to your records and to tell me if they are inaccurate.

I am registered as a 'data controller' under the General Data Protection Regulation (also known as the GDPR). My registration number with the Information Commissioner's Office is ... (provide your registration number).

Additional purposes for use and retention of information

I may store and use your personal information:

- for the purposes of communication with you
- for the purposes of discussing with my supervisor or other relevant professionals in an anonymous way.
- if you have been referred through a third party, such as through work, they may require the information.

CONTRACTING WITH THE UNSURE CLIENT

It is not unusual for clients to present for therapy arriving confused, uncertain as to why they feel the way they do, and bewildered about what to do about their problems. However, all clients share one thing in common: first and foremost, they want to feel understood and accepted. There is considerable research evidence to show that therapist warmth, empathy and unconditional positive regard are crucial for effective therapy (Norcross and Wampold, 2019a; Wampold, Norcross and Lambert, 2019). A therapist who ignores this and pursues a contract without first providing an adequate attuned 'play space' (Winnicott, 1971) for their client may well be experienced as unlikely to be able to provide a sufficient 'holding environment' (Winnicott, 1960b/1965b).

Furthermore, the goals clients initially set at the beginning of therapy may be determined by their script. For example: a client states clearly that a life goal is to find a partner and get married. During the course of therapy it emerges that the client has a strong sense that they should be married, on the basis of the cultural importance of marriage and the sense of not being a valid person if you aren't married, as held by parental and societal Parent introjects. It may transpire that this client then amends their goal to having the freedom to choose whether they want to actually get married at all.

Identifying clear goals for contracting can be especially problematic for clients with an undeveloped sense of self, and disorders of the self (Masterson and Lieberman, 2004). Indeed,

    DOI: 10.4324/9781003375890-55

for clients such as these, like a number of other clients, the initial working contract becomes 'finding a contract' (Steiner, 1974). Transactional analyst Frances Townsend proposes some useful questions for clients who come to therapy with vague exploration contracts to help translate these into specific goals; 'What do you hope to discover?'; 'How will discovering this change you?'; or 'What changes will you make from discovering this?'

It is perfectly fine for the therapist to suggest potential general contracts to unsure clients regarding the nature of the work they could productively work on. This could include increased self-awareness, greater capacity for emotional regulation, improved relationships, increased motivation, developing insight into their patterns and their origins, and so on. Indeed, good therapy is likely to cover most if not all of these suggestions as it unfolds, so suggesting them as potential areas of focus within the therapy could easily be used as standard practice with all clients, regardless of whether they are unsure or not.

A potentially problematic situation is the client who may reluctantly be attending therapy, perhaps at someone else's suggestion. This can include the client who has been referred to therapy, for example, by their family doctor, or at the urging of a family member, rather than purposely seeking out therapy independently. In such situations, engaging the client in a discussion about their ambivalence for therapy and what they can fruitfully get out of therapy and suggesting a broad exploration contract for a few sessions is advisable.

Finally, although it is common for TA therapists to ask clients at the beginning of the session if they have a particular goal, or something they specifically want to discuss, some people find this uncomfortable. Of course, some clients do have ideas, although for others, it can be worth the therapist suggesting potential areas to discuss, based on what has been discussed previously, and then checking with the client during the session if they are happy with the suggested focus. In fact, checking in with the client during the session if they are happy with the way the session is going, and if there is anything they want to do differently, or anything they want more or less of is good ethical practice, and is in keeping with research evidence which shows that therapist responsiveness and adjusting the therapy based on client feedback supports positive outcomes to therapy (Miller et al., 2016; Norcross and Wampold, 2019b).

USING HOMEWORK AND BEHAVIOURAL CONTRACTS

The design and introduction of behavioural contracts for specific between session behaviours or activities ('homework') are a common and highly recommended strategy used in TA therapy. There is a strong track record of behavioural contracting/homework within TA, with both Berne and the Gouldings making use of between-session homework to promote or consolidate change (Berne, 1966/1994; Goulding and Goulding, 1979; McNeel, 2010). As a treatment strategy it has much in common with cognitive-behavioural therapy. Clients have different reactions to it – some actively seek (and complete) homework, others ask for it, but don't complete it, and others very clearly say that they do not want homework. There is some research, mostly conducted by cognitive-behavioural therapists, that strongly suggests that homework and its completion are of great benefit to therapy.

'[M]eta-analysis ... showed that both homework assignments and homework compliance are positively related to psychotherapy outcome' (Tryon and Winograd, 2001: 387). They go on to say:

> Therapists who give patients homework assignments and who check on completion of these assignments achieve better outcomes than therapists who do not ask patients to apply what they learned in therapy in their daily lives. A study (Schmidt and Woolaway-Bickel, 2000) indicated that it is not necessarily the quantity of homework assigned, but the quality of the completed homework that leads to better therapy outcomes.

> (ibid.: 388)

DOI: 10.4324/9781003375890-56

I personally aim to give each client a 'homework' task (or 'development activity' or 'change booster', as I call them for clients who have negative reactions to the word 'homework') at each session. The homework task will either relate to what we are currently working on in the client's therapy, or to a specific therapy goal we have identified, or to initiate the change process for the next steps in the client's treatment plan. I explain to clients that therapy is only one hour each week, and what they do with the remaining 167 is important. I also explain that research has shown that clients who are active in their therapy process and engage in homework tasks, get better and quicker outcomes. Before setting any homework tasks, and probably during the client's intake meeting or their first therapy session, I have a conversation with them about their expectations regarding between-session tasks and also ask them what would be a realistic time commitment on their part. I explain that the homework tasks I am likely to give them typically require between 90 seconds and 20 minutes to complete each day. I also tell them that it is unrealistic to think they will do their tasks each day, and that task completion five days out of seven is fine, and that if that isn't possible, three days out of seven is sufficient to maintain momentum for change. I also explain that some tasks will show immediate benefits, whereas others might require some time and persistence before the full benefits are seen, in order to manage client expectations.

It is important that clients do not feel that the task is imposed on them, and that tasks are negotiated in a collaborative interaction. All behavioural contracts that are set should relate in some way to the client's case formulation or key script issues and need to be integrated into a coherent treatment plan. At the very least, the therapist needs a clear idea as to why they are recommending a particular behavioural strategy.

I recommend that the therapist keep some index cards, or slips of paper available, so that any homework contracts can be written down and the client can take them away to reduce the possibility that they will forget the contract. I encourage clients to make use of reminder apps on their smartphone to help them remember their tasks and also advise them that incorporating tasks into their daily routine will help them to complete them, and then have some discussion with them about when they think they might be able to include the task as part of their routine (e.g., doing some breathing or relaxation exercises after lunch, or keeping a gratitude journal as part of their bedtime routine). I also recommend that the therapist keep a record of the contract in their notes, so that they can follow up on the contract with the client in the following sessions. In the follow-up discussion of homework in subsequent sessions, it is advisable for the therapist to actively avoid taking a Parental position (especially when a client has not completed their homework), but to simply stroke the client for task completion and then invite them to discuss their experiences and reactions to the task. In the case of ongoing tasks, encouraging the client to stick with the task and persevere is also recommended.

52

DEALING WITH RESISTANCE OR NON-COMPLIANCE WITH HOMEWORK AND BEHAVIOURAL CONTRACTS

Sometimes, even when 'homework' contracts have been carefully planned and negotiated, the client does not complete them, or reports that the task was not helpful. Often, this tends to be something specific to that task that they did not like, or the client's circumstances (such as being too busy, or being unwell), or that the client did not understand the task and/or see its relevance to them. To some extent, this can be prevented by engaging the client in a conversation about the proposed homework task and ensuring the client understands what it is they need to do, and that its relevance and purpose are explained to them.

Any homework needs to be clearly linked to some kind of therapeutic objective in line with the client's goals, the current areas of focus in the therapy and the intended trajectory of therapy (treatment plan). Homework tasks often emerge from the content of therapy sessions, for example, the therapist might suggest some self-awareness/self-reflection/self-observation tasks based on what is being discussed, or they may suggest a tried-and-tested technique (such as relaxation exercises for anxious clients, or mindfulness for clients with depression), or a particular activity to support or enhance a piece of change work a client has done in session (e.g., facing their fears by doing a previously avoided activity, such as going to a social event for a client who has been socially anxious or withdrawn). When the task is relevant to the client's change process and feels achievable

DOI: 10.4324/9781003375890-57

to the client, then there is a much higher likelihood that the client will complete the task. It is also important that tasks are realistic in terms of what they require the client to do. Explaining to a client that an effective task requires some level or stretch or effort, but not too much so as to be unrealistic and then negotiating within-reach tasks works well.

The most common reasons given for non-completion are the client reporting that they either forgot or 'didn't have the time'. How the therapist deals with this is important, in that we need to account for how busy our clients are and for their need to rest and relax. In doing so, we need to support any movements towards change and also sensitively confront any sign that they are not taking good care of themselves. Forgetful clients can be encouraged to use reminder apps on their smartphones, or to engage the support of family or friends who can help to remind them. In the case of a client who repeatedly reports that they didn't have the time to complete agreed-on homework, then it is wise to ensure that homework is as brief as possible, or does not require much time or energy to complete, such as, 'Doing some breathing relaxation techniques for 90 seconds' or self-observation/self-reflection tasks, such as, 'Just notice when and how often you are being self-critical and giving yourself a hard time about something'. Taking a relaxed stance and avoiding Parental responses to non-completion are vital. If the client feels 'told off', or that the therapist is disapproving of them, this will put strain on the therapeutic relationship and may cause an alliance rupture (see Points 24 and 25).

The use of the word 'homework' alone can evoke quite strong reactions in our Child ego state, which can result in triggering a rebellious response associated with a range of experiences the individual may have had in relation to parents and teachers in childhood. Although exploration of such reactions can be fruitful, it may well be prudent to avoid this kind of reaction by finding some alternative word to home-work. 'Experiment' or 'development exercise' might be more acceptable and avoid the triggering of such resistance (see Point 51).

Some clients have high levels of psychological reactance (Brehm and Brehm, 1981). What this means is that some people are highly sensitive to feeling a threat to their freedom to choose, that they are being controlled, or pressured into doing something or that someone is making a decision for them, and in response they feel some level of anger and become resistant, rebellious or obstinate. Like all experiences of threat, the response is extremely rapid and automatic, and involves cognitive, affective, behavioural, relational and motivational components (Steindl et al., 2015). For example, I have quite high levels of reactivity, and I cannot stand it if someone tells me I 'should' or 'must' or 'have to' watch a particular movie/TV show, or go to a particular place, etc. I instantly feel annoyed and it activates what I call my 'fuck you driver'. Whereas, if someone says 'Oh, I think you might like …' Or 'If you love Barcelona and Madrid, I think you'll really like Lisbon', then I am much more receptive to the suggestion.

In TA terms, we would call reactance having a strong Rebellious Adapted Child ego state. This is often easily determined as clients with high levels of reactance will report being rebellious, or having issues with people in authority, or struggling with any sense of being controlled in any way, or having difficulty with following instructions or being told what to do (especially if they don't agree with or don't understand the reasons behind the task). Having a conversation with them about how you can both best approach between-session tasks is advisable. For clients with high levels of reactance, it is best to adopt a more reflective and non-directive approach in therapy and perhaps avoid the use of homework tasks altogether (Beutler, Edwards and Someah, 2018). Another way to approach this is to say something like, 'I don't know if this will work for you or not, but some people find (brief explanation of task) to be helpful' and then leave it up to the client to think about and decide if they want to engage with the task or not.

It is certainly true that for most people there is a part of the self that wants to change and another part that strenuously resists any change and complies with the script. Such ambivalence to change can be puzzling for both client and therapist, although, once understood, it can be worked with and addressed. If we take the view that all our script was developed in a relational context, and that our script represents some kind of means to preserve our attachments and ensure we are accepted or was developed to protect us or ensure our needs were met in some way or another, then we have ways of understanding the ambivalence to change more clearly. In these examples, our client may unconsciously fear change at some level because they feel that it might threatens to destroy the link with their internal objects/relationships (the attachment to their parents) and resistance can be seen as a means of survival. The Child logic is something like, 'If I hold onto this script belief, truly believe it, and act out my script, I can be sure to be loved and accepted.' Understood in this context, change would generate deep anxiety and fear of abandonment. This is just one possible explanation for resistance to change, and it is likely there are many different reasons why people are ambivalent to change (others, for example, include the emergence of impasses). The therapist is advised to maintain a spirit of enquiry and curiosity and acceptance towards the client's ambivalence and to invite the client into exploration of their ambivalence. It is unlikely that ambivalence or resistance will be resolved in one session, and will often need revisiting many times throughout the course of the therapy. This is particularly true for clients with complex problems or those with personality disorders or problems of a characterological nature.

It is generally sensible to assume that all clients feel ambivalent at some level about change. Raising this by saying something like, 'Most people feel a bit apprehensive, cautious, or even ambivalent about changing. Even though we need to change something, it can be daunting to put it into practice. I'm wondering what your concerns are in this respect?', or in the case of a change where a client needs to give something up (e.g., drinking too much alcohol), we might say something like,

> I know it's got out of hand and you've realized it's harming your health, but it's inevitable that over the years you've got enjoyment out of drinking, or liked the social elements of it. Or maybe you've used it to self-medicate when you've been feeling upset about something. I'm wondering what you might put in place to get those same benefits from healthier things. What do you think you could do instead of drinking that gives you those things without damaging your health?

I highly recommend all TA therapists acquaint themselves with the basics of motivational interviewing. Motivational interviewing is an evidence-based therapeutic approach which was specifically designed to deal with client ambivalence around behavioural change (Miller and Rollnick, 2013). The questioning methods and approach used in motivational interviewing are easily integrated into TA practice, and align well with TA contractual method.

53

THE 'GOOD ENOUGH' CONTRACT

Sometimes our contracts with our clients are not as 'tight' or clearly defined as we would like them to be. It is worth periodically revisiting the overall therapy contract(s) with your clients to see how they are progressing towards their stated aim(s) of therapy, and whether they want to change direction, or develop a more specific contract where the existing contract is more general.

In relation to contracting, do not get into contracts or set up promises that you cannot deliver on. If a therapist says they are willing to do something for a client, or sets up special arrangements, even on a temporary basis, they have to be prepared to do it for the long haul. This includes, but is not limited to, telephone contact between sessions, increasing session frequency, extending session length, and so on. It is far better not to offer such extensions than to offer them and then later have to withdraw them (Benjamin, 2006).

The approach and process of contracting can be reparative in itself. Seeking collaboration and clarification of wants, inviting the client to think for himself or herself and set their own priorities all demonstrate a respect for your client that may in turn invite them into self-valuing. In forming a contract, there is no need to get caught up in 'doing it right' or attempting to create the perfect contract. Developing a treatment contract with a client generally progresses through several stages of specificity. Each stage of contracting is revisited and developed through the course of the therapy. For example, a client may present with severe, long-standing depression. At the beginning of therapy the client may state their treatment goal as 'not to feel depressed'. To suggest a contract such as 'I will feel happy in myself' may seem unrealistic and far-fetched at this stage as it so dramatically contrasts with the client's existing self-image that the client will not consider such a contract to be possible. Furthermore, without spending some time building a diagnosis, the therapist may not have a clear sense of the client's prognosis, so to offer such a contract may be unethical. The therapist is advised in instances such as this to suggest a contract that the therapy will begin with exploring the client's patterns and the structure of their problems. Suggesting that alongside this, that you could also explore ways to improve their mood, or things they can do to help manage their feelings on a day-to-day level. After a period of therapy, focusing on the development of awareness, it may then change to 'not to give myself such a hard time'. Once a further period of therapy has taken place, focusing on the client not internally beating themselves up, the contract can be renegotiated to 'accept myself', which in turn may eventually be revised to 'self-love'. In this example, the contract is related to the client's diagnosis (severity of depression and loss of hope) and refining the contract becomes part of the therapist's ongoing treatment plan. At each stage the contract was 'good enough'. Each of these contracts may also be successively refined to include specificity and observable changes or actions (Stewart, 2007) as the work progresses and the client gains in awareness and vision. Working with progressive contracts such as these also allows for earlier termination of the therapy. For example, a client may decide that they have done enough for now, and may negotiate the possibility of returning to therapy in future, if they want to. There is no need for clients to stay in therapy in the long term unless they want to, or that they feel they are continuing to get enough benefits as to outweigh the time, effort and costs involved. Indeed, for many clients, long-term therapy is a luxury they cannot afford. I am an advocate of people dipping in and out of therapy as and when they need to, and using therapy effectively, rather than relying on it.

It is my experience that a large number of clients will actually stay in therapy that is broken down into smaller chunks and where success seems possible, rather than stay in therapy of an indeterminate length or leave with limited gains. In the case of a therapist establishing a loose contract (such as the depression example given above) with the intention of progression and refinement later in the therapy, it is important that the therapist regularly checks the existing contract and discusses any suggested amendments to the contract with their client.

54

CONTRACTING: PREPARING FOR CONFLICT AND NEGATIVE TRANSFERENCE

Contracting can pave the way for what is to come in therapy, and the changes the client is likely to experience along the way. From an ethical perspective, we have a responsibility to facilitate our clients making as informed a choice as possible about whether to enter therapy or not. Part of this negotiation and preparation needs to include reference to the turbulence that may occur as part of the change process. It is doubtful we can ever totally prepare clients for the reality of the disruption, both internally and interpersonally, that can occur throughout the therapy process. It is, however, possible to forewarn our clients of the turbulent, and sometimes conflictual nature of change. I suggest that such warning is both ethical and also provides a foundation for dealing with such issues as and when they arise. In my experience, contracting for this at the outset provides a clear frame for dealing with problems as they arise. The contract provides a guide for what to do when the client is experiencing intense transference or an alliance rupture with their therapist, and is something the client will likely hold in mind when they are uncomfortable about aspects of the therapy. This preparatory work is often remembered by clients at difficult times and can prevent premature termination by a client who simply got upset and didn't realize that conflict was not only to be expected, but a potential source of healing.

Sometimes clients can present for therapy with rather unrealistic expectations that once 'cured', they will lead completely harmonious lives and will never encounter conflict again.

 DOI: 10.4324/9781003375890-59

'Pain, ambiguity, paradox and conflict are inevitable in life. They are necessary in a deeply searching psychotherapy and, most importantly, can become vitalizing resources in living one's life' (Cornell and Bonds-White, 2001: 81). It is also wise to be honest about how the process of therapy can have an unexpected impact on other relationships in the client's life. It is not unusual for clients to end friendships or for close relationships to become tense for a period while everyone adjusts to the client's changes. Sometimes these changes are precisely what the client wants, or needs but sometimes they are frightening and take the client by surprise.

Just as it is prudent and ethical to forewarn clients that the therapy process can disturb their extra-therapy relationships, it is also wise to discuss the potential for alliance ruptures or the emergence of distress and negative transference in the therapy. My own method is to say something like the following at an appropriate time during the first few sessions:

> While I won't ever say anything to deliberately hurt your feelings, no one is perfect, and we all sometimes inadvertently upset or disappoint other people. It's important that you tell me if you do feel hurt or disappointed by something I've said or done so we can talk about it. That in itself can often be hugely therapeutic, as it's often a big change for a lot of people. Therapy works best when both people are frank and candid with each other. I might not always say what you want to hear, and sometimes I might really challenge you, but if I do so, I will be coming from a position of best intentions. If it's difficult, tell me and we can work it out.

> The feelings that people have in and about the therapy relationship can often be really important. Part of the way that therapy works is by having a different kind of relationship to the ones we normally have and a big part of that is openly discussing how we're experiencing each other. That can include being honest about any angry or hurt feelings so we can bring them out into the open and understand them. Also you might find there are times when you don't want to come to a session, or when you find yourself feeling reluctant or too embarrassed to tell me something. In situations like that, telling me you are having those

feelings is usually really important. We won't necessarily have to talk about whatever it is you're feeling embarrassed about, but just being open and honest about it will really help you get the most out of therapy. I realize that being so frank and honest can be really difficult. I can give you my word I will take your feelings seriously, but to do that, I'll need you to tell me about them. How does that sound to you?

Generally, clients respond positively to such statements, although they will commonly demonstrate some discomfort or unease at the thought of being so honest and dealing with conflict so directly. It is also very hard to imagine someone whom you have experienced as being supportive as being someone you might be angry with. In the case of such incongruity, it is useful to explore the client's feelings about their discomfort. My experience is that, in such situations, clients will express a general unease around conflict and managing unpleasant interpersonal feelings. Expressing difficult feelings and learning to manage conflict can then be brought into the therapeutic arena by the therapist, suggesting this as a potential area for change for the client through further contracting.

Part 5

TREATMENT PLANNING

COMPARATIVE TREATMENT SEQUENCES

Treatment sequence models are widely used in TA practice, as a conceptual framework to understand the types of stages and associated tasks that a client and therapist are likely to move through on the therapeutic journey. In practice, many transactional analysts develop their own synthesis of two or more of these sequences to understand the different stages of the therapeutic work. Although these models appear on the surface to be rather different from each other, they contain a number of similarities in that they all identify the beginning stages of therapy to comprise building a working alliance and then move to deeper, restructuring levels of work later in the therapy. Mostly they assume that decontamination precedes deconfusion, although this view of therapy has recently been challenged by a number of TA authors, primarily those from the relational approach, who consider deconfusion to be occurring from the very outset of therapy (Hargaden and Sills, 2002). These models can be helpful in giving the therapist a sense of the progression of therapy, and develop their patience in waiting for a client to be ready to move onto another stage of the therapeutic process, and in helping the therapist work out how to facilitate the client's movement into the next stage. However, they can be unhelpful, and even limiting in that they can give the impression that therapy is a linear process and that clients move through stages sequentially, when in reality therapy is more circular, or perhaps more accurately, spiral in its unfolding. If therapy is conceptualized as a fluid

Table 55.1 Therapy road map

Berne (1961/1994, 1966)	Woollams and Brown (1978)	Clarkson (1992)	Tudor and Widdowson (2001)
Establish working alliance	Motivation	Establish working alliance	Establish working alliance
		Initial contracting	Initial contracting
Decontamination	Awareness	Decontamination	Decontamination
	Treatment contract	(Treatment contract)	(Treatment contract)
Deconfusion	Deconfusion	Deconfusion	Emotional Literacy
		Internal Nurturing Parent	Internal Nurturing Parent
		Emotional literacy	Deconfusion
	Redecision	Redecision	Parent ego state work
		Parent ego state work	Redecision
		Rechilding	
		Reorientation	Reorientation
Relearning	Relearning	Relearning	
Termination	Termination	Termination	Termination

and an unfolding process, then these models can be helpful by providing a 'roadmap' of where one is in the therapy, and what might need to come next. Table 55.1 aligns four sequences. TA therapists can choose from, or combine these sequences to create their own 'therapy roadmap'.

FORMULATING INDIVIDUALIZED TREATMENT PLANS

Effective treatment planning is a key skill for transactional analysts, and yet there has been very little TA literature to guide transactional analysts with a framework for developing individual treatment plans. An individual treatment plan is usually devised in supervision, or on the basis of reflection about a client and their presenting issues. The method presented here is the one I teach to trainees and supervisees and has proven to be effective and simple to use.

STEP ONE

The therapist begins with reflecting upon the following two questions: 'What do I think this client needs to do? What changes do they need to make?' Answer your questions intuitively and write your answers using any wording you like. At this stage, you do not need to be precise. Your responses may be for global, large changes or for small changes. Include both in your list. If you are working with clients, I would encourage you to go through this process for each of your current clients now and discover for yourself how simple and effective this method of treatment planning can be. It is absolutely fine at this stage that these target changes are generated solely by the therapist. You may at a later stage share your ideas with your client for verification if you feel that to do so would be therapeutic for your client. Below is an example of possible responses to these questions. These are fairly common themes and you may be able to identify these in your clients:

 DOI: 10.4324/9781003375890-62

- Internalize a sense of self-worth.
- Learn to be assertive with their family.
- Stop trying to please everyone all the time.
- Stop feeling guilty about not being perfect.
- Stop giving themselves such a hard time about their real and imagined shortcomings.
- Learn to relax and let their hair down.
- Learn to manage and regulate their feelings.

The lists you generate for your clients might possibly be much longer.

STEP TWO

Take each item on the list and see how we can understand that particular change using TA concepts. To take the above example:

- to redecide script beliefs from 'I'm not good enough' to 'I am good enough';
- to be able to accept, ask for and give self positive strokes (self-worth);
- to redecide the 'don't be important' injunction;
- to use positive controlling Parent transactions to set limits when appropriate;
- to stop grandiosity about pleasing others and associated discounting of own needs and feelings;
- to stop overadapting;
- to interrupt and change critical internal dialogue between Parent and Child;
- to develop a more self-nurturing Parent ego state;
- to start accounting for successes and stroking self in celebration of personal strengths;
- to develop a realistic appraisal of self rather than seeking 'evidence' of script beliefs;
- to stop setting up situations and games whereby the script beliefs are 'confirmed';
- to use Adult resources to recognize when it is time to stop and relax.

You now have the basis of your treatment plan for this client.

STEP THREE

Now, take the list of target changes, and compare this with the client's goals for therapy and presenting problem. Indicate if any items do not correspond with the problem or your client's existing therapy goals. Any target changes that are not clearly accounted for by your client's therapy goals or are obviously linked to the client's intended direction of change are to be contracted for if they are to become part of the therapy. This can be done at any stage you feel it is appropriate to raise the issue with your client. The remainder of the issues are already covered by your existing contract and so can become part of your treatment plan. It is worth thinking at this stage about how you might facilitate these changes. If your client completed the Cooper-Norcross Inventory of Preferences (C-NIP) as part of the intake process, you can use this to guide your intervention plan.

STEP FOUR

Taking the list you compiled, highlight which are the three most important, or priority, target changes. Often certain changes will bring about other changes in an intrapsychic catalytic reaction. Using the example above, the three most important target changes might be:

- to redecide script beliefs about 'not being good enough' to 'I am good enough';
- to redecide the 'don't be important' injunction;
- to interrupt and stop critical internal dialogue between Parent and Child and replace it with a self-compassionate, Nurturing Parent internal dialogue

With these three changes, the other changes would be easier, or may take place spontaneously. It may be, however, that other changes can happen sooner, for instance, in this example, the script belief of not being good enough might be a very deep issue and only redecided after much therapy. Taking Adult control, evaluating situations and actively avoiding situations whereby the script beliefs are confirmed or even recognizing and changing these situations when they are taking place would weaken the strength of the underlying script beliefs and so may be a more realistic change to go for first. Take some time to work out which changes can happen first, or are 'live' in the therapy at the moment with your client. Explore in supervision which interventions you might make to help facilitate each of these target changes.

STEP FIVE

Indicate on your list which of the target changes are short-term and can be addressed soon, which will require ongoing attention and those which are long-range target changes, that would be more appropriate to introduce later on in the therapy process. You now have an individualized treatment plan for your client.

MONITORING AND REVISING TREATMENT PLANNING

Once you have identified a client's target changes and developed an individualized treatment plan, you will need to regularly revisit and revise your treatment plan. Ideally your treatment plan would be checked and revised after each session, but I would recommend that you review your treatment plan at least once a month for each client. It is important to continually monitor, review and track your client's changes over time.

An effective way to monitor changes in the process and in the client progress is by drawing up a table relating to your client's individualized treatment plan. In the process of change, often such central changes take place gradually with incremental change taking place over a period of time. One way of doing this is to write the list of 'target changes' on a single sheet of paper, and then, in columns corresponding to sessions, make a note of which changes were addressed. Do bear in mind that most changes will require repeated revisiting before the issue is finally resolved. Using the examples given in Point 56, we can develop the treatment plan 'tracker' in Table 57.1.

Take time to read your treatment plan before each session with your client, to refresh your memory of its contents. Keep your treatment plan in the above format with your client notes and make a note when each was tackled during a session. At the end of each session, simply marking which items from the treatment plan were addressed will enable you to keep a close track on the client's changes over time. Cross any changes off the list as they take place, indicating that the

216   DOI: 10.4324/9781003375890-63

Table 57.1 Treatment plan 'tracker'

Target change	Date:	Date:	Date:	Date:	Date:	Date:	Date:	Date:
Redecide script beliefs about 'not being good enough' to 'being good enough'								
Stroke economy – to be able to accept, ask for and give self positive strokes (self-worth)								
Redecide the 'don't be important' injunction								
Support use of positive Controlling Parent transactions to set limits when appropriate								
Confront grandiosity about pleasing others and associated discounting of own needs and feelings								
Confront over-adapting								
Interrupt and stop critical internal dialogue between Parent and Child								
Accounting for success and stroking success in celebration of personal strengths								

(Continued)

Table 57.1 (Cont.)

Target change	Date:	Date:	Date:	Date:	Date:	Date:	Date:
Promote realistic appraisal of self rather than seeking 'evidence' of script beliefs (decontamination)							
Game analysis of setting up situations whereby the script beliefs are 'confirmed'							
Stroke Adult resources for recognizing when it is time to stop and relax							

particular change has been fully made and add new items as relevant or as they emerge. Keep the three priority target changes under review and make notes on their current status. I usually keep a sticky note on the front of each client's notes, with the current priority targets for change or focus of therapy, any issues which I want to revisit, or which the client and I have discussed as something to focus on next. It is also really useful to keep track of the client's changes from outcome measure data (see Point 31). I also have another sticky note on the front of my client's notes with their initial score on CORE-10, PHQ-9 and GAD-7 and their latest score, so I can keep track on my client's progress and factor this into my short term treatment planning.

ACCOUNTING FOR THE IMPACT OF TRAUMA

A significant number of clients presenting for therapy have experienced trauma (Anderson, Howard, Dean et. al., 2016; Kessler et al., 2017). This is only to be expected, especially if one takes into account that most adults have experienced at least one traumatic event capable of causing Post-Traumatic Stress Disorder (PTSD) (Breslau and Kessler, 2001) and the prevalence of Adverse Childhood Experiences (ACEs) among the general population (Felitti et al., 1998). Indeed, many of the presenting problems clients bring to therapy have their aetiology in trauma, and so conducting therapy in a trauma-informed manner is best practice.

Working in a trauma-informed manner requires adaptations to how therapy is 'normally' conducted (SAMHSA, 2015; van der Kolk, 2015). First, being trauma-informed requires us to ask the question (implicitly or explicitly) 'What happened to you?' instead of 'What is wrong with you?'. This non-pathologizing stance is entirely in keeping with TA, where we view the client's presenting problems and symptoms as manifestations of their life script, which they developed in response to their life experiences. Trauma symptoms are, after all, a normal response to an abnormal situation (Courtois, Ford and Cloitre, 2009).

Traumatic events are emotionally overwhelming experiences which the individual perceives as life-threatening or significantly threatening, or where an individual witnesses injury or death to another person or learns about such experiences of a loved one. The main purpose of the human brain is to ensure survival, and one of the ways it achieves this

  DOI: 10.4324/9781003375890-64

is to avoid danger, based on its past learning. Threats and danger are associated with intense arousal, priming them for rapid assessment of future situations where the brain perceives danger. Traumatic events or prolonged stress effectively recalibrate the brain's threat response system into a more or less permanently activated state. Once activated, it will dominate the brain's functioning, making it difficult to activate deliberate and rational responses (Mobbs et al., 2009). If considered from a TA lens, this suggests a key principle in working with survivors of trauma is to soothe the Child ego state, so that the Adult can be activated.

Being trauma-informed means taking practical steps to minimize the potential for re-traumatization. Potentially re-traumatizing practices include (but are not limited to); mis-labelling client symptoms as disorders instead of traumatic stress responses, being overly authoritative or austere towards clients, heavy use of confrontation, making therapy conditional on the client conforming to the therapist's beliefs and definitions, making therapy conditional on the client complying with a blanket no-harm contract, minimizing or discounting the significance of the client's reports and experiences of trauma or abuse and being unaware of the impact that trauma can have on the life of an individual (for this, I strongly recommend all therapists find out more about the long-term impact of trauma, and particularly the long-term impact of ACEs on mental health). The trauma-informed therapist routinely screens all clients for trauma during intake (see Point 31). It is important to slow clients down and discourage them from disclosing details of any trauma before ensuring that they are sufficiently stabilized (see below). Some suggested dialogue for trauma screening is:

- I'm going to ask some questions now that are direct and intrusive. I don't need any details, all I need at this point is a yes or no answer, so I have a sense of what we're dealing with here.
- Has anything ever happened to you that might be considered traumatic?

- Did anything ever happen to you during childhood or adolescence that might be considered abuse?
- Has anyone ever behaved violently or aggressively towards you in a way that really frightened you?
- Have you ever experienced sex that was unwanted, coerced, or happened when you were asleep or too drunk or drugged to agree to it?

I also suggest that therapists ask all new clients to complete an ACEs questionnaire as part of the intake process (these are freely and readily available online).

Judith Herman's (1992) tri-phasic model has become the gold standard for treatment of trauma and as such is the the basic treatment one should follow when working with trauma. In summary, the tri-phasic model is:

1. Ensuring client safety and stabilization (i.e., establishing that the client is no longer in danger and that they can manage and tolerate intense emotions).
2. Trauma processing/remembering and mourning.
3. (Re)integration (enhancing relationships and promoting social reconnection).

Stabilization includes providing the client with psychoeducation about the nature of trauma and its effects (see above) and teaching clients grounding techniques and emotion regulation techniques so that they are equipped to deal with intense emotions (see Points 68 and 69). Helping clients identify and draw upon their own personal strengths supports the stabilization process. Stabilization alone is known to be highly effective for the treatment of trauma (even without the use of trauma processing techniques) (Eichfeld et al., 2019). It is important that the client can effectively regulate their emotions before they begin to discuss details of traumatic events. Disclosure of details of trauma needs to be done slowly, and ensuring the client remains within their 'window of tolerance' (Siegel, 2020) throughout. This is easier said than done, and so a cautious approach to disclosure (or referral to a therapist trained in trauma therapy) is recommended. Although the tri-phasic model is presented as a linear series of stages, in reality, the (re)integration stage generally occurs throughout therapy. As TA is rich in models regarding interpersonal relationships, most TA therapists are good at helping clients to enrich their relationships, manage boundaries, and reconnect socially.

A detailed discussion regarding trauma processing is beyond the scope of this book. Furthermore, as the vast majority of counselling and psychotherapy training only provides a basic and general introduction to trauma, under-taking further training and CPD on working with trauma are strongly advised.

TREATMENT PLANNING FOR EXPERIENTIAL DISCONFIRMATION

In my research (Widdowson, 2013), I identified a previously unnamed process that the therapists were using with the clients who had the best outcomes. I named this process systematic experiential disconfirmation (Widdowson, 2014). I find it to be the quickest and easiest method for facilitating redecision. Needless to say, as a technique, it works best in the context of a solid therapeutic relationship where the task and goals of therapy are agreed and where there is a good enough emotional bond between the therapist and client. The process of redecision is essentially re-evaluating and discarding or changing a script belief (and script patterns), such as ways of relating, behaviour, or typical emotional expression. If we see a life script as a network of beliefs, attitudes, values, implicit rules, expectations, that guide how we live, and how we relate to others and the world, then script beliefs are relatively stable, once the individual has developed them. Some will change during the course of the lifespan, through maturity, education, exposure to new people and new situations, falling in (and out of) love, heartbreak, work, achievement, suffering. Others, especially an individual's most 'core beliefs' will remain, fairly unchanged, and potentially stronger from years of 'confirmation of their validity'.

The method I attached to systematic experiential disconfirmation was memory reconsolidation (Ecker, Ticic and Hulley, 2012) as it seemed to offer a pre-existing, research-based framework for facilitating change around implicit emotional learning and core beliefs. As transactional analysts, we recognize that our clients have an array of sophisticated mechanisms to maintain their script, and to filter out anything

DOI: 10.4324/9781003375890-65

which challenges their script. This preserves an internal sense of equilibrium, or homoeostasis. When they come to therapy, they are vulnerable and asking for help; their previous ways are no longer working for them, and so they are (at least on the face of it), receptive to help. Fortunately, most clients these days are sufficiently therapy-savvy to realize that the therapist will likely challenge their thinking and call out counterproductive or damaging behaviour. This makes contracting for disconfirmation experiences much easier. I often say to clients in the early stages of therapy that I am likely at some stage in the therapy to invite them to do something which seems counterproductive, and that they are welcome to question what I am doing, although I may well ask them to simply 'trust me on this one. It is part of a plan, and not just something I have made up on a whim.'

Memory reconsolidation has been developed into a therapy approach called coherence therapy (ibid.). As a constructivist therapy (like TA), coherence therapy views all of our client's symptoms as making sense *at some point in their history*. So, for example, the symptoms of a client with social anxiety and who is terrified at the prospect of speaking to other people make sense when we see that their fear of others started at a time when they were being badly bullied at school. When people who were nice to her, one day, joined in with the bullying the next day, and none of the teachers intervened to stop it. This process of identifying clear, and reasonable inferences about the historical cause of our client's problems is something every transactional analyst does at least once a day in practice (if not more), and so this way of thinking is entirely in keeping with TA.

Discoveries on memory reconsolidation – based on neuroscience and psychology research – have found that when memories are activated, they become malleable, and amenable to change. This is of particular significance when we consider that most of our client's symptoms and distress is indeed held within their implicit memory system. During the assessment phase of TA therapy, we identify a series of 'shorthand' statements to summarize our client's script: injunctions, script beliefs, and so on (see Points 35 and 79). These statements have stood the test of time because they identify fairly typical responses a child might have in response to distress, confusion and the need to preserve their attachment relationships.

The way memory reconsolidation is used in therapy is first by identifying an implicit learning (or script belief, or injunction, and so on), and bringing it into the client's awareness. The client needs to be able to resonate with the message we have put to them (or worded as an injunction). If they can, we have effectively shed light on some of the client's implicit learning (which made sense at the time) which now has a central role in their current problems and symptoms. Memory reconsolidation occurs when a person brings the implicit learning into awareness, while having an experience which disconfirms the client's belief (Ecker, 2018). As life script largely sets a template of expectations, this mismatch then triggers a mechanism of prediction error and expectancy violation. This then triggers a process whereby the old belief/learning is updated, or replaced with new learning. It is important to note that the disconfirming experience can be something relatively small, if it violates the expectation and/or the implicit emotional learning, while the belief is in conscious awarenness, the old script belief will be changed, or redecided.

So one way of incorporating this into a treatment plan would be to invite a client to reflect on their identified script beliefs and injunctions after sessions, and to pay particular attention to times when they would usually impact on them negatively. Invite them to notice what their usual script expectations are and what actually happens. Of course, when done in this way, the process is not targeted, so may lack some of the surgical precision we can see with targeted memory reconsolidation. It makes sense to frequently ask clients to tell you what their expectations are of themselves, others and different situations. Ask them what they imagine will happen and how they will end up feeling. Recommend that they keep their initial expectations in mind when in the situation, but be willing to go with the experiment, in order to see evidence there still is for their belief. When the experience does not confirm their beliefs and there is a mismatch between expectations and reality, prediction error will occur and the old belief will be updated. Whenever you and a client identify an additional script belief, you can also begin to address this in the same way.

Whenever a client tells you of something which disconfirms their script (often as they describe the events of their week), whether or not the experience was by chance or planned, there is value in picking up on it in the session, draw the client's attention to it then keep the experience and how it disconfirms their script in their attention for a few minutes. This is to block their usual discounting mechanisms which have prevented them from previously disconfirming their beliefs and maintained their script beliefs (see Point 88). In this sense, working with disconfirming script beliefs can be kept 'on the agenda' as a potential strategy at any given time, as part of the broader therapy contract.

Often clients have several particularly powerful and especially limiting script beliefs, which can be seen as the keystone, which holds the entire script structure in place. I encourage you to think about corrective experiences your client could potentially have which might disconfirm these beliefs. To some extent, many of our client's script beliefs are gently challenged in an ongoing and implicit way as part of the therapeutic relationship. For instance, a client who does not feel worthy and who has a 'don't be important' injunction will have an experience which does not match with these in therapy. Where the relationship has provided a mismatch, it can be used at critical moments to create memory reconsolidation.

For example, Jess, an anxious and highly conscientious client with terribly low self-esteem became tearful and agitation early in a session when I asked her about the previous week's homework. She explained that she hadn't done the homework tasks we had agreed because her daughter was back home from university for a week and her husband was ill and so had been unable to contribute to household chores. She added: 'I expect you're disappointed and cross with me for not sticking to the agreement and wasting your time. I hope you don't think I'm not putting enough effort in and decide to throw me out of therapy!' In response, I smiled warmly and said: 'Jess, just look at my face for a few moments. Do you see any signs of disappointment or anger? Please, tell me what you see.' She moved around in her seat a little and said, 'No, you don't seem cross.' I nodded and said: 'I'm not at all cross or disappointed with you. I know you are committed to therapy and you have always done therapy homework carefully. This week has a bit different for you personally and you've prioritized family relationships by spending quality time with your daughter and taking care of your husband. I think that sounds great, and I'm sure spending time with your daughter in particular has been lovely.' I think I invited her to elaborate on the fantasies she had about my expected reaction. I then asked her how she has experienced my actual reaction and if it matched her expectation in any way. She stated that it had not, but she still felt as if she had disappointed me (feeling like a disappointment to others was a familiar feeling for Jess). We then spoke a little about her strong feeling that if she wasn't perfect, then she would disappoint people and that would be terrible. I paused for a moment and asked her if she thought it was terrible that I was ten minutes late for our previous session. 'Oh no, not at all,' she said. 'You were stuck in traffic and you let me know you were going to be late. These things happen.' I said that maybe it could be seen that I had done a terrible thing, or that I might have disappointed her. 'No, I wasn't disappointed,' she said. I commented that it seemed that she had two sets of rules, one for everyone else, and different and much more stringent ones for herself. I wondered out loud why she was treating herself unfairly and not applying the same standards. I then followed this by saying, 'So there is a part of you who believes you must always be on time and do everything perfectly or it will be terrible, and you also have this experience of me not being perfect last week and of that not actually being terrible at all.' We then continued the discussion for a little while about being perfect and making mistakes, and we both shared some silly and minor mistakes we had made which made us laugh. She concluded that 'Nobody is perfect. Things happen. And maybe it's not so dreadful after all.' (Another example of using memory reconsolidation can be found in the case of Alastair, see Widdowson, 2014.)

Sometimes, only one or two disconfirming experiences (which are then discussed and held in the client's awareness) are sufficient. However, deeply ingrained script beliefs which a person has carried around for many years are likely to need many disconfirmations to weaken their grip over the person's psyche. When planning how a client can seek our dis-confirmation, it is important to bear their 'window of toler-ance' in mind. If the disconfirming experience is very powerful, or too intense, the client may discount it somehow as the challenge to their script will be too much at that moment in time. Certainly in the early phases of therapy, a light-touch, fairly gentle disconfirming experience is enough to begin to apply some oil to the cogs of the client's life script to get things moving. Some change to script (even if it just questioning it) is better than no change.

It is worth noting that research indicates that the period of 4–5 hours after a session is critical to the consolidation of learning from the session (Pedrera, Pérez-Cuesta and Maldonado, 2002). This is because of the neurological changes that take place in the client's neural networks during a therapy session. For this 'golden window of opportunity' period of time the client's memory systems and synapses are still very malleable while they continue to process the session. In light of this, I usually recommend that clients consider things they could do after therapy for 'decompression time' and I encourage them to focus on physically and mentally healthy activities during this time. This might include having a quiet evening reading and with no TV, making something nutritious for dinner, seeing a supportive friend, or going for a walk, which are all good ways to ensure that the re-consolidation period is handled optimally. I also encourage clients to 'speak to themselves kindly' for the rest of the day and to offer themselves the patience and understanding they would offer to another person they cared about.

TACKLING 'THE SPLINTER' AND 'THE BENT PENNY'

In his typically creative character of writing, Eric Berne came up with a number of analogies and metaphors to explain the development, maintenance and treatment of human problems. Two of these are his 'splinter' analogy (Berne, 1971) and his 'bent penny' metaphor (Berne, 1961/1986). As concepts, not only do they help us and our clients make sense of how they have come to be in the situation they are in, but they also encourage us to develop ways to address them so that our clients can move to a place of greater well-being.

As a model, TA places great emphasis on taking an individual's development into account in order to understand the formation of their life script (and, by extension, their presenting problems). Berne used a metaphor of a stack of pennies to represent the development of the psyche, with a new penny being added to the stack each day. Over time, a large tall stack would accumulate. Berne invited us to imagine that trauma, adverse childhood experiences and such like would cause a bent penny to be added to the stack. One bent penny would skew the stack, however, a large number of bent pennies caused by repeated trauma/mis attunement, etc. would result in the stack being unstable. The task of the therapist can then be viewed as a kind of psychological *Jenga*. As part of the therapy we are metaphorically identifying which pennies are bent (by identifying the early scene), carefully removing them, hammering them flat and placing them back without the stack collapsing, through carefully attuned, well-judged and well-timed and incisive interventions.

DOI: 10.4324/9781003375890-66

If we use this metaphor for both assessment and treatment planning purposes, Berne's message is clear. He suggests that as transactional analysts it is our job to continually consider where our client's bent pennies are, and how we might flatten them out to cause greater stability to our client's 'stack'. This can be applied to treatment planning, particularly on a session-by-session basis. So, think about your clients, and ask yourself, both before and during sessions, 'Where are their bent pennies and what am I going to do to help flatten them out?'

In his splinter analogy, Berne (1971) used the example of a patient visiting their doctor with a sore back. The ineffective doctor would prescribe painkillers and send the patient away, whereas the effective doctor would notice that the client was limping slightly when they walked into his office, ask the patient to remove their shoes and socks, and notice that there was a splinter in their foot. The doctor would then simply remove the splinter and prescribe something to reduce the inflammation and clear any potential infection. The patient would then find that their back pain was resolved due to being able to walk freely and evenly. If we take this analogy and consider how it relates to therapy, our task can then be considered to find the psychological equivalent of the splinter and remove it. However, this is easier said than done. With psychopathology (perhaps with the exception of trauma), there are usually no clear-cut single causes of the client's problems. The splinter analogy presupposes that there is one splinter, whereas in reality there are likely to be a number of them. Recent research on psychopathology suggests that a series of small changes start to interact, amplify each other and become self-perpetuating (network theory). We also have to account for potential genetic vulnerabilities, the client's temperament and their interactions with their environment, and possibly the impact of structural oppression. Additionally we need to take into consideration the tendency of the human brain to prioritize negative information and to draw conclusions which will promote attachment and therefore survival.

When considering multiple splinters, transdiagnostic processes identified by Harvey et al. (2004) propose that all forms of psychopathology involve distortions/disturbances in attention, flexibility, perception and interpretation of stimuli, memory, expectancy, reasoning, thought process, emotion regulation, and behaviour. It is reasonable to assume that our clients will have 'splinters' in several of these domains, if not all, and that these will be intrinsically connected to their script.

For example, most disorders involve negative affectivity to some extent or another. Efforts to help promote emotional regulation (as in, down-regulation of negative emotion and up-regulation of positive emotion) will help shift a client's overall mood. If we combine this with efforts to help change their negative expectations, negative memory bias and negative ways of interpreting events, we not only help the client to change their script, we also help the client to adjust their overall frame of reference (Schiff et al., 1975) to a more flexible, optimistic and realistic orientation which promotes greater movement towards health. By looking for and identifying multiple splinters, the therapist can construct a comprehensive treatment plan that reflects the complexity and interactive nature of a client's process and presentation, and which systematically addresses their script and supports the emergence and activation of their *physis* (Berne, 1971), their intrinsic drive towards health and growth.

AWARENESS, SPONTANEITY, INTIMACY, AUTONOMY AND HOMONOMY

Within TA, autonomy is viewed as the freedom to choose how one lives, without the constraints of one's life script. The late Petruska Clarkson is reported to have wryly commented: 'Autonomy is doing something *even if* your parents approve of it.' Berne defined autonomy as being characterized by the release of three capacities: awareness, spontaneity and intimacy (Berne, 1964). Stewart (2007: 34) has summarized the trans-actional analyst's role in the slogan 'confront script – invite autonomy'. In addition to addressing the client's script issues, the TA therapist proactively utilizes methods that will promote the development of awareness, spontaneity and intimacy. The movement towards enhanced awareness, spontaneity and inti-macy can be used as an alternative treatment planning method that focuses on health rather than pathology (Cox, 2000), or can be combined and used simultaneously with a script-challenging approach as a dual process model. In contemporary TA, we also see the promotion of homonomy as being a vital part of the client's change process.

AWARENESS

In Berne's descriptions, awareness is similar to the method of phenomenology which involves: bracketing, or the putting aside of one's assumptions, biases and prejudices; a description, in staying with the most initial, simple description that is suffi-ciently explanatory, rather than digression into speculative, overly complicated and theoretical explanations (Occam's razor);

DOI: 10.4324/9781003375890-67

and equalization, that is, giving equal value and significance to each descriptive component. Phenomenology, like true awareness, is concerned with what is experienced and how it is experienced (Nuttall, 2006). Awareness requires an uncensored openness to and noticing of new experiences and a sense of presence in the here-and-now. Awareness can be promoted in a range of ways, including mindfulness techniques which invite a flow of present-centred awareness. Other methods include challenging the client's script-based frame of reference to support their capacity to experience the world 'as it is' and the discounting mechanisms they use to distort reality (see Widdowson, 2021).

SPONTANEITY

Spontaneity involves an attitude of curiosity and adventurousness and experiencing the world as a continual new moment (Cox, 2000). It does not mean being impulsive or never planning anything. Instead it involves cultivating an openness to experience, and a willingness to experiment and try out new things, and new ways of being. Creative experiments designed and used in the therapy room promote spontaneity. Clients in therapy are seeking to rid themselves of the constrictive, limiting nature of their script so invitations to respond differently can be exciting and liberating. For therapists, spontaneity in the therapy room is difficult in that we have to maintain a continual reflexive stance in relation to our impulses rather than acting them out. Being open to our experience and our full range of awareness and judiciously experimenting with our awareness and different ways of responding to transactional stimulus may enhance the client's experience of spontaneity in the therapy. Furthermore, interventions which are designed to help the client develop the personality trait as openness to experience are likely to be supportive of greater spontaneity. It is likely that the unpredictability of spontaneity can be unsettling and anxiety-provoking for some of our clients. Inviting a sense of curiosity, an acceptance of this lack of predictability and an attitude of experimentation, cultivating the openness to new experiences may also result in increased and welcomed spontaneity.

Similarly, encouraging clients to experience and push through their anxiety can support their movement into greater spontaneity (Gentelet and Widdowson, 2014).

INTIMACY*

Intimacy permeates the therapeutic relationship. Greater intimacy is promoted by the therapist's authenticity, warmth and honesty and sense of trustworthiness within the relationship. This also highlights that as therapists we have a duty of candour, in our relationships with our clients. It is also supported by the appropriate use of humour and our willingness to experience our own vulnerability and accept our own imperfections and psychic wounds in relationship with another. Considered self-disclosure and frank disclosure of countertransference that does not burden our clients with the therapist's experiences or personal issues also deepen intimacy. Also, the therapist's consistent use of of permission, protection (Crossman, 1966) and potency (Steiner, 1968) promotes greater intimacy.

HOMONOMY

Recent developments in TA have introduced the concept of homonomy as a balance to the over-emphasis of the individualistic potential of autonomy (see Points 9 and 17). To promote greater homonomy, interventions which support and enhance the client's relationships relational capacity with others and promote greater attachment security are likely to be helpful. Also, helping the client to develop a sense of the interconnectedness of all things (such as the delicate balance of ecosystems) and the experience of a sense of shared and common humanity promote homonomy. Similarly, interventions that deepen the recognition that humans are social animals, and that we cannot survive alone, and it is only through relationships and social cooperation that we thrive also support homonomy.

Part 6

AVOIDING COMMON PITFALLS

62

BEING REALISTIC ABOUT TREATMENT LENGTH

I have previously commented that it seems that in many cases TA training appears to largely be teaching white middle-class people to provide long-term therapy to other white middle-class people (Widdowson, 2022). This is based on my observation that many people in the TA community seem to hold the erroneous assumption that long-term therapy is superior to short-term therapy. With a few exceptions, this position is not supported by the research evidence. To be clear, I am not against long-term therapy – after all, it does have its place. However, I am against considering long-term therapy to be superior and the default option. I am also against poor practice in contracting regarding expected treatment duration.

Over the years, extensive psychotherapy research into the 'dose-response effect' or, how many therapy sessions are necessary has shown that short-term therapy is effective. My own research on the effectiveness of TA psychotherapy for depression found that as few as 16 sessions of therapy can be effective (Widdowson, 2013; 2016). The dose-response effect research indicates that around half of all people will have achieved their therapy goals by session 20 (typically between 13–18 sessions). Of course, this means that the other 50 per cent of clients are still struggling, and will likely need 35–52 sessions to improve (Hansen et al., 2002). These findings were supported by a meta-analysis by Lutz et al. (2021) which found that 50 per cent of clients with clinical-level symptoms had achieved clinically significant change by 21 sessions, with 75 per cent achieving clinically significant change by session 35. A study by Stiles, Barkham and Wheeler (2015), based on

DOI: 10.4324/9781003375890-69

data from over 26,000 clients, found the average number of sessions was 8.3, with 60 per cent of clients reaching clinically significant recovery by the end of therapy (therapy was mostly fewer than 25 sessions) with a further 19 per cent meeting the criteria for 'improved'.

Most clients follow a fairly common trajectory: either rapid change at the beginning of therapy (which tends to slow), those who are steady improvers, and those where the picture is more up and down throughout the course of therapy. The dose-effect response generally shows that for most clients, improvements slow after 18 sessions, suggesting that most of the changes that are likely to occur will have already taken place by that time. The routine use of outcome measures allows therapists to monitor their own clinical effectiveness by monitoring how many of their clients achieve clinically significant change within the time frames listed above.

Even arguments regarding the superiority of long-term therapy for personality change do not stand up to scrutiny. The kind of radical complete restructuring and change in personality we might hope for rarely occurs as change tends to occur in specific traits. Indeed, most people do not actually want to change their personality drastically, even if it is problematic for them (Tyrer, 2018). There is a good amount of research to show that significant change can occur in personality traits in a relatively short period of time, with change occurring in as little as between two and ten weeks (Allen et al., 2018; Steiger et al., 2020). Specifically the research has identified clear changes in the traits of emotional stability, extraversion (including increases in positive affect), conscientiousness, openness to experience in response to short-term interventions and completion of daily between-session homework tasks.

It is poor practice and unethical to engage a client in long-term, open-ended psychotherapy without explicitly contracting with the client that the therapy will be conducted in that format. While it is impossible to entirely predict exactly how long therapy will take, it is possible to give the client a rough estimate based on the type, duration and severity of their problems. In my own practice, I contract with client for therapy of up to 20 sessions in duration. If during the course of therapy it becomes apparent that the client may need longer, I initiate a conversation about it at the first opportunity to do so. Based on the dose-response effect research discussed above, it would be realistic to contract with most clients that they can typically expect therapy to last up to 40 sessions.

There are certain situations where therapy of a longer duration may be required. These include clients who have complex PTSD (WHO, 2019) or dissociative identity disorder as a result of prolonged, severe childhood abuse, who may require therapy of around two years in duration (possibly longer). Clients with eating disorders, those who have a history of psychosis, and clients seeking treatment for alcohol or drug addictions may also all require longer therapy, however, this should only be conducted with the agreement of the client's psychiatrist (and in the case of addictions, after the client has undergone a medically-supervised detox). Clients with personality disorders also tend to require longer in therapy (Castonguay, Constantino and Butler, 2019).

As a general rule of thumb, the greater the duration of a client's problems, the longer they are likely to need therapy. Similarly, the greater the degree of the client's functional impairment, the longer they will need therapy. Indeed, some poorly functioning clients may need (and want) long-term supportive therapy.

63

DIRECTIONALITY AND AVOIDING THERAPY DRIFT

Directionality is a concept derived from existentialism that human nature is focused on 'going somewhere' (Cooper, 2019). The TA concept of *physis* – our innate tendency towards growth and healing is similar to the concept of the actualizing tendency in other humanistic psychologies. Indeed, there is a view among many humanistic practitioners that if we give someone the right environment, they will inevitably and naturally grow and heal. However, in some ways, this can be a problematic stance in that it assumes that people can step out of long-standing, ingrained and limiting or harmful patterns, and that sometimes even when we know what we *should* be doing, we still stand in our own way. Nevertheless, the notion of directionality is a useful one to consider in relation to psychotherapy, as ostensibly, clients come to psychotherapy in order to metaphorically or figuratively *get somewhere*. Despite this, there is a real risk – especially in longer-term therapies – of therapy drift, or getting stuck in therapy that isn't actually going anywhere.

Of course, there are some exceptions to the notion that therapy needs to actually have a clear and well-defined outcome. For instance, some clients want longer-term exploratory therapy and are happy to have a regular reflective space and a comfortable therapeutic relationship with a therapist who knows them well. There are other instances where long-term supportive therapy is indicated, such as with clients who have little available Adult ego state, clients where there is little realistic prospect of significant improvement, and clients who have had very difficult lives, who struggle to function

DOI: 10.4324/9781003375890-70

and who have little to no social support. Supportive psychotherapy largely focuses on the provision of a warm, empathic relationship, and taking a non-structured, non-goal-directed stance in favour of supporting the client's self-esteem and emotional functioning. It tends to work primarily in the realms of positive transference and avoids the exploration of unconscious conflicts (Grover et al., 2020). Shorter-term supportive psychotherapy can also be incredibly helpful for bereaved clients, who often only need an empathic and supportive space to give voice to their grief with someone who will listen to and validate it.

There are a number of potential reasons why therapy ends up drifting or getting stuck (Waller and Turner, 2016). First, it is possible that the client is not fully engaging with therapy, or is attending therapy each week but not committing time and energy between sessions into actions which will support their process of change. Another reason for therapy drift is insufficient skills or knowledge on the part of the therapist. While we all need to stretch our ability, it is important that the therapist continually seeks out opportunities for professional growth and expansion of skills and knowledge. Sometimes therapists have a romanticized view of therapy, believing that somehow their own intuition and good intentions will be sufficient to (eventually) generate change. This is often associated with a refusal to engage with psychotherapy research and evidence-based practice, on the grounds that somehow they and their clients are special, or that the research does not fit (I have actually heard this given as a reason for lack of engagement with research findings, although how the statement could be justified, given that the individual refused to read research and find out if it was true remains a mystery). Another potential reason for therapy drift is the therapist not actually having any information on their own clinical effectiveness and having an unrealistic and over-inflated view of their own abilities (see Point 90). One reason I have also heard given for therapy drift is to allow time for unconscious processes to unfold. While there is some merit in this argument, it seems to overlook the possibility that unconscious processes are arguably always present and occurring from the outset of therapy.

As therapists, we have an ethical and moral obligation to critically examine our practice, and to continually examine whether we are actually making a difference to our clients' lives. In cases where therapy appears to be drifting, then we have a responsibility to tackle this one way or another. This might requires us to refer the client on, we may require additional training, supervision or further reading, or we may decide to re-contract with our client, perhaps reviewing their goals and the tasks of therapy, or indeed switching to long-term supportive therapy. Long-term supportive therapy or exploratory therapy are perfectly viable options, and are the best choice for number of the clients we see, however, they need to be clearly contracted for and explicitly stated in terms of their purposes, aims and intended outcomes.

64

REDUCING THE RISK OF IATROGENIC SHAMING

Iatrogenic illness is an illness that is caused by medical treatment. Wordnet gives the definition 'induced by a physician's words or therapy' (http://dictionary.reference.com/browse/iatrogenic). This definition is closer to what I am referring to here.

Many clients present with core issues related to shame and shame-based identity (Cornell, 1994; De Young, 2021; Erskine, 1994; Nathanson, 1994). One goal of the therapy for such clients is the reduction and resolution of shame issues. Unfortunately, therapists can induce or exacerbate shame in their clients by not paying attention to their use of methods. Other ways in which a transactional analyst can inadvertently induce shame in their client is through their use of language, their demeanour, and their attitude, all of which can subtly, yet powerfully, convey an 'I'm OK – you're not OK' position to their client. This can be true, despite the best of intentions on the part of the therapist, and a client may nevertheless experience the transactions as being 'not Ok' (regardless of how they are delivered by the therapist), according to the script and internal process of the client. Iatrogenic shaming can inadvertently be activated through the poor application of a great number of therapeutic concepts, but within TA, the potential for iatrogenic shaming seems to occur most frequently through lack of skilful application of the following concepts or tools.

CONTRACTING

Contracting can be used excessively, particularly in the early sessions when clients are often still uncertain of the potential of therapy, the scope of what will happen in sessions and uncertain of their goals (see also Part 4, Contracting). An excessive focus on generating specific goals can leave clients feeling bad for not knowing exactly what they want, that they know what needs to happen, but they can't manage to make the changes, or that they don't know how to get what they want. Coming on too strong with behavioural contracts can back clients into a metaphorical corner, and if for whatever reason the behavioural contract was not completed, the client can feel shame. Indeed, 'sometimes the process of contracting may itself suggest that the person is not OK' (Lee, 1997: 99). Managing this tension is not easy, as clients (ostensibly) come to therapy to change, yet enthusiastically embracing the idea 'you must change' can reinforce the message that the client needs to experience some kind of transformation to be OK. The Gestalt therapists describe the paradoxical theory of change (Beisser, 1970), whereby in accepting ourselves and who we truly are we liberate the capacity for change. Taking a stance of promoting the acceptance of who one is, and of changing what isn't working can minimize the risk of shaming through contracting.

DECONTAMINATION

Attempting to do decontamination through exhortation (Berne, 1966/1994) or an excessively 'educational' approach to the therapy can be experienced by the client as being Parental (although the therapists using this approach would quite possibly swear they were 'offering Adult information'). Exhortation occasionally works as a therapeutic approach but does not promote the client's autonomy and freedom. It can leave the client feeling small and stupid, or patronized, particularly when they intellectually grasp the exhortation, but cannot yet make the internal change needed, or change their behaviour to fit.

GAME ANALYSIS

Games are by definition an unconscious process. Games may be very obvious to outsiders, but not to those who are mired in the experience of the game. Pointing out a client's games can be very shaming. Indeed, the word 'game' is often taken to imply a degree of conscious manipulation (which will, of course, usually be strenuously denied!). There is no virtue in feeling satisfied and clever after pointing out a client's games while they sit and feel bad about themselves for their 'stupidity' or 'manipulativeness'. Raising the idea of secondary gain can also be profoundly shaming, and needs to be done sensitively, and gradually over time. Do not use game analysis for 'blame storming', an exercise whereby the participants shift and assign blame for a situation.

DISCOUNTING

Once more, discounting is by definition an unconscious process (Schiff et al., 1975), and therefore is not immediately amenable to direct, conscious thought. The phrase 'you are discounting' may well be met with a denial, or with a shame response which may in turn reinforce the client's script messages such as 'I am so stupid'. The areas in which a client is discounting can be enormously illuminating, and indeed not confronting the discount can reveal a lot of information regarding the client's patterns of defence. Confrontation of discounting needs to be done carefully to prevent the client from hearing the message 'You are wrong to think how you think, think how I think instead.' Any kind of diagnostic pronouncement whereby the therapist tells a client what they are doing using TA theory has the potential for weaponizing of TA concepts and of inducing shame.

'POLLYANNA-ING'

A desire to soothe, to hurry the client into feeling better, to 'do something useful' and fear about the potential of exploring profoundly painful feelings can seduce therapists into defensively focusing on the positive or providing simplistic answers for the client. It is often very difficult to 'be with' and contain the depth and extent of our client's pain. Ignoring the profundity of the 'psycheache' of a client who feels very down is experienced by the client as an empathic failure. The resultant cognitive dissonance the client experiences, while feeling alone due to the empathic failure, can reinforce script beliefs and result in shame.

This list is not exhaustive but is meant to give the practitioner some examples of how unskilful and insensitive application of TA tools can be damaging rather than healing and, as such, runs counter to the therapeutic principle of 'do no harm'.

It is worth being alert for any signs that the client might be experiencing shame, and for checking this out with the client at various points throughout the therapy. For example, if the therapist has challenged the client, asking, 'I just want to check something out with you – do you feel at all "told off" by me by what I've just said?' If the client responds that they do feel told off, the therapist is advised to apologize, and back off. There is a lot of benefit in making a habit of checking out with all clients in each session how they are experiencing the therapy, and if it is the right balance for them. Analysis of transactions can be helpful in minimizing iatrogenic shaming. The stimulus that triggers shame can come from the therapist and can be extremely subtle, and may be outside of the therapist's awareness. It is also possible that the stimulus can be partially internally generated in that there is something about how the therapist has responded (or initiated) with the client that has some kind of resonance for the client, in terms of their implicit memory. The wise TA therapist is prepared to examine, non-defensively, their transactions with their client, and to accept their own contribution to this stimulus (and consequent shift). Refusal on the part of the therapist to see their part in the sequence can give the psychological-level message to the client that the client is somehow 'wrong' and that the source of the interpersonal problems is located solely in the client. Such a process would be likely to reinforce the negative script beliefs the client may have regarding how 'self' and 'other' operate in relationships.

In summary, the therapist needs to be attentive to their way of relating to their client, and to account for the impact of their communication upon the client to minimize the potential for reinforcing script through iatrogenic shaming.

AVOIDING 'RACKET OKNESS'

It is not unusual for people newly introduced to TA to embrace the philosophical principle of 'people are OK' enthusiastically. They go around 'being OK' with others, adopt a positive view of people and challenge others whom they experience as behaving or viewing others in ways which might be considered 'not OK'. Although this can certainly make for a more pleasant world and is the beginning of developing an accepting therapeutic stance, congruent with a humanistic model, if used rigidly and uncritically, it can also develop into a deeply problematic position.

What can happen that turns this into a problematic position is a seductive pull to ignore the less-than-pleasant aspects of our emotions and emotional responses to others. That is, the pull to disavow or discount our 'shadow side' in the pursuit of 'OKness'. In the service of this desire to 'maintain OKness at all costs', a racket of OKness develops. If we take the definition of a racket to mean the adopting of a substitute, permitted feeling covering a forbidden feeling (English, 1971), then certainly 'OKness' can be seen at times to be a racket.

In the case of the development of an 'OKness racket', the neophyte transactional analyst in their zeal to 'be OK' may begin to significantly discount the existence (Mellor and Schiff, 1975) of emotional data that feel unpleasant or uncomfortable in some way, or emotional reactions towards their clients which are not 100 per cent positive. Of course, this discounting process becomes problematic because shutting out these emotions means shutting out a resource that can be of profound use to both therapist and client. Our understanding of the development of rackets is that the individual buries disavowed and disallowed emotions, and covers them with an inauthentic emotion (see Widdowson, 2016, for a discussion of this, and the renaming the concept of rackets as 'secondary emotions'). The conventional view of rackets/ secondary emotions is that this process somehow links to the individual's script and the racket/ secondary emotion reinforces important aspects of the individual's script. If this is the case, how can 'OKness' be rackety? Clarkson (1992a) described the 'counterscript cure', the 'flight into health' as one potential means of transformation, whereby the client (in this case, the TA trainee) adopts a position which, on the surface, appears to run against their script, but in some ways is actually a modified version of their script, and is an adaptation to another introjection. It could be, for example, that in burying their 'not OK' feelings, the individual is seeking belonging – belonging to the TA community – and is actually adapting to an external source in a similar way to how they adapted to their parent's frame of reference. I suspect this is a particular threat to those who come to TA with an 'I'm not OK – you're OK' life position, in that it is relatively easy for them to see others as OK, and they want to believe that by repeating the mantra they can truly believe that they really might be OK, thus fulfilling a magical transformation fantasy. Adapting to the racket 'OKness' position would also, using Hargaden and Sills' (2002) conception of the self, allow the individual to identify with the A1+ self-identity system, and in doing so disavow and repress their 'not OK' feelings towards self or others. By maintaining a positive identification with the 'OKness', the individual can maintain a fragile identity of being 'one of the good guys'.

I am proposing that, as transactional analysts, we develop a more realistic position in the teaching and practising of the concept of 'OKness', and one which accounts for the existence of negative, unpleasant feelings. In his seminal paper, 'Hate in the countertransference', Winnicott (1946/1987) paves the way for the therapist to allow themselves to experience the 'unpleasant' and 'unkind' thoughts and feelings they have towards their client, and to see them as a normal and possibly even as a central aspect of the therapy. Maroda (1994/2004) takes this position further by urging therapists to use their affective responses towards their client as a potent therapeutic tool. Maroda advocates regular, but carefully timed and carefully worded, disclosure of the therapists' affective countertransference towards their client, even when the feelings are 'unpleasant'.

Projective identification is a particular transferential phenomenon that can induce a range of unpleasant feelings and thoughts within the therapist. In projective identification the client is thought to be projecting certain intolerable feelings into the therapist, so the therapist can process, metabolize, detoxify and transform these feelings for the client who can then in turn re-own them. Ogden (1982) identifies four primary functions of projective identification: (1) a defence against experiencing unwanted, disavowed aspects of the self; (2) a means of communicating – if one's feelings are experienced by another, this creates a profound sense of being understood; (3) a way of relating to the other person, and maintaining relationship; and (4) a method of psychological change – the feelings are changed by the other, and we also learn new, more productive ways of transforming and containing our own intolerable feelings. Considered in this light, projective identification can be viewed as having great potential for therapeutic change, and as being a creative means for the client to communicate their feelings and their needs.

> Where the patient has need, the therapist must have capacity. In other words, where the patient has need to defend herself against all sorts of unacceptable feelings, the therapist must be able to tolerate the presence of such feelings within herself – or, at the very least her own potential to have such feelings. The therapist must be able to do (for the patient) what the patient cannot yet do (for herself) – that is, the therapist must have the capacity to sit with bad feelings without needing to disavow them.
>
> (Stark, 2000: 274)

Not acknowledging the unpleasant feelings that might be projected does not mean that they don't exist for the client, or indeed within the therapist, but what it does mean is that the feelings are not available for re-working in the therapeutic relationship. By adopting a stance of racket 'OKness' and refusing to see ourselves as anything other than infinitely patient, tolerant and understanding, we can rob the client of this powerful opportunity to reintegrate previously intolerable emotions. Indeed, disavowal of these feelings by the therapist is likely to reinforce on an unconscious level for the client that such feelings are inherently dangerous and therefore should be disowned, discounted and projected out. For clients who experience themselves as being inherently bad, being with a therapist who is in a racket OKness position can feel profoundly lonely and isolating, and can reinforce on an unconscious level the client's script beliefs of being intrinsically bad or unworthy. Maroda (1994/2004) also warns against the tendency of therapists to adopt a racket OK position, making the observation that it is when bad feelings are disavowed that they can exert intense unconscious pressure upon the therapist (and consequently their client) and can get acted out destructively, despite all wishes to maintain the 'good' position.

Berne recognized the significance of these 'bad' feelings, and the importance of acknowledging their existence:

> He who pretends that these forces do not exist becomes their victim. His whole script may be a project to demonstrate that he is free of them. But since he is most likely not, this is a denial of himself and therefore of his right to a self-chosen destiny.
>
> (Berne, 1972: 270)

The transactional analyst is invited to make space for their own unpleasant feelings to emerge; to give themselves permission to feel all of their feelings – no matter how unpleasant. Accepting negative feelings and welcoming them as a source of useful information are both a challenge and an important developmental step in the process of becoming an effective transactional analyst.

AVOIDING MARSHMALLOWING

Many clients presenting for psychotherapy experience strong internal 'stroke filters' (Woollams and Brown, 1978); discounting positive strokes, disbelieving them or redefining them in some way to neutralize them. The tenacity of these stroke filters and their imperviousness to simple stroking and contradiction can be quite startling. Positive stroking can hit up against the client's resistances, especially when the client believes only bad things about themselves and has an extensive negative self-belief system in their script.

There can be a tendency among some inexperienced transactional analysts to excessively stroke their clients, as if stroking will somehow magically transform them. This heavy use of strokes can appear to clients to be disingenuous, partly as a result of its being a culturally dystonic way of interacting (Steiner, 1974). An overly stroking approach can also appear false, patronizing, and can have a tone of infantilizing the client, or can be experienced as such by the client. This is in contradiction to an approach that seeks to strengthen and promote Adult ego state functioning. Furthermore, heavy use of stroking can also promote symbiosis (Schiff et al., 1975). I have had a number of clients who stopped seeing previous therapists because they felt the therapist was 'too nice' and overly permissive. In almost all of these cases, the client reported that they experienced the therapist's use of stroking to be false or unrealistic and left the client feeling that the therapist was reluctant to confront them. There is also the possibility that, for clients with dependent or avoidant personality traits, a 'stroke-heavy' approach keeps the client stuck in script, and dependent on the therapist to provide them with their quota of strokes,

DOI: 10.4324/9781003375890-73

rather than challenging the underlying neediness. Such a collusive relationship is not one that is conducive to therapeutic change.

While there is a great deal to be gained by ensuring the client experiences the therapist as warm and accepting, and providing their clients with encouragement, praise for making changes, and feedback on how the therapist experiences them, the intensity of stroking must be carefully matched to the upper limits of what the client can tolerate at that moment in time. Giving the client a gentle stretch; not too much that they reject the stroke completely, but enough to support some movement out of their script is the optimal approach. When strokes are given to a client, it can be productive to ask the client to 'really hear' the stroke and notice what happens. The therapist can then ask them if they took it on board, or did something else with the stroke.

Clients occasionally solicit their therapist's reassurance, either directly or indirectly. Eager to demonstrate their understanding and acceptance, and fuelled by the desire to 'be useful', inexperienced therapists can succumb to this pull and offer the client their sought-after reassurance (i.e., accept the game invitation). Not providing a stroke to a client can sometimes facilitate the client to become aware of their neediness or desire for approval. By not giving a stroke, the client's need is brought to the surface, where it is amenable to change, rather than lying buried, but motivating the client's behaviour and way of interacting with others.

EXAMPLE

A client was discussing a problem with a male colleague in her small team who often acts dismissively and whom the client feels does not appreciate how she helps him out. This then moved into a discussion of the client's fear of her (male) boss and lack of confidence around men in positions of authority. The atmosphere of the session was becoming tense, and the client went on to say: 'I think he thinks I am stupid. In fact, sometimes I wonder about that, and I think I am stupid.' The tension in the room was almost palpable. Her (male) therapist felt that the psychological-level message in the client's last transaction was 'and you think I'm stupid – tell me I'm not'. After a long pause, the client said, slowly and carefully, 'I sometimes think that you think I'm stupid.' At this point, it would have been easy to stroke the client and refute this belief. However, her therapist responded with an empathic interpretation, 'It must be very difficult spending all your time looking for approval and reassurance.'' This hit the spot and the client nodded agreement and wept for several minutes. The therapist sat silently, witnessing the client's distress, eventually saying, 'It seems like what I said hit upon some truth for you. How was it for you to hear that?' The client nodded and, recognizing the psychological-level message, said, 'I was wanting you to say that you approve of me, and that you think I'm smart.' Her therapist replied, 'Would you have believed me, even if I'd said so?', to which the client responded, 'No, I wouldn't have. Not deep down.'

By not providing the initially sought-for strokes, the therapist created an atmosphere where the client's neediness for reassurance was brought to the surface. In doing so, the mechanisms that led the client to seek for, but not believe, positive strokes were delivered directly into the therapy.

Certainly there is a place for stroking in therapy. We all need strokes to some degree or another. Clients, supervisees, trainees and colleagues all need strokes, and we certainly should offer strokes. However, sometimes, 'less really is more'.

Part 7

REFINING
THERAPEUTIC SKILLS

67

BALANCING CHALLENGE AND SUPPORT

It is easy for therapists to become over-reliant on a particular preference in relation to challenge or support, which often relates to their own personality and needs. This, however, may become rigid and consequently not be appropriate for a large number of clients. Challenge and support can be considered as two ends of a continuum and the therapist needs to attune to the required level of challenge and support needed for each client at any given moment. High levels of support can be very important for clients who are feeling profoundly emotional, or who are experiencing painful transitions, or while dealing with the emergence of repressed feelings. High levels of support can, however, be problematic when overdone or misattuned and can effectively impair the therapist's potency and render the therapeutic relationship a cosy, collusive space where little change takes place. Low levels of support can be helpful in promoting resilience in the client and inviting a client to take Adult responsibility, but can be experienced as persecutory or withholding by the client, who may well leave therapy if they feel their needs are not being sufficiently attended to and who may experience the therapy as an unsafe place to explore deeper levels of affect.

Challenge also needs to be carefully attuned. Again, low levels of challenge promote a climate of collusion, and do not contain the required leverage to facilitate change. If challenge levels are too high, clients will feel persecuted and the potential for iatrogenic shaming is high. This is particularly true in the early stages of therapy if the therapist makes extensive use of confrontation or discounting (Schiff et al., 1975). Most clients

DOI: 10.4324/9781003375890-75

presenting for therapy realize that a degree of challenge will be necessary for the work, and many welcome the therapist's challenge (at least at the social level) as a catalyst for change, provided it is sensitively balanced with sufficient levels of support: 'The therapist's task is to challenge habitual assumptions and relationship patterns and create sufficient turbulence for new structures to emerge' (Holmes, 2001: 17).

68

DEVELOPING EMOTIONAL AWARENESS AND GRANULATION

One of the aims of TA therapy is deconfusion of the Child ego state (see Point 74). Although Berne developed the term, he never defined it clearly, or explained what confusion of the Child ego state is. It is important to remember here that although TA uses commonplace language, it tends to be used in a different way, and with a different meaning to its usual dictionary definition. In this instance, confusion is not an experience of cognitive confusion or puzzlement, but instead is an emotional experience. I see confusion of the Child ego state as occurring when either the Child experiences intense, overwhelming and dysregulated affect which it cannot effectively process, and/or when the Child experiences emotions, impulses, desires, and so on which the child experiences or believes are either disapproved of or are unacceptable within their family. In this instance, the emotions are disavowed or repressed, resulting in a mismatch between what is experienced and what is acceptable and what is expressed. This process (which is based on psychodynamic concepts of dynamic repression) results in a confusion within the Child ego state and an impairment of the ability to fully understand and express one's emotional states.

There is now a growing body of evidence which suggests that impaired ability to identify one's internal emotional state is a feature of many mental disorders. There is also considerable research evidence which has shown the benefits of enhancing emotional awareness. Moreover, research has found that promoting emotional granulation – or the ability to distinguish between different emotions and to identify subtle nuances of emotional experiencing – benefits mental health and therefore can be a useful component of effective psychotherapy (Lazarus and Fisher, 2021).

Therapeutic work and psychoeducation to help clients develop their emotional awareness and granulation can be especially useful when integrated into treatment plans for the first few sessions of therapy. In my experience, clients who have greater emotional awareness and a wider emotional vocabulary make quicker gains in therapy, and proceed through deconfusion more smoothly and rapidly than clients who have lower levels of awareness and ability.

A simple intervention to support emotional awareness is to invite clients to think about different emotions and come up with different words to describe variations in intensity of each emotion (the emotions I suggest are Paul Ekman's list of six core emotions; Anger, Sadness, Fear, Enjoyment, Surprise, and Disgust (Ekman, 2004). For example, in British English, anger might range from feeling irritated or annoyed through to being livid or raging. This often makes a useful between-session homework task, and some people find that this is a fun task to complete with friends and/or children.

One model specifically designed for emotional granularity is the valence-arousal circumplex chart. The model has two axes: one for emotional valence (pleasure-displeasure), the other for arousal, or emotional intensity (high arousal-low arousal) (Feldman Barrett, 2006; Lindquist and Feldman Barrett, 2008). The diagram (which can be found online) can be used to help clients distinguish between subtle differences in emotional state. For example, a client may report having felt 'depressed' all week. By using the model, the client might be helped to identify that they have also felt sad, bored and tired taken from the displeasure-low arousal quadrant of the model.

Another model which helps promote emotional awareness is the feelings wheel (Willcox, 1982). Although it was originally published in the *Transactional Analysis Journal*, diagrams of the model are in wide circulation and can readily be found online. It is a popular model which is used by many therapists worldwide. I usually have a number of printed full-colour copies available in my therapy room, and often use it in one of the first few sessions with clients whom I think might benefit from developing these emotional skills. Prior to introducing the client to the diagram, I have usually explained to my client about the value of developing emotional awareness and granulation, and checking to see if they are interested in using this as a tool within their therapy. If the client agrees (and therefore we have a contract for emotional awareness work), I show them the diagram and point out that the inner circle represents 'large emotions' and that the outer circle uses different words to identify variations on the 'larger emotions'. I invite them to notice what they are feeling right now, and to select as many words as they need to in order to describe how they are feeling.

Either the valence-arousal circumplex or the feelings wheel can be used for between-session homework tasks. For example, clients can be invited to ask themselves at least twice, and preferably several times a day 'How do I feel right now?'. Frequently, simply naming the emotion makes it feel more manageable and can reduce its intensity. It can also be used to identify potential action to help regulate the emotion, such as by inviting the client to ask themselves 'What do I need right now? What would help me with this feeling?' once they have clearly labelled their feeling(s).

69

SOOTHING THE CHILD EGO STATE WITH EMOTION REGULATION TECHNIQUES

The most common presenting problems psychotherapists encounter in their practice all involve emotional distress: depression, anxiety, trauma, grief, relationship problems. Helping clients to develop strategies to regulate their emotions and manage their distress has a rapid beneficial effect and contributes significantly towards the client's process of change.

The distress that many of our clients are experiencing when they first begin therapy is so powerful that therapeutic movement can be slow, unless they can find ways of reducing the intensity of their emotions. The most effective therapeutic work is done when the client is in a moderate state of emotional arousal, and within their 'window of tolerance' (Siegel, 2020). If there is too little emotional arousal, the work will largely be cognitive, if there is too much emotional arousal, the client will feel too overwhelmed to process their experiences and think clearly. Moderate levels of emotional arousal promote the kind of experiential cognitive-affective processing where the most effective change work takes place (Widdowson, 2016). From a TA point of view, emotional distress deactivates the Adult ego state and the Child ego state has dominance. Therefore we need to soothe the Child ego state before engaging the Adult ego state. Fortunately there are many simple-to-use emotion regulation techniques which can be part of your therapeutic repertoire.

When introducing emotion regulation techniques in therapy, always demonstrate them in session. After demonstrating and explaining the technique, repeat it and invite your client to join

DOI: 10.4324/9781003375890-77

in and gently guide them in how to use the technique. This gives the client an in-session experience of the technique so they immediately learn its beneficial effects, and also prevents clients from leaving the session unsure of how to perform the technique (which mostly results in clients not engaging with techniques between sessions). After demonstrating techniques and guiding clients on their use, it is sensible to discuss with your client how they experienced the technique, how they feel after using it, and to explore different situations in which they might use it outside of therapy.

Many emotion regulation techniques are based on activation of the parasympathetic nervous system, or 'rest and digest' systems which in turn lowers activation of the sympathetic nervous system, or 'fight and flight' system. Two such techniques are what I refer to as 'soothing rhythm breathing' and 'self-soothing touch'. Soothing rhythm breathing involves breathing in through the nose for the count of four, pausing for a second, then breathing out through the mouth for the count of six and pausing for a second before inhaling again (making the out-breath longer than the in-breath is key to activating the parasympathetic nervous system). People who have breathing difficulties or cardiovascular diseases should be advised to speak to their doctor or specialist nurse before using this technique. Self-soothing touch simply involves placing the palm of one hand on the upper chest, and the palm of the other hand on the solar plexus/diaphragm area and just allowing the hands to rest there for a while. After a few moments, you can guide your client towards noticing a comforting warmth spreading from their hands through their chest and abdomen. This swiftly soothes the client's Child ego state, and enables them to re-engage their Adult. Both techniques can be used as often as one wishes, although I usually advise clients to practise them twice a day, for 90 seconds each in order to reduce baseline levels of distress and to develop their ability to self-soothe when needed.

A popular technique used for grounding and emotional regulation is '5, 4, 3, 2, 1'. This exercise directs attention towards sensory information in order to 'get grounded' in the present moment. An element of distraction from distress is also likely to be a factor in its ability to regulate affect. The instructions for this technique are: 'notice five things you can see ... (pause) ... four things you can hear ... (pause) ... three things you can feel through your skin ... (pause) ... two things you can smell... (pause) ... and one thing you can taste ... (pause).' If you are guiding a client through this in session, it is useful to ask them to nod, or indicate when they have noticed the specified number of sensory information. It can sometimes take a few moments for someone to notice different noises, for example, so be patient. Sometimes people struggle with identifying things they can smell or taste. In this instance, guiding them to smell their clothing, skin or hair may help. Even if a person cannot locate a particular taste, they will always be able to taste their own saliva. The sustained focus on here-and-now sensory information is usually sufficient to automatically activate and engage the Adult ego state and reduce levels of unpleasant emotion.

The use of gratitude journals is a well-established and well-researched intervention to increase positive emotions and promote social connection (Kirca, Malouff and Meynadier, 2023). To keep a gratitude journal, all one has to do is to take a few minutes each evening to write down between three and five things, preferably from that day, that one is grateful for. Paying attention to, feeling and holding on to a sense of gratitude while one completes the journal entries give this activity its full effect. If considered from a TA perspective, it seems likely that keeping a gratitude journal shifts a negatively-biased frame of reference (Schiff et al., 1975), such as one might see in depression and anxiety, to a more positive orientation. The effects of keeping a gratitude journal are not immediate, but will gradually build over a number of weeks as the frame of reference reorientates itself towards noticing the good in the world.

70

DEEPENING AFFECT

A large majority of clients presenting for therapy are seeking a means of regulating their emotional states. Often their feelings are intense and overwhelming, or they feel detached and confused by their emotions and the emotions of others. Leader (2008) argues that there is a culturally prevalent model whereby individuals avoid any intense or distressing emotion and that these unpleasant emotions are 'medicated away'. He discusses how individuals, rather than learning key emotional skills, seek to live in a sanitized, non-distressing world. This avoidance of distress risks the loss of the vitality and richness of experience that these emotions bring. Part of the task of the therapist can then be seen to be to enliven and revitalize, promoting healthy acceptance and expression of emotions. Indeed, for some clients, supporting distress tolerance is an important therapeutic task.

Deepening affect is not the same as catharsis or cathartic methods, although such deepening may well have a positive cathartic result for the client. By facilitating the deepening of affect, the emotional intensity may stimulate the emergence of an impasse. The redecision school of TA employs heighteners for this purpose (McNeel, 1976). The heightener deepens the affective charge of the piece of work and facilitates the triggering of a redecision.

Deepening affect in therapy sessions can be used to promote emotional literacy (Steiner and Perry, 1999). For clients who have very low levels of emotional literacy, the therapist can assist by helping the client verbalize their internal experience, and decode it into the language of feelings. This process develops emotional differentiation (ibid.). In some respects, this

DOI: 10.4324/9781003375890-78

process of identifying and decoding emotional experience parallels the developmental processes parents engage in with their children (Stern, 1985). This may be particularly important for clients who did not have parents who were able to decode effectively. The subsequent containment (Bion, 1970) and affect regulation role the therapist engages with here can be an important part of the therapeutic process. It is possible that this process may even stimulate change in neural pathways, particularly within the orbito-frontal cortex, the area of the brain concerned with affective regulation.

Swede raises the distinction between discussion of feelings and expression of emotion:

> Discussion is concerned with events that are removed from the present in time and place, including discussions of what happened at earlier therapeutic sessions. This is usually an evasive maneuver. Description is an intellectual way of handling feelings. The Adult tells the therapist what the Child is feeling, but the Child himself does not show in the description. This is often an evasive maneuver into pastimes. Expression is the direct expression of affect concerning the here and now at the time the affect is felt. This may be gamy or it may be intimate. The therapeutic goal is the expression of intimacy.
>
> (Swede, 1977: 23)

Deepening affect has many potential therapeutic outcomes. Any therapy that promotes greater experiential awareness and phenomenological exploration and processing may well generate insight and promote Adult awareness. It is possible that in deepening the emotional charge of an issue that *physis* is mobilized, and the client experiences a sense of organismic disgust, and spontaneously seeks redecision, such as may happen with the use of heighteners. Similarly, maintaining relational contact, empathy and responsiveness during heightened affect promotes the client's ability to process and rework transferential aspects of the therapeutic relationship (Fowlie and Sills, 2011).

Systematically deepening affect in sessions, facilitating its effective and appropriate expression and then following this with analysis and processing of the emotional experience may well also contribute to increasing affective tolerance. This is particularly so with an open, accepting and mindful stance in relation to the emotions, rather than seeking catharsis for its own sake. It is wise to avoid 'over-nurturing' in relation to feelings, or rushing in too early to resolve the feeling which does not promote affective tolerance, but can infantilize and promote dependence. The Child ego state of the client may well need to experientially learn that they can experience intense emotions, tolerate distress, express the feelings appropriately and that they and others around them will survive the experience. The most effective change work takes place when there is a moderate level of emotional arousal in the session. If there is too much emotional charge, the client may feel overwhelmed or have insufficient available Adult ego state to integrate the work. If there is not enough emotional charge, the therapy can lack potency or just be a process of intellectualization where very little change happens.

Some authors advise 'striking while the iron is hot' (Luborsky, 1984), that is, selecting the most affectively charged aspect of a client's communication (particularly ones which may highlight parallels in the therapeutic relationship) and intensifying them to make affective links between different feeling states (ego states) and the client's present experience. The advantage of this approach is that highlighting such links in an affectively charged way minimizes the possibility that the client may intellectualize the experience. This approach should not, however, be used in a blanket manner, and several authors also advise 'striking while the iron is cold' (McWilliams, 1994; Pine, 1985; Yalom, 2001), that is, raising such discussions at a time when the client is calm and in a different feeling state and has sufficient available Adult ego state to process the experience. This second approach is more appropriate for clients who have a greater degree of disturbance, such as clients with personality disorder, or clients who may experience the therapist's intervention in the midst of an intense emotional experience as shaming or as criticism.

CONTRAINDICATIONS

Interventions that deepen affect should not be used where the therapist is not able to provide sufficient containment and protection for the client. Clients who have poor tolerance of affect need any work on expression of emotions to be done gradually. Rapid or intense deepening of emotions can be experienced as profoundly overwhelming and does not provide sufficient protection for such clients. This is particularly true for clients who struggle with affective regulation, such as clients with borderline personality disorder, who, rather than increasing the affect, need a therapeutic approach which promotes regulation and containment of emotions and one which helps them develop appropriate means of expressing them. Clients presenting with trauma also need a period of stabilization before accessing deep and intense emotions (see Point 58).

Sometimes deepening affect or facilitating the expression of emotion can result in 'script backlash' in that the client may experience a worsening of symptoms or some kind of internal attack, following the breaking of some unconscious rule. The intrapsychic repercussions and unconscious significance of deepening affect need to be considered, before, during and after interventions that seek to deepen the affective charge in order to maintain client protection.

Interventions that deepen affect include empathic responding and enquiry into the affect the client is expressing, or those which focus on the affective aspect of a client's experience, even in reporting on or discussing prior events. A well-timed interpretation can also deepen affect, particularly hidden feelings or those being defended against. An example of this is 'I understand that you feel sad. I wonder if a part of you also feels angry.'

71

PROMOTING HEALTHY EXPRESSION OF EMOTION

Traditionally, transactional analysts have either not stroked (acknowledged) racket feelings, or have confronted them (Stewart, 2007). This presupposes that the 'therapist knows best' and can accurately identify a feeling as a racket or not. In practice, this ability to detect in the moment is not so easy, nor is it necessarily helpful to either ignore a feeling or to confront a particular feeling a client may be experiencing. Furthermore, traditional TA models around feelings restrict 'authentic' feelings to a list of four emotions: anger, sadness, fear and joy. Developments in emotion psychology and neuroscience have demonstrated clearly that humans have a much greater range of universal basic emotions. Indeed, one group of researchers at Berkeley University (Cowan and Keltner, 2017) identified 27 distinct emotions, each with their own pattern of neurological activity and physiological reaction. Paul Ekman's six emotions – anger, sadness, fear, enjoyment, surprise and disgust – are easy to remember and sufficient to explore with clients in sessions on how they experience and express these emotions.

When clients arrive for therapy, they are seeking a safe space where they can explore. When clients are disclosing their feelings, they initially need all of their feelings to be accepted, and for the therapist to understand them – to understand the client's frame of reference and to begin to see why the client feels the way they do. It is important that as therapists we bear in mind that this process can be painful, difficult and daunting for clients, who may never have expressed this level of emotional vulnerability before. Once these initial presenting feelings have been empathically accepted, then the client may feel safe enough to explore the underlying feelings. Here we need to be mindful that the expression of these deeper and previously repressed emotions may well feel somehow unacceptable or forbidden. It is likely that at an unconscious level, the client's Child ego state may be afraid of disobeying the Parent by expressing the emotion:

> The client … needs to feel heard at this 'racket' level of communication before feeling safe enough to go deeper. It is important initially to respond to the client's felt meaning … Eventually the empathic bond makes it possible for the client to feel secure enough at an 'unthought' level to revive unmet needs and suppressed developmental needs. For her to feel safe enough to do this she has to inherently trust that the therapist is capable of understanding her most profound emotional states (Clark, 1991).
>
> (Hargaden and Sills, 2002: 33–34)

This process of consistent empathy and validation, combined with work which supports greater awareness, granulation and expression of emotion, will support and maybe even act as a catalyst for deconfusion.

Facilitating the healthy expression of emotion in terms of Steiner's emotional awareness scale (Steiner and Perry, 1999) promotes the movement from numbness, physical sensations and primal experience by moving across the verbal barrier to differentiation and causality, where the individual can recognize emotional states and identify their origin (see Point 68). Clinical experience would suggest that a great number of clients are afraid of emotional expression, conflating it with being 'out of control', which may be reflective of the internal chaos the client feels at some level in response to their early life experiences and their awareness of the oceanic feel of their repressed emotions which may emerge through the process of deconfusion. A common example of this is the fear many people experience in relation to anger that is often confused with aggression. Sensitive and gradual re-educational work that invites an awareness of the difference between the two states and which emphasizes personal responsibility for the expression of emotions can be relieving for such clients. In working with this, the therapist might enquire if the client felt any sense of anger about a particular situation or event (perhaps in with other emotions the client can more easily access). The therapist can validate the client's anger and then explore with them how they might express their anger in a way that is appropriate to the situation. This may include providing information around emotions in general, or the development of assertiveness skills.

The expression of emotion is, to some extent, culturally determined. Some cultures emphasize and encourage emotional restraint, and the minimizing of emotional reactions. Other cultures emphasize strong, exaggerated emotional expressiveness. When working with clients we need to be conscious of the impact of the client's cultural background and context on their level of emotional expressiveness.

Thomson (1983) emphasizes the problem-solving function of emotions that are located within the appropriate time frame, and that, although often uncomfortable, such feelings should be welcomed and allowed space to be worked through to their natural resolution. Moiso (1984) invites analysis of the emotion in terms of its message: fear tells us of present danger, anger of damage being done, and sadness speaks of loss. Joy obviously speaks of pleasure. Each emotion has an instinctive action and a social request: fear requires escape from the danger, and help or reassurance from others. The action of anger is to attack or protect and it requires a change in the environment or from another person. Sadness requires a withdrawal of energy into one's self, and consolation and compassion from others. Joy impels us towards others to connect and share our joy (ibid.). Basic analysis of transactions can be tremendously helpful in promoting healthy expression and the subsequent resolution of emotions, as it is not unusual for people to unwittingly communicate in unclear ways that do not invite a positive response from the environment. By facilitating positive, appropriate, and clear communication and using their own affective responses to the client (social diagnosis), the therapist can help the client relate to others in more growthful and intimate ways.

72

TRACKING WHERE THE CLIENT IS OPEN, AND WHERE THEY ARE DEFENDED ON A MOMENT-BY-MOMENT BASIS

The Ware sequence (Ware, 1983) is a commonly taught piece of TA theory, and one which has immediate appeal in its simplicity, and also its sense of being systematic, and guiding the therapist in their interventions. Yet, in practice, it has limited usefulness as a model and, in my view, can be obstructive to the therapy process. For a detailed critique of the Ware sequence and the personality adaptations model, see Tudor and Widdowson (2008). Here I offer an alternative to the Ware sequence that uses the same therapeutic skills, but in a way which tracks the client's process on a moment-to-moment basis.

The division of a client's experience into thoughts, feelings and behaviours is in many respects a false 'trichotomising' (ibid.) which does not account for the complex and multi-faceted nature of a client's experience, which will at any given moment include thoughts, feeling and behaviour as a whole. Focusing on one aspect of the client's experiencing also does not pay sufficient attention to the client's unfolding phenomenological process in the moment.

Also, designing interventions according to a pre-determined sequence significantly limits the therapist's flexibility, creativity and affective resonance with the client. It could be argued that this in itself is not helpful in that following a sequence will by definition impair the therapist's capacity to utilize awareness, spontaneity and intimacy (Berne, 1964) in the therapeutic

DOI: 10.4324/9781003375890-80

encounter – the very capacities which are characteristic of autonomy, and as such ones we need to promote in the therapy.

The three 'doors' of the Ware sequence are the open door, or where the client is most receptive, the trap door or where the client is most defended, and the target door or the area where the most change will take place. Following a set sequence in working with any client will significantly limit the therapist's capacity to attune to the client on a moment-to-moment basis. What I have found helpful is *to consider where this client is open and receptive, at this moment, and to consider where this client is most defended, at this moment.* Analysis of the areas of receptivity and defence will reveal that it is only certain thoughts and feelings in relation to specific things that are limited. These configurations will change repeatedly throughout the progress of the therapy, and indeed throughout a single session.

In some respects, it could be argued that feeling is always the 'open door', in that all stimulus we receive is initially processed via the amygdala and the emotionally-driven limbic system. We process on an emotional level before we engage cognition. However, affect and cognition are not easily separated as both operate simultaneously within the individual. All affective experiences are appraised using cognition, and all cognition is affect-laden and motivated by affect (O'Brien and Houston, 2007; Stern, 1985). At any one time an individual will be experiencing on an affective level, and even the most affective-defended person will at some level be experiencing emotionally. A key task for the therapist is to attune to this affect, regardless of how buried or repressed it is, and to incorporate that into the therapy either via empathic transactions or interpretation.

To be empathic and attuned (Erskine et al., 1999) requires that we set aside any preconceptions about the client and their experience. In this respect, it is crucial that to fully attune to our clients we set aside any notion of a preconceived, limited (and limiting) fixed sequence to their process.

73

ENCOURAGING JOURNALING TO PROMOTE SELF-AWARENESS AND SELF-REFLECTION

Journaling is a popular personal development activity which can be used to support the therapy process. It is certainly worth asking a client if they already keep a journal, or if it is something they would consider doing. Several processes take place in TA therapy that written methods can effectively enhance. Regular reflective time will develop the client's reflective capacity, enhance mentalizing and promote greater awareness of the client's own internal process. This can include greater awareness of the internal dialogue between ego states. Additionally, reflective writing promotes contained affect expression and affect analysis (Yalom, 2001). Written techniques can be used at any stage of the therapy and can clarify, deepen and accelerate various processes, such as contracting (by focusing on the client's goals and wishes), decontamination (clients may recognize hitherto implicit contaminations and challenge them without therapist intervention), emotional literacy (emotional awareness, affect expression and analysis), deconfusion (recognition of repressed emotion), reinforcement of redecision, right through to helping process feelings on an approaching ending of the therapy.

REFLECTIVE JOURNALS

The simplest method of using writing in therapy is by inviting your clients to keep a journal. I often suggest to clients in their first session that they get a notebook for this purpose. I suggest that they set aside around 15–20 minutes, once or

 DOI: 10.4324/9781003375890-81

twice a week for journaling. The journal can be used to record their feelings and reflect on why they feel the way they do. It can be used to capture particular insights they might have between sessions, or to make notes as a reminder of material they want to discuss in therapy sessions. They can also be used to 'diary' specific events, situations, interactions with people and the feelings they experienced at the time and the reflections they trigger.

The use of journals as a therapeutic tool was pioneered by James Pennebaker. In a series of research studies, he found that journaling about a distressing event for four consecutive days significantly reduced distress (Pennebaker, 1997). His findings have been replicated in a number of subsequent studies which have all shown that therapeutic journaling is a reliable method. The technique is simple and can be easily explained to clients. It is important that before suggesting this method as a homework activity that the client has sufficient ability to manage and regulate any emotions which arise from the exercise. It is also wise to advise your client that they start by choosing an event which they feel is manageable; in other words, suggest that they do not go straight to the most traumatic event of their life.

The instructions for Pennebaker's therapeutic journaling method are:

- Choose a distressing event from your past to write about (it is best if the event was more than six months ago, in order to ensure that there is sufficient 'distance' from the event).
- Write about the event for 15 or 20 minutes each day for four consecutive days.
- Write about the event in as much detail as possible, including what you thought and felt at the time for the full 15–20 minutes. If you finish before 15 or 20 minutes, start again and use up the whole time without stopping.

Invite your client to report back on their experiences at their next session.

Reflective learning journals are a key component of the course-work of most psychotherapy and counselling training programmes – there is good reason for this. Regular, structured journaling will enhance your development as a therapist by promoting development of reflective capacity. They can be used to reflect on your own life, your reactions or counter-transference in particular sessions, and also for professional development by identifying key learning points from the therapy of a number of clients. A particular favourite reflective learning method of mine was developed by Daryl Chow (2022). Chow recommends that therapists set aside 15 minutes each week to look back through their diary and reflect on each session conducted that week. The next step is to identify a learning from that week. The learning may be from something that went well or had a good outcome, or it may be from a blunder, mistake or error. He advises providing some brief contextual information and keeping the journal entry brief, and limiting it to around 100–140 words. He advises that it is best if each entry is given a title, and is numbered and dated so that the therapist can periodically review their learning, and that the entry title makes it easier to track themes or connect learnings from cases.

DIFFERENCES BETWEEN DECONTAMINATION AND DECONFUSION

Decontamination and deconfusion are therapeutic processes frequently discussed by transactional analysts, which, along with redecision form the 'backbone' or central tasks of TA therapy. Decontamination and deconfusion are two discrete, yet often interlinked and overlapping processes. Beginners to TA therapy sometimes struggle with understanding the difference between the two concepts and the processes involved in them. Structurally speaking, decontamination is a process involving the Adult ego state, and deconfusion is a process involving the Child ego state.

Berne developed his ideas around the Adult ego state independently, but parallel to discoveries in cognitive therapy (Schlegel, 1998). A contamination of the Adult ego state involves the individual mistakenly accepting some Child or Parent content for Adult ego state (Stewart and Joines, 1987). An example of this would be an unchallenged belief that has no rational basis, and one which falls apart under rational scrutiny and dialogue. As the formation of a contamination happens in the context of the whole individual, it is very likely that a double contamination will occur, that is contamination of the Adult by both Parent and Child. For example, a parent figure may repeatedly tell a child they are stupid, and the child unquestioningly accepts this and believes it to be the case (perhaps using their poor spelling as 'evidence' of their stupidity). These beliefs are often held at an implicit, preconscious level and TA therapists seek to uncover these implicit beliefs and engage the client in scrutiny and challenge of their here-and-now validity.

Much of what transactional analysts describe as decontamination has a great deal in common with the methods of cognitive therapy. Decontamination can be considered in many ways a cognitive therapy process, and indeed a number of cognitive-behavioural methods can be used successfully for decontamination. It is, however, important to recognize that the Adult ego state is not just a rational data processor: the Adult ego state is the ego state which is adapted to the reality of the here-and-now situation, therefore methods which invite full here-and-now awareness, such as many gestalt therapy techniques or methods drawn from mindfulness approaches (Kabat-Zinn, 2001, 2004) can be used successfully for decontamination.

Deconfusion. on the other hand, was clearly described by Berne as a psychoanalytic process (Berne, 1961/1986). The process of deconfusion would therefore be more likely to be similar to processes normally used in psychodynamic therapy, and would include methods such as transference analysis (Hargaden and Sills, 2002; Moiso, 1985).

> Deconfusion is the process by which the therapist facilitates the patient to connect with her internal Child ego and bring experiences, feelings and sensations … into the therapeutic relationship … The treatment plan involves the therapist's capacity and ability to be attentive, thoughtful and skilful in understanding her counter-transference responses … The methodology for deconfusion consists of an analysis of the domains of transference together with the therapist's use of empathic transactions.
>
> (Hargaden and Sills, 2002)

> The aim of deconfusion is the transformation of unconscious processes such as archaic, dormant and conflicted aspects of self, into a more conscious, vibrant and mature dynamic.
>
> (Hargaden and Sills, 2003: 188)

Another way of thinking about the difference between decontamination and deconfusion relates to the process of development of script decisions. How we conceptualize script beliefs being formed in TA can be roughly summarized as follows: the child has an experience and he experiences feelings connected to his experience. He develops fantasies, or draws conclusions connected to these experiences and feelings in order to make sense of them, and these fantasies or conclusions become 'fact' (to the individual).

Experience → Feeling → Fantasy/Conclusion → Fact

If we are using Berne's principle that decontamination precedes deconfusion, the process of resolution (treatment direction) of associated script decisions can be considered to run parallel to this, but running in the opposite direction.

Experience → Feeling → Fantasy/Conclusion → Fact
Deconfusion ← Deconfusion ← Decontamination ← Decontamination

This diagram shows the connections between decontamination and deconfusion and different aspects of the process of the development of a script decision, but does so in a linear fashion which does not necessarily represent the process of decontamination and deconfusion. Some TA authors see the process as a progressive one, with decontamination being an earlier stage of treatment than deconfusion (Clarkson, 1992a; Woollams and Brown, 1978). However, some authors have recently presented the idea that deconfusion can begin right from the moment of meeting between therapist and client (Hargaden and Sills, 2002). In many ways, this matches my experiences, in that the formation of the therapeutic relationship requires a degree of containing of the client's affective state, and the emphasis is on empathic transactions (Clark, 1991). Using empathic transactions will inevitably involve a degree of deconfusion, so to draw a distinction between the two as a linear process which follows a set sequence is in some ways not representative of the therapy process in practice. It is likely that the TA therapist will be working on multiple aspects of experiences, feelings, fantasies and cognitive construal in a fluid way.

What is important is for the therapist to have a clear sense as to which ego state they are predominantly working with at any given time, and to be clear about their intentions in terms of whether they are promoting decontamination or deconfusion, and their rationale behind their intervention choice.

DISCONFIRMING SCRIPT BELIEFS

The life script is a psychological set of conclusions, beliefs, expectations, rules, and so on which is developed in order to make meaning out of life and all its experiences. It is essentially a process of learning, albeit one which is flawed. This is because not only is the development of life script an internal, personal, and usually implicit process, but it is one which is based on the mental capacity one has at the time of forming any given script conclusion, or script belief. The script then influences how we perceive things, how we make sense of and interpret events, and it puts a lens over what we remember and our memory of events. Moreover, we look for, pay attention to, interpret and remember information which is consistent with our script beliefs in a process which is known as confirmation bias. Information that is not consistent with, or that challenges script, tends to be discounted, ignored, rejected or explained away, therefore, the script becomes self-perpetuating.

An individual's script beliefs are usually experienced as self-evident and true. Even when presented with a logical argument against the script belief, the belief tends to persist. Script beliefs are changed in a process which is known in TA as redecision. Possibly the most effective method for redecision is *experiential disconfirmation* (Widdowson, 2014). This means that the therapist needs to pay attention to experiences the client reports during sessions, or that the therapist either makes use of or creates experiences – either in sessions or through the use of specifically selected homework activities – which will in some way disconfirm the client's script beliefs. It is particularly important to highlight the disconfirmation or draw the client's attention to it, and to hold it in mind for a period of time to minimize the chances that the client will discount the experience.

An example of drawing on events from a client's life for the purpose of disconfirming script beliefs is from a client of mine who had a 'Don't be Important' injunction, and script beliefs of not being good enough and of not being likeable or loveable. My client told me, almost in passing, that on the previous Saturday her next door neighbour brought her a homemade cake for her birthday, and that on the Sunday, she had met a friend for lunch and found several other friends had joined them as a birthday surprise. I commented that I thought these were lovely things for her neighbour and her friends to do, and that clearly they had put time and effort into doing something to make her feel special and appreciated, and that perhaps this meant that they really did like her. She responded with, 'Yes, they are nice people. They were probably just doing it to be nice.' I asked if she thought they would go to such effort for someone they didn't like. My client went quiet for a few moments, and it seemed as if she was trying to find some reason to dismiss what I had said. I then commented that in the past she had told me that two of the group of friends who had surprised her are known for 'speaking their minds' and 'telling people what they think of them'. She confirmed that this was the case. I then said that this all seemed to indicate that perhaps they did like her after all, and that even if she didn't think she was likeable, that other people clearly did, and that perhaps she might want to think about that over the coming days. Over the course of the next few sessions, I picked up on any reports of positive interactions my client had with other people and said to my client that the evidence seemed to suggest that she was not as unlikeable as she believed.

Another way of facilitating experiential disconfirmation is by asking clients what their expectations are or what they predict will happen in a particular forthcoming situation. By asking the client to explicitly state their script-based expectations or predictions, this brings them into conscious awareness and therefore makes them more easily challenged.

The client can then be asked to approach the situation open-mindedly to see if their expectations or predictions are accurate or not, and to report back on what happens in the next session. This draws on a process known as prediction error (Papalini, Beckers and Vervliet, 2020; Winkler et al., 2022).

An example of stimulating prediction error to trigger experiential disconfirmation can be found in the case of Alastair (Widdowson, 2014). As a child, Alastair had been taught that boasting was distasteful, and that people who expressed self-pride were disliked by others. Consequently, as an adult, he felt unable to show any signs of being pleased with himself or of telling others about his achievements, which was having an adverse effect on his career. I invited Alastair to hold in mind during the course of the following week his belief that people who expressed pride were not likeable. He did so, and during a meeting at work noticed that a colleague who was well-liked was speaking openly and with great pride about some of the good work he had been doing. Alastair realized that expressions of pride did not necessarily lead to being disliked, and he tested his new learning out by disclosing some of the work he had done which had resulted in a substantial cost saving to his company. Not only was he widely praised for his work, but he also received a large pay bonus for saving the company a significant amount of money. All of these experiences combined provided Alastair with sufficient experiential disconfirmation of his script beliefs around not boasting or expressing pride and fear of being disliked that he was able to redecide these beliefs and replace them with more realistic views.

As many of our clients script beliefs are (at least from our perspective) clearly lacking in any kind of supporting evidence, it is often fairly easy to identify potential situations where they may be able to consciously test out the validity of their script beliefs or script-based expectations and instead have an experience which disconfirms the 'truth' of these outdated beliefs and expectations.

USING ALLIANCE RUPTURE AND REPAIR FOR DECONFUSION

The process of relational repair begins with identifying the relational rupture. Ruptures can be identified by the recognition of a rupture marker – some behaviour on the part of the client which the therapist notices and interprets as indicating a rupture (see Point 25). When ruptures occur, the client activates their protocol regarding their 'response of self' – a characteristic way of responding in anticipation of not having an underlying wish fulfilled, and the 'response of other' – the response the client expects from the projected, transferred Parent as part of their protocol. Safran and Muran (2003) identify two primary types of relational rupture markers: withdrawal and confrontation. The ultimate goal is for the client to express underlying repressed feelings – usually feelings that were repressed and forbidden during childhood. Thus rupture and repair form a potent method of deconfusion involving the expression of repressed emotions and the gradual healing of the relational wounds associated with the repression. Unfortunately, the way the client responds to ruptures can actually subtly invite the expected 'response of other' – particularly so with confrontation markers which can invite a defensive or rejecting response in the therapist and thus confirm for the client the need to protect their vulnerability with hostility. When withdrawal markers present, the therapist needs to be attentive to any underlying repressed anger and hostility and subtly and sensitively invite its expression. With confrontation markers the aim is to invite the expression of any repressed feelings of vulnerability and hurt that lie underneath the overt hostility. Safran and Muran (2003) offer two different

 DOI: 10.4324/9781003375890-84

processes, one for each type of relational rupture. I have adapted their model here and synthesized the two processes into one. Please note that this is not a linear process with easily identifiable stages, but an overlapping and often cyclical process whereby different parts may be worked on simultaneously, or re-worked over and over in the process of repairing the rupture. Although this model uses two types of rupture markers, each with a particular underlying feeling, it is important to remember that there are in reality more than two types of rupture markers, and any rupture marker may have any underlying feeling. The ones presented here are, however, common markers and common repressed feelings.

The process of deconfusion can be a slow and gradual one. The therapist is advised to utilize their countertransference responses to inform them as to what might be going on. Using metacommunicative transactions (Widdowson, 2008) (see Point 77) to bring an awareness of the relational enactment that is taking place into the here-and-now of the therapy deepens this process. In this process, the client will be contacting deep emotional pain and so the therapist must maintain an empathic stance throughout and keep an awareness of what is (potentially) going on for the client behind the apparent social level of the message to inform their responses. The therapist also needs to account for their part in the enactment, remain non-defensive and not respond from a position of blaming the client. Metacommunication can assist with staying present and in contact and also exploring the significance of any enactment.

To move forward, the therapist invites the client to say more about how they are experiencing the therapist. Particularly with confrontation ruptures, it is absolutely crucial that the therapist is willing to hear the client's feedback – no matter how hard it might be for them. The therapist needs to take seriously and empathically affirm the client's experience. The therapist needs also to seriously consider the 'grain of truth' in what the client is saying and make a serious attempt to acknowledge their part in any enactment. The rupture repair does not necessarily require disclosure from the therapist, nor does it require a position which takes full responsibility for the problem, but it does require the therapist to admit their oversights and errors. With both types of marker, the therapist's task is to invite the client into full expression of their underlying, repressed feelings. Safran and Muran (2003) note that clients who began with a withdrawal marker may begin to express feelings of anger or hostility here, but often 'pull their punches', by qualifying their statements, or by becoming hesitant.

Clients with a confrontation marker are invited to explore the underlying feelings of vulnerability their hostility is covering. Again, the client may well defend against the emerging vulnerability. The therapist can use metacommunicative transactions to highlight the process that is occurring when clients retreat from expression of underlying feelings. Another possibility here is to invite the client into an awareness experiment, whereby the therapist invites the client to state their feelings (which may be still partially repressed) more stridently – for example, 'As an experiment would you try saying "I feel a little worried about how I'll cope over the next few weeks" and see how it feels?' The client's response is then explored – if they take part in the experiment, the therapist explores the feelings; if the client refuses, their reluctant or anxious feelings are explored. Remember, the client's pattern of withdrawal or confrontation was developed as a defence against some kind of pain and so the relinquishing of the pattern is likely to be a slow process. The deconfusion takes place gradually as the client expresses their feelings and underlying needs. This may take a considerable amount of time, and will probably require repetitive cycles of rupture and repair before the deconfusion is complete (or at least partially resolved). The client's feelings here may well be clouded by rage or despair and terror of abandonment, which reflects the underlying pain of the original affect. The therapist needs to remain potent, and stay empathically attuned to the client throughout this process, particularly in cases where the client expresses a request to their therapist that their therapist is unable or unwilling to gratify.

USING METACOMMUNICATIVE TRANSACTIONS

Metacommunications are based on the therapist's subjective sense of what is happening in the therapy in the here-and-now. The therapist relies upon direct observation of the client, continual observation of their own internal state and observation of their subjective sense of what is happening in the relationship on a moment-to-moment basis. The therapist then invites a dialogue with the client about their experience and the process of how therapist and client are relating. For example, the therapist may notice the client looks uneasy, that they are feeling slightly tense and they have a vague sense of distancing between themselves and the client, and so the therapist uses these three experiences to construct a statement which is offered to the client for mutual analysis. 'I notice you're looking around the room, and I'm feeling a little tense. I get a sense of distance between us right now. Does that make any sense to you?'

> A metacommunication is an intervention that utilizes the therapist's countertransference in the here and now of the therapy together with exploration of the here-and-now process of the therapy in a collaborative engagement with the client so as to explore the relational significance for the client of what is occurring in the therapy ... Metacommunicative transactions usually contain a process observation, that is, an observation about the unfolding process, or the many unfolding processes, that are happening between the therapist and client.
>
> (Widdowson, 2008: 58)

Metacommunicative transactions are in many respects direct interventions that incorporate the characteristics of autonomy:

awareness, spontaneity and intimacy. As interventions, they embody a spirit of enquiry, curiosity and collaboration. In exploring the therapeutic relationship in an ongoing fashion the therapist and client can gain significant information about the client's subjective ego state shifts, their transactions (and ulterior transactions), their games and their script.

Construction of metacommunicative transactions require that the therapist pays close attention to directly observable events, such as shifts in the client's position, but also to less tangible shifts in the energetic quality of the connection between them, their sense of relative closeness or distance and their sense of the client being relationally open or closed and withdrawn at any given time. The therapist uses their observations and intuitive sense of the energetic flow within the session and comments on their experience, and invites the client into a dialogue about their experience, and the significance and meaning of the experience. Metacommunicative transactions can also name a relational dynamic that is happening between the therapist and client, such as a sense of being overly cautious, a competitive edge, a sense of longing, a cosy atmosphere of stroking. This requires that the therapist pays close attention to their feeling states and repeatedly checks their 'relational barometer'. To do so, the therapist will need to be striving to continually develop their self-awareness, particularly in relation to how they interact with others, and also to have done considerable personal therapy to give them a foundation that enables them to begin to disentangle their own issues and projections from the client's. All of this requires a profound honesty and openness, both to self and others (including sometimes hearing difficult feedback) that facilitate the therapist's use of self and the use of the therapeutic relationship as a vehicle for exploration, change and growth.

THERAPY OF GAMES

Alliance ruptures can be conceptualized in relational TA terms to signify the possibility of a game enactment between the therapist and client. Therapists who work relationally with the transference and countertransference as a major therapeutic tool do not consider the enactment of a game to be intrinsically bad, but rather an inevitable process whereby the client's unconscious process or core conflictual relationship theme (Luborsky, 1984) surfaces in the transactions and relationship with the therapist. Such a relational approach sees that it is not the enactment of a game which is problematic, but rather that the emergence and enactment of the game provide the therapeutic dyad with an excellent opportunity to re-work the underlying script or protocol issues from which the game originates.

As therapists, we have two main options in dealing with games in the therapy room – watch for the game and confront (at the opening con), or be receptive to the game and allow ourselves to be engaged in the unfolding of the client's unconscious processes. Whereas confronting or interrupting the game may be useful in certain situations, in other fields of application of TA, making space for the game to emerge can be a crucial feature of an in-depth TA therapy. There are proponents within the TA psychotherapy world who advocate the early confrontation of, or avoidance of games (Goulding and Goulding, 1979). A psychodynamic or relational approach views staying out of games not as an optimal therapeutic stance and that 'confronting or aborting a patient's game [is] not therapeutic' (Woods, 2000: 94). The exception to this is the therapist participating in a third-degree game, which therapists of all persuasions would agree is anti-therapeutic. Indeed, the therapeutic stance is to become aware of the game and interrupt its flow, and work with the underlying conflicts before the game pay-off is reached. In cases where first-degree games have reached their pay-off, the therapist engages the client in an analysis of the interactions and seeks to understand and repair any rupture in the relationship. Stark says 'the optimal stance is one that involves semipermeability – the therapist allowing herself to be impacted upon but not completely taken over' (2000: 109). She describes how the therapist needs to be receptive to the client's projections to give the client

> the experience of delivering all of herself into the room and discovering that both she and her therapist can survive. The therapist must allow herself to be responsive to the roles imposed on her by the patient, so that the patient can have the opportunity to master her internal demons.
>
> (ibid.: 109)

Another relational psychoanalyst, Karen Maroda, also describes the therapeutic stance and the importance of the therapist's semi-permeability:

> I have learned that my role is not to refuse to be stimulated in this way. My role is to help the patient understand what he is doing and, toward this end, allow myself to be incorporated into his historical play by being responsive. The therapeutic objective is not necessarily for the therapist to feel differently from the others; it is for the therapist to handle his feelings more constructively than did the patient's significant others. Ultimately this enables the patient to be aware of his own feelings and behaviour and take responsibility for both.
>
> (1994/2004: 129)

Working with games using a relational TA lens requires that the therapist adopts a non-defensive position regarding their own contribution to the game enactment. In basic TA terms, a game is not possible without two players (Berne, 1964), therefore, it is unhelpful and theoretically inaccurate to consider that one person (i.e., the client) is 'playing a game' with another (i.e., the therapist) in isolation and with no contribution to the situation from one party. The power differential in the therapeutic relationship is in many ways (at least on an emotional level) a direct parallel with the client's early relationships with their parents (who are more emotionally powerful than their children). As such, the client is likely to take on the responsibility for the enactment of the game, thus reinforcing script beliefs, for instance, beliefs about 'being bad'. Effective therapy and repair of such alliance ruptures require the therapist to be self-aware regarding their own particular relational vulnerabilities (and engagement in therapy to resolve these issues).

Therapists also have an unconscious, and one which is not immune to proactively issuing game invitations. Clients can respond to the game invitations of their therapist, and in some respects will be particularly vulnerable and susceptible to responding to such invitations due to the nature of the power imbalance in the relationship. As therapists we need to be particularly vigilant for how our own issues are acted out in the therapeutic arena, and to commit to ongoing personal development and thorough personal therapy (see also Points 26, 27, 43, 96 and 97). Following Berne's recommendations, it is wiser for the therapist to reflect upon the question 'What game am I in?' rather than 'Am I in a game?' (Berne, 1966/1994).

Games are an unavoidable aspect of human interactions, including psychotherapy. The role of the psychotherapist is not to avoid them completely, but to seek to understand what this game means for this client at this time as a manifestation of the client's unique unconscious. Similarly, the therapist can productively learn about what this game means for them as a manifestation of their own unconscious. Finally, the therapist's role is to reflect upon what the participation of both them and their client means at this time, and upon how the game was co-created (Summers and Tudor, 2000).

79

THERAPY OF INJUNCTIONS

Injunctions provide a summary of themes present in an individual's internalized prohibitions (see Point 35). Injunctions are considered pre-verbal, implicit aspects of a client's script: the child develops their injunctions in response to reactions and behaviours from primary caregivers. In this context, injunctions can be considered to be relational in origin in that they provide a set of rules that the individual needs to follow in order to preserve relationships and thus maintain a (script-bound) sense of 'being OK'. Holmes describes this process from the perspective of attachment theory:

> The key point about defences from an attachment perspective is that they are interpersonal strategies for dealing with suboptimal environment. Their aim is not so much to preserve the integrity of the individual when faced with conflicting inner drives, but to maintain attachments in the face of relational forces threatening to disrupt them.
>
> (2001: 25)

From this, we see that injunctions serve a purpose in that the child develops their injunctions to make sense of their world, and to develop rules for living which will ensure that their attachments are preserved. They act as 'internal safety rules' that the individual can follow, and thus keep key caregivers around. Unfortunately, as we know, these injunctions are limiting in later life and can represent the essence of an individual's script that we are seeking to resolve in TA therapy.

The Gouldings' list of 12 injunctions provides a useful shorthand, but needs to be considered carefully for each client, as using a defined list of 12 injunctions can miss

 DOI: 10.4324/9781003375890-87

both the subtleties and variations of an individual's childhood experience and meaning. It seems both theoretically accurate and therapeutically useful to encourage clients to find their own words to express script conclusions, to articulate their own 'meaning-making'. It is also crucial not to restrict the analysis of script to negative, restrictive decisions.

(Cornell, 1988: 279)

That notwithstanding, the shorthand of the injunctions can be a useful tool for the therapist to begin their process of formulation of understanding the client's process and experience using a series of common themes. Redecision therapist and colleague of the Gouldings, John McNeel has expanded the Gouldings' original list of injunctions to 25 injunctive messages (McNeel, 2010). McNeel has generously made his work available on his website: www.aspiringtokindness.com

Injunctions are tenacious aspects of an individual's script and need to be repeatedly addressed, implicitly and relationally for effective resolution. The Gouldings developed elaborate redecision therapy methods that tackled the injunctions directly. However, all TA sources on redecision methods emphasize the need for ongoing reinforcement of the redecision. It is important in seeking redecision of injunctions that the therapist is mindful of the attachment-preserving intention of the injunction and the desperate fear the client may feel in their Child ego state at the possibility of disobeying an injunction. Resolution of injunctions is a gradual and relational process and one that the therapist needs to pay attention to over time. Often the very processes of psychotherapy provide a direct challenge to the client's injunctions. With planning, the therapist can seek to repeatedly challenge their client's injunctions in an indirect fashion, in addition to any direct methods they may also utilize.

80

INTERVENTIONS AND APPROACHES TO THERAPY OF INJUNCTIONS AND INJUNCTIVE MESSAGES

John McNeel (2022) places the therapy of injunctive messages firmly within the context of a supportive therapeutic relationship by emphasizing the need for therapists to provide *affirmation* (or validation) of the client's experiences and present suffering, *acceptance*, *empathy* (as opposed to a conversation where one attempts to 'fix' another's problems) and *invitation* to find new, more resourceful ways of living. McNeel also notes that the process of therapy of injunctive messages takes time and requires considerable behavioural change and reinforcement of changes. In many ways, the therapy of injunctions can be considered an ongoing process, as it is unlikely that a single piece of therapy will result in an immediate and permanent resolution of an injunctive message. In the spirit of considering the therapy of injunctions/ injunctive messages as ongoing processes which are embedded within a therapeutic relationship, the following interventions are offered as examples which the therapist can use to trigger their own creative and individualized ways of working with clients injunctions.

DON'T EXIST

In many respects, therapy in and of itself is a potent confrontation of this injunction. Clients are reminded through the empathic relationship that they exist, and their existence is validated. Acknowledge their pain, and their struggles with life. Support clients' engagement with life and help them to

DOI: 10.4324/9781003375890-88

identify people, places and things which enliven, and invigorate them and which nourish their soul.

DON'T BE YOU

Encourage and support self-definition and expressions of individuality. Validate the client's perspective, their uniqueness and their history. By promoting the development of a 'coherent narrative' (Holmes, 2001), the client's sense of self is developed and validated.

DON'T BE CLOSE

Pay careful attention to the level of 'felt closeness' with your client. Sensitively and gently enquire into their experience. Pay attention to how the client 'avoids' or fears closeness in sessions. Support clients in finding new and more satisfying ways of relating to others and in forming, maintaining and deepening their closest relationships.

DON'T BELONG

Understand twinship transference (Hargaden and Sills, 2002; Kohut, 1984) as signifying the need to 'belong'. Help the client to identify and celebrate ways in which they are similar to others. Invite the client to reflect on how they feel accepted in therapy, which cues they pick up on to let them know that they are OK with you. Explore the client's wider social relationships. Encourage them to 'find their tribe' and to give themselves permission to feel a sense of belonging.

DON'T BE IMPORTANT

This is often a very difficult injunction to treat and will need repeated attention as subservience and the desire to 'not be selfish' is culturally reinforced. Encourage your client to allow others to treat them as special and important (perhaps considering a gift to others, as many people enjoy making others feel special). Gently confront the client 'talking about others' in their session and enquire as to how they feel receiving all of your attention in sessions. Support your client in feeling pride and self-satisfaction.

DON'T SUCCEED

Cultivate a positive but realistic attitude in respect of goals. Show interest in the client's goals and interests. Encourage your client to think about and work towards short-term, medium-term and longer-term life goals. Celebrate any successes or achievements – no matter how small. Recognize and take to supervision (and perhaps personal therapy) any envy that you may feel towards your client.

DON'T GROW UP

A variation on this is 'don't be separate'. By consistently emphasizing the client's autonomy and capacity to change and individuate, the therapist challenges this injunction. The therapist can also address the client's fear of acting autonomously, and their fear of taking responsibility. Repeatedly affirm for the client that they are indeed grown up, and able to make independent decisions about their own life.

DON'T BE A CHILD

A variation on this is 'don't be dependent'. In my clinical experience, 'don't grow up' and 'don't be a child' often occur together, creating a difficult double bind for the individual. Validate the client's childhood experiences, their ways of making sense of the world and survival strategies, but not in a 'marshmallowing' or overly enthusiastic way. Stroke playfulness and fun. Normalize relational needs of 'having the other initiate'. Also in therapy of this injunction, there may be need to develop a prolonged idealizing transference and work with the client's dependency needs. It is important the therapist has also begun examining their own dependency needs in their own therapy.

DON'T BE WELL/DON'T BE SANE

Stroke effective problem-solving and emphasize health. Often the fear of being well or sane is the fear of the responsibility this brings, or the fear that if they are well, then they won't get looked after, so strategies which invite your client to identify that they want to be taken care of and then going about and getting age-appropriate ways of being taken care of can be supported. Encourage your client to problem-solve and also to engage in positive healthy lifestyle changes.

DON'T FEEL

Provide a permissive atmosphere where all of the client's feelings are acceptable within the therapy room. Repeated attention to feelings, empathic transactions and promoting healthy expression of emotions are all effective methods of gently confronting this injunction. Facilitate the development of emotion regulation skills.

DON'T THINK

Invite expression of the client's own thoughts and reflections. Sometimes the client may need to disagree with the therapist, to develop their own independent thinking; in this case, stroke the client for thinking for themselves. Help clients learn that it is fine for people to have differing views and perspectives. Stroke clarity of thinking and clarity of planning. Support your client in taking their time to work out a problem, come to a conclusion, or to figure out an answer to something.

DON'T (DO ANYTHING)

Stroke positive action and movement out of procrastination. Celebrate spontaneity.

ESCAPE-HATCH CLOSURE REVISITED

There are two linked, but different procedures within the TA literature that directly address tragic script outcomes: escape-hatch closure and no-harm contracts. The key difference between escape-hatch closure (even time-limited closure) and no-harm contracts is that an escape-hatch closure is, by definition, a decisional process, and is 'taken by the client for him/herself, with the therapist as witness, and is inherently non-changeable (the unconditionality is part of the decision). A no-harm contract, like any other contract, is agreed between client and therapist and is changeable' (I. Stewart, 2008, personal communication).

Although these definitions suggest that there are distinct differences between the two procedures, the differences seem somewhat semantic and in reality, the process is virtually indistinguishable. Indeed, in a paper often cited as the source for no-harm contracts, the procedure is identical to that of escape-hatch closure (Drye, Goulding and Goulding, 1973). Escape-hatch closure is a process whereby the individual verbally makes a commitment to her/himself with the therapist acting as witness that no matter how bad things are, they will not kill or harm themselves, kill or harm others or go crazy (see Stewart, 2007, for a full description of this process). Stewart asserts that escape-hatch closure has the potential to be therapeutic for all clients, although the process must be carried out at an appropriate time in the therapy, and not done 'for the sake of it' without sufficient preparation (ibid.).

Attachment theory offers some interesting perspectives for consideration of escape hatches. An attachment perspective would suggest that an individual keeps their own escape hatches as an internal secure base (Holmes, 2001). It would stand to

DOI: 10.4324/9781003375890-89

reason from this position that an individual will not be ready to close their escape hatches until they have internalized a new secure base, which will normally be the therapy and the therapist. This emphasizes the need for the development of a good working alliance before escape-hatch closure is contemplated. Part of the function of a secure base is as a provider of internal self-soothing and as a means of tolerating intense affect. So in addition to ensuring that escape-hatch closure is not raised until there is a sufficient working alliance, the therapist needs to ensure that the client has begun to develop new, positive means of self-soothing and developed the capacity to tolerate intense affect. The primary means of learning to tolerate affect is widely accepted to be the experiencing of an empathic relationship. If the client can regulate their emotions effectively and can tolerate distress, then there is no need to pursue escape-hatch closure.

Raising escape hatches prematurely in therapy can provoke alarm and confusion in the client. In situations where the therapist raises the issue of escape hatches without any clear discussion that the client may be at risk (such as when it is raised during intake), the client can feel alarmed and unnecessarily distressed by the therapist's introduction of escape-hatch closure. Heavy-handed or premature focus on escape-hatch closure can lead clients into adapting to the therapist, and 'going through the motions' of closure, without intrapsychic closure or can raise the issue of harm in a client who is not yet ready to discuss or resolve these issues. Certainly, insistence on escape-hatch closure is not only inappropriate, it is incredibly poor practice.

In my view, escape-hatch closure and no-harm contracts are deeply problematic. First, they are often used reactively by therapists who see potential or actual emergence of suicidal ideation in their client. In such instances, jumping on escape-hatch closure as a means of addressing this does not adequately explore the client's emerging suicidality. As such, it can give the client the impression that their suicidal thoughts are unacceptable and shameful, which is likely to compound their difficulties even more (Ayres, 2006; Mothersole, 1996). As psychotherapists, it is our job to tolerate human distress, not to push it away or create further distress because we are afraid of our clients' 'dark thoughts and feelings'. If a client believes that their suicidal thoughts are unacceptable to the therapist, they are likely to avoid discussing them in therapy, which can give the therapist the impression that the client's suicidal ideation has been resolved, when instead it is simply being remaining unspoken about in a process of over-adaptation (Schiff and Schiff, 1971).

Just because a client has verbally stated in a session that they will not kill or harm themselves, anyone else or 'go crazy' does not mean that any of those scenarios will be prevented, and it is absurd to think that they would. If a client is in a state of such distress where any of these three options seems attractive to them, then they are unlikely to have sufficient functioning Adult ego state to stick to the escape-hatch closure, again, highlighting that emotion regulation and distress tolerance work are more suitable.

Sometimes escape-hatch closure or no-harm contracts are pursued by therapists as a defensive manoeuvre in order to provide them with some kind of protection in case a client does pursue one of these tragic script outcomes. Such thinking is misguided; if a therapist documented that they had pursued escape-hatch closure with a client who was at risk, effectively the therapist has documented that the client was considered to be at risk, that no action was taken and that the therapist simply took the client at their word that they would not act upon their urges to harm. Such a scenario would not protect a therapist in a malpractice complaint and in fact would be evidence of negligence.

There is no evidence to support the use of escape-hatch closure or no-harm contracts (McConnell Lewis, 2007), and indeed there is some evidence to suggest that they can be counterproductive and actually increase suicide risk (Drew, 2001). Therapists who want to pursue an evidence-based way to attending to client safety and protection are advised to develop good risk assessment and management procedures and to collaboratively create safety plans with clients. Fortunately there are many excellent and accessible guides to creating safety plans available online, such as www.stayingsafe.net.

CLIENT PROTECTION

There is a range of considerations the therapist needs to take into account in ensuring there is sufficient protection for their client and also for managing their own needs. Resourcing yourself as a therapist is a vital aspect of protection. Obtaining adequate and regular ongoing supervision is a key part of ensuring there is sufficient support and protection available for the therapist, but also for the client in terms of quality assurance and the ethical management of the therapist's caseload. Commitment to reading, attending workshops and other aspects of continual professional development form part of the resourcing of a therapist, and ensure that the therapist's skills and knowledge continue to develop.

TA therapists resource themselves through their own engagement in personal therapy, which seeks to resolve aspects of their own script which may get in the way of their work. Personal therapy for therapists also has a part to play in the therapist developing their capacity to experience, contain and deal effectively with intense and unpleasant emotions. A therapist who is not in touch with or is unable to handle their own anger, or profound grief, or be the recipient of the intense emotions of others is unlikely to be able to provide adequate protection or containment of a client who is experiencing similar intense emotions.

Obtaining a client history, particularly with regard to any previous suicide attempts or self-harming behaviour or violence, is important. A previous history of acting destructively to self or others or of impulsivity provides a strong indicator that the client may not be able to contain the intense feelings that psychotherapy can unleash. In the case of a client presenting with such a history, it is important that the therapist seeks supervisory advice on whether to work with the client or to refer on. All therapists have a responsibility to be familiar with at least basic risk assessment methods and strategies for dealing with increasing or imminent risk of suicide or violence. Alongside this, the therapist needs to determine how each client deals with acute distress and contains their impulses. Clients who do not handle strong feelings well may need to develop the capacity to regulate their emotions and learn key self-soothing strategies or impulse control strategies before the therapy work can progress safely (see Points 68 and 69).

The pacing and timing of the work are important also in providing protection. The pull to delve too deeply too quickly can be strong in early sessions. This is particularly the case with clients who have some insight, and who feel a huge pressure to 'offload' the intense emotions they are struggling with, or those with strong urges to tell their story. In my experience, when we rush things, we invariably have to go back and re-do them. The difficulty in therapy is that once an issue has been covered, particularly in the early sessions, it can be hard to go back and go through it once more later on. In the early sessions we have to strike a careful balance between getting to know the client and find out about their history, while also attending to the content and process and facilitating the integration of material as the client settles into the therapy (see also Point 18). Providing a degree of containment can be vital in instances of strong emotions that threaten to overwhelm the client, leaving them feeling disorganized or fragmented. Knowing when to slow down, or even stop a client is an important therapeutic skill, and is more an 'art' to master than a skill which is easy to develop. Rothschild makes a similar point in the context of describing working with trauma survivors. Her principle is that one should 'know where the brakes are, and how to use them, before one applies the accelerator' (2000: 79).

Diagnosis is also a central aspect of determining client protection. The most fundamental question each transactional analyst has to answer about each client is, 'How much available

Adult ego state does this client have?' Identifying tendencies towards destructive acting-out is essential, as is accurate assessment of any major psychopathology. Taking time to examine your diagnosis is important as the therapist can pre-empt issues and provide protection by way of things such as specific contracts according to the client's diagnosis. Stewart (1996) also cautions against using dramatic or cathartic techniques until a clear contract is in place, the therapist has completed their diagnosis and some preparatory work has taken place. Familiarity with psychiatric disorders, their features and manifestation is important here, as is the ability to recognize potential rapid escalations of feelings, for instance, increased agitation moving towards incapacitation or violence (Schiff et al., 1975).

83

POTENCY AND PERMISSION

The 'Three Ps' of potency (Steiner, 1968), protection and permission (Crossman, 1966) are central to the practice of effective and ethical TA psychotherapy. Having discussed client protection in Point 82, I focus here on potency and permission.

POTENCY

The potency of the therapist lies in the capacity to contain despair, uncertainty, doubt, meaninglessness, hatred, rage, shame and anxiety, both within the therapist and their clients. Potency also includes the therapist's sense of emotional and psychological resilience. Potency relates to the therapist's ability to provide sufficient intensity and strength in the therapy for the client to disobey Parental injunctions and scripting (Berne, 1972). The therapist's potency is also increased by the use of the therapist's training, skills and knowledge in the service of the client, and by the therapist having a clear sense of why they are doing what they are doing (treatment planning) (Stewart, 2007). Ongoing personal and professional development work, recognizing and accepting the need to take regular breaks and holidays from work, and attending to personal needs all model good boundaries, self-care and, by extension, therapeutic potency. Our potency as therapists also involves an awareness of our own personal strengths and resources, and an acceptance of our personal limitations. In my doctoral research (Widdowson, 2013), clients were clear about what they experienced as features of the therapist's potency. Each client articulated that therapists who had confidence in their ability combined with a sense of curiosity, a clear sense of direction for the therapy, an ability to

DOI: 10.4324/9781003375890-91

be authentic and real, and, interestingly, a sense of humour, were experienced as having high levels of potency.

PERMISSION

At its most basic level, permission in therapy involves the therapist creating an atmosphere in which it is OK to say the unsayable, give voice to fears, shameful thoughts, fantasies and deeds, to express oneself and to be real. Permission is an interesting concept, and one which, in my view, needs careful consideration. Historically, a number of TA therapists took a parental stance and literally gave clients verbal permissions, often in the form of verbal affirmations in sessions. This approach has all kinds of inherent potential problems, not least the risk of infantilizing adult clients. It is also unclear to what extent a client will accept a positive verbal message from a therapist when their internal self-experience is highly negative and critical. In this instance, it is possible that the direct giving of verbal permissions can exacerbate the client's sense of internal badness and isolation. I do, however, believe there is a place for the provision of encouragement, support, strokes and the replacement of negative, limiting script beliefs with more positive and resourceful beliefs in the therapy. However, the means by which this provision takes place needs careful thought and discussion in supervision, and should not be just automatically churning out positive statements for the client. The developmental and transferential implications of gratifying and providing permissions need to be considered carefully. Although some people have had dreadfully restrictive upbringings and are hungry for permission and may require encouragement and invitation to begin to live in more flexible and expansive ways, permission-giving can serve the therapist's needs far more than the client's:

> When one of my supervisors commented that I see everybody as hungry, thus confronting my tendency to project my depressive issues on all my clients, I was able to start discriminating between

> those who needed to be emotionally fed and those who needed to
> be asked why they had not learned to cook.
>
> (McWilliams, 1994: 230)

In approaching clients who need to be asked why they have
not learned to cook, TA therapists can use a more psychodynamic approach. This approach, rather than directly giving
permissions, is one which affirms the client's autonomy in a
way which is congruent with TA philosophy. The method
involves noticing when the client is implicitly seeking permission, or whether the client appears to 'need' permission in
some area and to attempt to amplify the client's desire for
permission and facilitate the client's expression of their
neediness. Once this desire is in conscious awareness, and the
client has articulated it as a direct statement, the therapist can
invite the client to explore the significance of asking for permission and how they stop themselves from taking permission independently.

84

IMPASSE THEORY REVISITED

An impasse is a stuck point, where there are equal and opposing forces present. The Gouldings first elaborated impasse theory following their work with Fritz Perls, the originator of gestalt therapy who understood internal conflict as being an internal battle between the 'topdog' and the 'underdog' (Perls, 1969). The Gouldings took this understanding and applied TA structural theory to understand the conflict as a conflict between ego states (Goulding and Goulding, 1979). Ken Mellor (1980) later developed impasse theory to create a consistent model (the Gouldings' model mixed structural and functional ego state models) that incorporated some child development theory. It is Mellor's conceptualization of impasses which is most widely used among TA practitioners at present (Figure 84.1).

Students who are new to TA often confuse an impasse with the client feeling 'stuck'. Whereas an impasse will always involve a sense of stuckness, stuckness is not necessarily indicative of the presence of an impasse. For an impasse to be diagnosed, there need to be equal and opposing forces in conflict. Impasse diagrams must also show the two sides of the conflict, as an impasse is often confused (diagrammatically) with internal dialogue between ego states. Describing the dialogue for type three impasses can be particularly problematic, as these are global, impressionistic and developmentally early conflicts which are often experienced on a somatic level. They have a timeless quality in that clients will often report having 'always felt that way'. Describing these impasses is usually done by way of describing the general themes of the impasse, for instance, a type three impasse around existence may simply hold the words 'die' and 'I want to live', or may be connected to

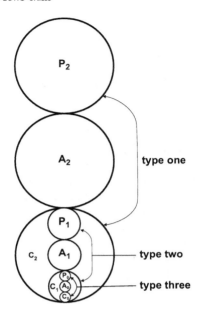

Figure 84.1 Impasses
Source: Mellor (1980).

themes such as abandonment, engulfment (Gobes, 1985; Lee, 1997), and so forth.

Often the emergence of an impasse is indicative of a move towards greater health on the part of the client. The early stages of therapy are often characterized by a Parent-led process in that the client's intrapsychic process is following the 'instructions' of the Parent ego state. When the client's Child ego states resist these Parental wishes and desires and their Child ego states have been activated, then an impasse may emerge as the two opposing sides conflict with each other.

Recent TA authors have begun to explore the relational dimensions of impasse theory, and the role of impasses in explaining seemingly intractable stuck points in therapy. Petriglieri (2007) proposes impasses as necessary points of repose and reflection whereby the individual experiencing the impasse collects their thoughts and reconfigures them in a process of meaning making. Cornell and Landaiche (2006) consider the interpersonal aspects of the impasse and explore how therapy often works with the deepest, unconscious impasses – those at type three level (Mellor, 1980) – and how the very work of therapy pushes both the therapist and client to their relational edge.

Indeed, many transactional analysts now view the process of impasse resolution in very different terms from those of the Gouldings, who focused on the use of two-chair methods for impasse resolution (Goulding and Goulding, 1978). Current TA therapy tends to view the resolution of type three impasses as being a relational process, and linked to deconfusion. There is great interest in integrating body psychotherapy methods to work with such early and often somatically based processes.

Commonly, practitioners seek a rapid resolution of an impasse once an impasse is identified. My experience would suggest that prematurely seeking resolution of an impasse results in a hollow and short-lived victory: the impasse will either return, intact, or the impasse will emerge in a different presentation. Impasses are complex intrapsychic processes with complex dynamics and are mostly not amenable to rapid resolution. Practitioners are advised to spend a great deal of time in the process of impasse clarification with clients, which will often lead to a spontaneous impasse resolution. The process of 'being with' the impasse can be incredibly frustrating for both therapist and client, but taking time to complete the process effectively will avoid the need to revisit material at a later date, and may well provide space for the integration needed for the impasse to be resolved.

My own practice has changed considerably over recent years in how I work with impasses, in that I no longer pursue impasse resolution but instead seek impasse acceptance. First, I step out of seeking to valorize one side over another. Therapists typically take sides with the client's Child ego state, thus creating an internal loyalty battle with the client's Parent ego state, which in many ways makes the impasse more entrenched. Instead, I highlight the impasse, acknowledge the dilemma this poses for the client, and encourage the client to accept that they have this internal conflict and to find a way to live with these two equal and opposing internal forces. I have found that once the struggle is removed through the process of acceptance, that the impasse often seems to dissolve or no longer troubles the client.

USING CHAIR WORK IN TA: SOME GUIDELINES

Chair work techniques have a long history in transactional analysis, particularly in working with Parent ego states and in promoting resolution of difficulties between Parent and Child ego states. These methods were introduced into TA by the Gouldings (Goulding and Goulding, 1979), who were taught these methods by Fritz Perls. They have been subsequently developed by a number of TA authors, including John McNeel's Parent Interview method (McNeel, 1976) and Richard Erskine (Erskine et al., 1999).

Chair work is a highly active experiential technique. Essentially, in all forms of chair work, the therapist invites the client to imagine that a particular person (such as a family member or school teacher) is sitting in an empty chair that is in the room. They are then guided to have an imaginal dialogue with that person, moving between seats as they switch 'speaker'.

Over recent years, I have noticed a reduction in the number of TA therapists who are doing chair work, which is a real shame. Chair work is an incredibly powerful method, and it is not unusual for it to be the a major turning point in someone's therapy. Despite the fact that the number of TA therapists doing chair work seems to have declined, chair work has actually grown in popularity in other therapies. Chair work is a major technique in process-experiential therapy, and also in schema therapy and is also being used in CBT. As all three of those therapies are considered to be evidence-based, and that research has been conducted on the effectiveness of chair work alone, there is convincing research of its usefulness in therapy.

DOI: 10.4324/9781003375890-93

Scott Kellogg (2015) has identified five major types of chair work: (1) external dialogues; (2) internal dialogues; (3) dreamwork; (4) corrective dialogues; and (5) role playing. Within TA, chair work tends to be used to external dialogues or internal dialogues.

External dialogues can be used to deal with 'unfinished business' that a client has with a person who is dead, or who is no longer in their life, or in cases where expression of emotion may had adverse consequences (such as telling a manager 'where they can stick their job'). By expressing long-held pain and saying the things they would have liked to say long ago, it is believed that this allows the client to process these past events, by, for example, expressing outrage, and anger and explaining the impact on their life by mentally confronting an abuser, or another person who hurt them. Similarly the process of expressing grief, and unspoken thoughts and feelings to a person now deceased can facilitate the processing of 'stuck grief' and enable the person to move on in their life. Although expression of 'unfinished business' is, strictly speaking, a gestalt intervention and not a TA intervention, it seems to have a powerful effect on the equilibrium of ego states and can represent or facilitate a movement out of script. Another common use of external dialogues in TA in the Parent interview (McNeel, 1976). Here, once the chair work is underway, the client moves to the empty chair and speaks 'as if' they were their parent, with the therapist conducting a conversational interview with the client's Parent ego state. This is almost always a highly intense process, with clients expressing a considerable amount of emotion and usually coming away with some new insight into their Parent which supports healing. Also the use of external dialogue can also facilitate the client in expressing compassion, warmth and love to their Child self. Although also usually very emotional, the process tends to be more gentle, just as one would be with an actual child who was distressed or confused.

The primary focus with internal dialogue chair work is the expression of an internal conflict the client experiences, with the client placing each side of the conflict on one of the chairs and again, moving back and forth between them as the session unfolds. Typically within TA, the conflict is seen as being between the client's Parent and Child ego states, such as is seen in an impasse (Mellor, 1980).

Another way internal dialogues can be used is in addressing self-criticism and the part of the client which attacks them. By switching chairs, the client is supported by the therapist to fight back and counter the self-critical part's argument. Interestingly, it often becomes clear that the self-critical part's (original) intention for the client was positive, such as wanting the client to be able to 'fit in' socially, or wanting to motivate them into doing things, such as studying, or household chores. If a positive intention can be identified, the client can then easily let the self-critical part know that it is no longer needed and that the client will manage just fine without its constantly undermining the thought process.

INITIATING A PIECE OF CHAIR WORK

Starting a piece of two chair work is often remarkably simple. Usually it can be instigated whenever a client starts commenting on how they 'wish they could only say … to …', the deceased or someone from their past. It can also be started when two conflicting parts of the client's psyche have been identified, or when the therapist and client think it would be useful to explore one of the client's parental introjects further. At such moments, I might gesture towards the empty chair in my therapy room and say, 'What would you like to say to …? If they were sitting right here, right now, and could hear you, what would you say?' Often in such situations clients will respond to their therapist, however, with a little encouragement will often enter into the chair work quite quickly. I say, 'I invite you to respond as if they were here, right here, right now, and say all the things you've been wanting to say. I realize this might seem strange at first, however, that will soon pass. It's a technique based on imagery and emotional expression.' I explain to clients during the initial contract phase of therapy that I use mental imagery techniques, and that if I ever invite them to use such a technique, that I'd really encourage them to be open-minded and go with it and see where it takes them. I may again gesture towards the chair and say, 'Would you be willing to say that to him, right now?' Usually this is more than sufficient to start the process. It is not always necessary to use an empty chair – slight modification of the method can have the same result and can feel substantially easier for some clients. Clients who are likely to feel silly talking to an empty chair can be asked to close their eyes and mentally imagine seeing the parent in front of them. Clients who struggle visualizing can be invited to imagine hearing the dialogue instead.

FACILITATING THE PROCESS

If possible, the therapist is advised to turn slightly towards the empty chair and to break eye contact with the client to encourage the client to engage with the process. Encourage the client to speak in the first person, and to make clear statements, and use prompts such as, 'Tell him how you felt. Tell him what is was like for you all to live with him …' or 'What I want to tell you is …' or 'What I need from you is …'. To keep the work moving along, whenever something clear, emotionally significant or where a response is called for, simply invite the client to switch chairs. 'I wonder if you'd be willing to switch chairs for a moment, and respond as if you were your dad. This is usually quite illuminating.'

Be mindful of the internal sense of loyalty a client will experience towards their parents, no matter how abusive their parents were. Inviting disagreement or 'fighting' with the Parent can be extremely destabilizing for a client and can set up strong intrapsychic resistance (Clarkson, 1988). It is important that the Parent ego state does not feel threatened but feels respected and has an opportunity for healing. Often the Parent will spontaneously move into strong affect or reveal information regarding their own personal history. This may pave the way for the Parent resolution process (Dashiell, 1978).

ENDING CHAIR WORK

It is wise to end a piece of chair work as soon as a significant statement has been made or when the client has reached some insight. Chair work can be tiring, so keeping it brief is wise. It can be ended simply by stating, 'That seems like a good place to stop.' Ensure that you spend plenty of time debriefing after using two-chair methods. The debriefing should also include some discussion of how the experience felt for the client.

86

USING VISUALISZATION AND MENTAL IMAGERY IN TA

Mental imagery is known to be an effective tool in the psychotherapy of mood and anxiety disorders (Skottnik and Linden, 2019). Not only can it be used to generate temporary mood states, but also it can have longer-lasting effects. Recent research has shown that repeated positive imagery can reduce negative interpretation bias among people with depression (Blackwell et al., 2015), suggesting that the use of imagery can have long-term therapeutic effects on an individual's frame of reference.

The Gouldings used different variations on mental imagery techniques to address traumatic early scenes (see Goulding and Goulding, 1979), many of which involved some element of changing or rescripting the original scene. Imagery rescripting is a recognized technique for the treatment of post-traumatic stress disorder (Bosch and Arntz, 2021). With imagery rescripting, a distressing memory is recounted, and then the narrative is changed in an imaginary way, such as by the Adult self of the client entering the scene, confronting a perpetrator and taking the Child to a place of safety (one client imagined his adult self, me and a police officer intervening and physically throwing his father out of the house and thereby protecting his Child self from an attack), or by introducing a superhero (another client imagined Conan the Barbarian chasing some school bullies away and then coming back to take him to a place of safety).

The calm place technique, which was originally developed in Eye Movement Desensitization and Reprocessing (EMDR) therapy (Shapiro, 2018) can be easily integrated into TA therapy for its usefulness in soothing the Child ego state. In this

 DOI: 10.4324/9781003375890-94

technique, the client is guided towards identifying a memory of a calm place, preferably one they have visited. They are encouraged to picture a particular scene without the presence of other people and to activate the memory as strongly as possible and relive the experience with as much rich sensory detail as they can generate. This can be used daily as an emotion regulation or relaxation strategy. Clients who are prone to nightmares or bad dreams often find that the use of this technique just before going to sleep significantly reduces the frequency and intensity of their nightmares.

Mental imagery techniques can also be used to help clients to develop healthier Structuring and Nurturing Parent ego states (Lapworth and Sills, 2011), by drawing on experiences and memories they already have. One procedure is a variation on resource development and installation (RDI) used in EMDR, which is known to be effective in the stabilization phase of therapy for people with complex trauma (Korn and Leeds, 2002). In this, the client is encouraged to identify a particular quality, resource or personal strength which would help them to manage their current difficulties. This might include qualities such as resilience, confidence, flexibility, or resources such as being able to manage their emotions, and so on. The client is then asked to identify a person or persons from any point in their life (family members, friends, neighbours, teachers, therapists, etc.), or role models (famous people, fictional characters, etc.), who possess this particular quality. The client is then guided to building up a rich multi-sensory mental image of the person and of the person emanating the desired quality and of the client absorbing it and allowing it to fill their being. Encourage the client to remain with the image and felt sense of the quality for a period of time, and to repeat this as often as they desire.

The positive Parent ego state can be built similarly by drawing on memories of individuals or creating a composite ideal Parent using a combination of memories and imagery. This can be done by asking the client, 'Who were positive influences for you when you were a child? Who behaved in a caring or loving way towards you?' Ask the client to remember these positive interactions and activate a felt sense of the presence of the caring person. If your client really cannot remember any positive interactions, they can imagine them based on what they have seen from other people or what they know about good caregiving to children. Invite the client to feel and develop the presence of those positive interactions/memories/images of a person. Help them to locate a felt sense within their body and to build a clear visual image and ask that they instruct themselves that they can bring this particular felt sense back into their awareness at any time they want to.

87

WORKING WITH THE CHILD EGO STATE TO RESOLVE TRAUMA

Clients who have experienced childhood trauma will usually hold deep wounds within their Child ego state. This intra-psychic wounding will show its presence when our client has a strong and disproportionate emotional reaction to situations (or even no emotional response where one might be expected or reasonable). There are many ways in which a TA therapist can work with the Child ego state to facilitate healing, many of which have similarity to Muriel James' (1974, 1981, 2002) method of self-reparenting.

One method is therapeutic letter writing, where the client writes a letter from their Adult ego state to their Child ego state. The aim is for the Adult ego state to offer compassion and a healing, corrective experience to their Child. Therapeutic letter writing can be done in session, although often works well as a between-session homework task. The formula I use is to invite the client to begin the letter with 'Dear XXX, I am writing to you because I know you are hurting. I know what happened to you because I was there …'. I encourage the client to validate the Child's emotions, and to explain to the Child that what happened was not their fault, and that they deserved to be protected and cared for. It is important that this does not shift into blaming, but instead communicates a simple message to the Child that they no longer need to take responsibility for the mistakes of others. I invite my client to tell their Child self all of the things that they needed to hear, but were never told; that they are loveable, that they are good enough, that they are stronger than they think, that things can and will get better. To finish the letter, I suggest that the client uses a statement such as, 'I love you and I will never leave you because I will carry you inside of me forever.'

There are many potential variations of this exercise. It could be done as a two-chair dialogue or as a piece of mental imagery work in session. Also, the client may find it beneficial to engage in a letter exchange between the Child and Adult ego states. Adrienne Lee's mirror exercise (Lee, 2003) is an incredibly powerful technique which works with the Child ego state. In this technique, the client is guided to visualize looking into a full-length mirror and seeing their Child self reflected back at them. The therapist facilitates a healing dialogue where the Adult ego state tells the client whatever they needed to hear or know (similar to the method described above), and the exercise concludes with the Adult ego state reaching into the mirror to hold the Child, and then bringing the Child ego state towards them and into their heart to merge with them.

Clients who often felt afraid as children, or who were punished for their natural playfulness and spontaneity or clients who reported a lack of nurturing can be encouraged to do things and 'take their child self with them'. A client recently found going for a long walk in the park, feeding the ducks and then buying an ice cream (all the while, engaging in some internal dialogue with his Child ego state) to be a highly enjoyable and therapeutic experience. Another client transformed several usual movie nights into therapeutic opportunities through changing their intent and purpose. She set the scene by changing into her pyjamas, and then settled down on the sofa with a blanket and snacks to watch the kind of movies she would have loved as a child, again, doing this consciously and engaging her Child self in some dialogue throughout.

Although these techniques may seem rather gimmicky and superficial, there is a good amount of scientific evidence to support their use. We know that activating feelings of compassion and care – including self-compassion – triggers the release of oxytocin, which promotes feelings of calm, safety, trust and connectedness. Research has also shown that self-compassion focused imagery reduces the levels of the stress hormone cortisol in the blood (Rockliff et al., 2008). By activating the client's Child ego state and providing it with an experience of care and compassion, it seems highly likely that the Child ego state will indeed experience a reduction in distress and an increase in positive feelings, including the sense of being cared for and of social connectedness, therefore reducing the ongoing impact of childhood trauma.

88

REVISITING DISCOUNTING: INCORPORATING COGNITIVE BIASES INTO TA THEORY

Each person creates their own subjective reality, based on their own individual psychology and influenced by their frame of reference and life script. Developments in psychology research over the years have discovered the ubiquity of cognitive biases, which are distortions in the perception of or interpretation of reality. It is believed that these are connected to our limited information-processing capacity and the need to make decisions quickly.

It is estimated that at any given moment, the brain is processing around 11 million pieces of sensory data. Somehow, in that cacophony of signals, it has to determine how to prioritize and filter so that salient information can be identified and acted upon (where relevant) and data which is seen as irrelevant can be discarded. It is in this perception and interpretation of data where cognitive biases create a distortion of reality. The science of cognitive biases is consistent with TA theory on discounting and, through incorporating cognitive biases into TA discounting theory, we can expand and update TA thinking on discounting and firmly link it to the substantial amount of research into cognitive biases, thus enhancing the evidence base for TA theory and practice.

Discounting is 'unawarely ignoring information relevant to the solution of a problem' (Stewart and Joines, 2012). Although cognitive biases may not necessarily be about the solution to a problem – indeed, they may in actual fact be the *cause* of many problems.

DOI: 10.4324/9781003375890-96

'The person who discounts believes or acts as though some aspect of the self, other people or reality is less significant than it is' (Mellor and Sigmund, 1975: 295). Similarly, discounting can involve either minimizing some aspect of self, an other or the reality situation or magnifying it (grandiosity) (Schiff et al., 1975). Here I discuss several cognitive biases and will briefly explain how they work, in the hope that you, the reader, can see how these can be integrated into TA thinking and hopefully will develop insights into how these can be used in practice.

We all have an *egocentric bias*, which is based on the fact that we can only know the world from our own unique perspective. In many respects, each of us experiences ourselves as the centre of our own universe. Of course, problems can occur because of a mismatch whereby we forget, or fail to see that we are not the centre of other people's universes also. Our own beliefs, thoughts, values, and so on all make perfect sense to us, because they are the creation of our own thought processes and *naïve realism* means that we assume that their logic is self-evident and that any sane or rational person would see things the same way. Because we are the centre of our own universe, we believe that others are paying more attention to us than they actually are, such as when we walk into a restaurant, we notice people glancing at us (this is likely a non-conscious survival-based response on their part to notice movement and a change in the environment). This is called the *spotlight effect*. And because we are all too aware of our own internal state – especially when it is unpleasant, such as when we feel anxious or ashamed, we believe that others can see how nervous we are, or that others can see 'shame and guilt written all over our face' with the *transparency effect*.

We pay attention to and notice things that are familiar with *attentional bias*, and those things that confirm our existing beliefs and we reject information which challenges these beliefs through *confirmation bias*. We also have a tendency to create stories or narratives which not only fit our own frame of reference but which discount the intentions and motivations of others. Possibly the clearest example of this is *fundamental attribution error*. With this cognitive bias, we interpret other people's actions as having some kind of negative motive or intention behind them. So if our partner is late to meet us, we can interpret it as being because they don't care, or don't respect us (of course, there could be a whole number of cognitive biases which led them to be late in the first place!). In the example of our partner being late, one reason for their lateness might be the *planning fallacy*, which refers to the tendency people have to routinely underestimate how long a task will take. Of course, our inability to get as many tasks completed as we had planned can very easily feed into a person's script beliefs, or can fuel disappointment, annoyance or irritation which in turn can trigger all kinds of games and unhelpful processes.

Humans also have a *negativity bias*, whereby we privilege and prioritize information which is negative, in terms of what we pay attention to, how we interpret things and events, and how we recall information. This is very likely a survival mechanism as there is a greater survival advantage for remembering something which is negative, or unpleasant over something which is positive or pleasant. There is also a distinct survival advantage in perceiving information negatively and reacting to it as a potential threat. However, this evolutionary relic is a significant contribution to our tendency to feel depression, anxiety and other disorders of negative affect. All of these cognitive biases (and more) interact, and shape and maintain our frame of reference and life script. Because we cannot see what we cannot see, clear feedback from another can help challenge and rectify these distortions of reality. As therapists, if we are aware of the existence of these cognitive biases and their role in the creation and maintenance of life script, we can help our clients to recognize them and find new, more adaptive, realistic and balanced ways of perceiving, interpreting and remembering the events of their daily lives. Of course, a note of caution is wise here: we too are subject to cognitive biases, and they will inevitably influence what we pay attention to and how we respond to information in the course of our work as therapists. Through careful and honest ongoing self-reflection, the application of critical thinking, personal therapy and supervision, we can mitigate against them to some extent. However, it is important to remember that these are pervasive and persistent parts of human experience and so there is an ongoing need to be vigilant and mindful of their influence.

CONFRONTATION

Confrontation is a loaded word; it carries such negative conno-
tations of 'being told off', of angry conflicts, and so on that a
number of people, therapists included, shrink inside even when
the word is mentioned. In spite of all of this, sensitive and well-
timed confrontation remains a potent therapeutic method. In
discussing the need for confrontation to be made from a position
of empathy and care, Masterson recommends the following:

> Confrontation must be done intuitively and empathically and
> must 'fit' the clinical material the client presents. It requires the
> therapist confront from a neutral, objective, emotional stance
> because it is clinically indicated, not out of anger or from his or
> her own personal needs, that is, to be aggressive and assertive, to
> direct, control, or admonish the patient.
>
> (1981: 136)

Hahn (2004), in using the Masterson approach, offers the
following four areas as particular aspects of the client's process
to attend to and confront problematic distortions in the
treatment of clients with borderline personality disorder:

1. Limit setting.
2. Reality testing.
3. Clarifying the consequences of maladaptive thoughts,
   feelings or behaviours.
4. Questioning the motivation for maladaptive thoughts,
   feelings or behaviours.

This approach is not incongruent with a TA approach, in
that TA therapists should always confront third-degree

DOI: 10.4324/9781003375890-97

script/game behaviours (Stewart, 1996) and effective confrontation strengthens reality testing and Adult ego state functioning (Schiff et al., 1975). Strengthening Adult ego functioning would also include developing the capacity for reflexivity and thinking through the motivations and consequences of one's actions.

Confrontation can act as a strong invitation for the client to cathect Adult. One difficulty with confrontation is that even with the best will in the world, a confrontation can be heard by the client as being Parental. In the case of confrontation that is (or is perceived as) Parental, the intervention is likely to be ineffective. Berne (1966/1994) identified confrontation as an intervention used for decontamination purposes. Berne also added that confrontation should not be used 'when it makes you feel smarter than the patient' (ibid.: 236).

Berne suggested that confrontations should be followed up later in the therapy with confirmation. A confirmation is one of the therapeutic operations that is designed to 'reinforce the ego boundaries still further' (ibid.: 240). The confirmation basically reinforces the original confrontation and prevents the client from slipping backwards, so to speak. Confirmation also strengthens decontamination: 'for the Adult, confirmation has a strengthening effect because of its logical force' (ibid.: 240).

'In systems theory there is an acknowledgement of the importance of creating a crisis in order to find the necessary turbulence or disruption or destructuring from which new growth and healing can arise' (Clarkson, 2003: 53). Indeed, as Berne described, after confrontation 'the patient is stirred up and his psyche is thrown out of balance' (Berne, 1966/1994: 235). Striking the right balance with the degree of confrontation is not easy. Confrontation can, with some clients, provoke extreme reactions, which may be as a result of the confrontation putting the client in touch with an internal vacuum (Bateman and Fonagy, 2006). It is perhaps wise for a therapist to bear this turbulence in mind and provide opportunity in the therapy for the confrontation to be processed and integrated by the client before moving on to something else.

I frequently use a relatively gentle form of confrontation (which I would call 'challenging') in sessions where I ask a client if it is OK if I play 'Devil's Advocate'. If the client agrees, we have a contract for me to use this form of confrontation. I then offer the client a perspective which challenges their thinking, intentions or ideas about the outcome of a situation, and then tell the client I am stepping out of the Devil's Advocate role, and ask them how it was for them to hear me be so challenging and what their thoughts and feelings were in regard to what I said. I find this approach reduces the risk of alliance ruptures, client defensiveness and enables me to temporarily step into confrontation and then out of it and back into an empathic stance.

EVALUATING YOUR CLINICAL EFFECTIVENESS

People become therapists, in part, because they want to help others, and all of us want to do a good job. And yet, there is no denying that some therapists are simply more effective than others. Unfortunately, the evidence shows that therapists are not very good at determining their own clinical effectiveness and tend to overestimate their abilities. This is not particularly surprising; the *Dunning-Kruger effect* is a well-known phenomenon in psychology (Dunning et al., 2003). Basically, it refers to the tendency people in general have in considering their skills, knowledge and ability to be above average. A number of well-constructed research studies have confirmed that the Dunning-Kruger effect is endemic among psychotherapists. In one study by Bickman (2005), a staggering 65 per cent of respondents rated themselves in the highest categories, and none rated themselves as below average. Of course, this is impossible, by definition, approximately half of all therapists will be average. Some therapists cite their years of experience as evidence of their effectiveness, and yet this does not provide any guarantee, with a number of studies indicating that experienced therapists perform no better than trainees, and worryingly, in some studies experienced therapists show lower performance than newly qualified therapists (Goldberg et al., 2016).

Miller, Hubble and Chow (2020) have identified three core activities which they state create a personal 'culture of excellence' for psychotherapists. These are: '(1) Establishing a baseline of effectiveness; (2) obtaining regular, ongoing performance feedback; and (3) spending time outside of daily work in focused, systematic efforts to improve.' These first two activities will be discussed in this present point, and the third will be discussed in Point 91.

Establishing a baseline of effectiveness requires measurement of one's outcomes, which, in practical terms, means routine use of outcome measures in clinical practice (see also Points 31 and 62). There is now overwhelming evidence to show the benefits of the use of outcome measures from increased positive outcomes to reduced drop-outs (Miller et al., 2007). Moreover, using outcome measures enables therapists to determine each individual client's progress and improvement during therapy and also, by systematically gathering data on the improvement rates of their clients, the therapist can determine their own clinical effectiveness rate. This can be done by using a simple benchmarking strategy where the therapist's recovery rates can be compared to those from large-scale research studies. Based on the meta-analysis by Lutz et al. (2021), an average rate of recovery therapists should aim for is 50 per cent of clients with clinical-level symptoms achieving clinically significant change within 20 sessions, and 75 per cent of clients achieving clinically significant change by session 35. It is important to add some caveats to this: a number of factors are known to slow down progress and speed of recovery. These include (but are not limited to) greater initial functional impairment, comorbidity and personality disorders. However, clients with depression, anxiety (except those with chronic anxiety and highly negative self-attributions), trauma, OCD and relational problems often do very well in short-term therapies (i.e., therapies of 35 sessions or fewer).

In terms of which measures to use, in my own practice, I use CORE-10, PHQ-9 and GAD-7 for routine session-by-session use. CORE-10 covers global distress and functional impairment, PHQ-9 measures depressive symptoms and GAD-7 addresses anxiety symptoms. These three measures collectively cover a wide range of symptoms from a vast array of disorders (most disorders have some depressive or anxious symptoms). They are freely available online, and are easy to administer and score. Most clients can complete them quickly at the beginning of the session without using up precious time from the session. The clinical cut-off point for each of these three measures is 10, with scores above 10 being in the clinical range and scores below 10 being non-clinical. Severity bands go up in fives, so scores of 10–14 are in the low range of severity, with 15–19 being moderate, and so on. This congruence between the three measures means that therapists can rapidly assess severity of client problems and improvement on a week-by-week basis. Essentially, what the therapist needs to look for is a reduction in scores each week. In cases where scores increase slightly, the therapist can easily check with the client to see if anything has occurred during the week which can account for the worsening. If there is steady worsening or a lack of improvement after a number of sessions, the therapist needs to seek supervision on their work with that particular client and have a conversation with the client about how the therapy might be adjusted to better suit their needs.

Seeking client feedback is also known to have a beneficial effect on psychotherapy outcome. This can be done in several ways; informally and verbally by checking in with the client towards the end of each session as to how they feel the session has gone and if there is anything they would like to change; or formally through the use of a feedback measures such as Scott Miller's Session Rating Scale (this can be downloaded, together with tips on its use, from www.scottdmiller.com). The benefits of actively seeking client feedback will readily become apparent. Although with most clients, things go smoothly and there is little required in terms of feedback, for clients where the path of therapy is less smooth and more bumpy and uneven, obtaining feedback can make all the difference.

91

USING DELIBERATE PRACTICE TO ENHANCE THERAPEUTIC SKILLS

Transactional analysts commonly audio-record sessions with clients, particularly trainee transactional analysts, who are seeking to obtain audio recordings suitable for presenting in the Certified Transactional Analyst examination. Listening to audio recordings of sessions is often fruitful in enabling the therapist to notice patterns of language and how they are making their interventions, which is information which they can use to considerably sharpen up their skills. For example, a frequent mistake of beginning therapists is talking too much, or making long, cumbersome interventions. Listening to audio recordings will help to make such errors apparent. Systematic use of audio recordings in personal reflection and self-supervision, and also in individual and group supervision can result in the therapist considerably sharpening their skills, and also developing the capacity to reflect in action, as well as reflect on action (Schön, 1983). Listening to audio recordings of one's work does take some persistence and requires enduring some cringe-worthy moments, and getting used to the sound of one's own voice (which due to bone conductance sounds differently on a recording to what one expects it to sound like).

Tony Rousmaniere (2016, 2018) has developed a solid, research-based method for improving therapeutic skills centred around the notion of deliberate practice. His website has many useful resources and instructional videos to help explain the background and method of deliberate practice (see www. drtonyr.com and www.dpfortherapists.com). Essentially the method requires the therapist to identify a specific skill or cluster of skills they want to systematically improve. This could

 DOI: 10.4324/9781003375890-99

be identified by reflection on practice, from reviewing audio recordings or through supervision. Rousmaniere notes that although most therapists can cognitively understand the value of deliberate practice, very few persist with it and will often find reasons or excuses not to engage with it. Because of this, it can be useful to contract with a supervision group to use deliberate practice, or trainers may wish to integrate it into skills practice (for a superb example of this, see McLeod, 2022).

SUGGESTED AREAS FOR DELIBERATE PRACTICE:

Reflect on your skills in the following areas, and, where possible, obtain honest and realistic feedback from your supervisor or peers on your strengths and areas of weakness. Identify a priority area of focus, and develop an action plan of activities you can do to strengthen your ability in those areas. Where possible, construct SMART goals with clear markers for evidence of achievement of improvement.

Here are some interpersonal (Anderson and Patterson, 2013) and therapeutic skills to practise.

FACILITATIVE INTERPERSONAL SKILLS

- Verbal fluency
- Facilitating hope and positive expectancy
- Persuasiveness and influencing
- Emotional expressiveness
- Warmth, acceptance and understanding
- Empathy
- Alliance bond capacity
- Alliance rupture responsiveness
- Alliance rupture repair.

THERAPEUTIC SKILLS

- Basic counselling skills (e.g., active listening, open questions, use of silence, reflection, summarizing)

- Contracting and collaboration (e.g., goal setting, negotiation of task, identifying therapy contract, enhancing client motivation, setting homework tasks)
- Assessment and treatment planning (e.g., conducting assessment sessions, clarity and accuracy of diagnosis, identifying key issues, identifying client strengths, treatment planning, structuring and sequencing of interventions)
- Structuring sessions (e.g., initial sessions, starting sessions, contracting, identifying a session focus, maintaining focus, pacing and intensity, closing sessions)
- Relational skills (e.g., authenticity, potency, permission, immediacy, metacommunication, challenging, deepening client experiencing, providing corrective emotional experience, self-disclosure)
- Decontamination (e.g., challenging, increasing cognitive dissonance, Socratic questioning)
- Deconfusion (e.g., empathy, transference interpretation, promoting emotional granulation/ regulation/expression)
- Redecision (e.g., two-chair work, impasse clarification, disconfirming script beliefs)
- Other therapeutic skills (e.g., use of mental imagery work, risk assessment and management)
- Self-management and self-care (e.g., regulation of own emotions during sessions, management of counter-transference, management of case load, ensuring adequate breaks, between-sessions, self-care activity, ongoing professional development activity, developing therapeutic skills/knowledge).

Another method that can be used is through listening to recordings of sessions and identifying sessions that went well and sessions that didn't go so well. With sessions that did go well, see if you can identify what features, skills or activities seemed to facilitate the session. With sessions that didn't go so well, see if you can identify key moments where you could have intervened differently. At these points, pause the recording, and construct an alternative intervention which might have been more effective. Rousmaniere (2016, 2018) recommends rewinding the recording, pausing at these points and then saying the alternative intervention out loud and repeating this process several times, perhaps introducing slight changes to the tone or wording to identify an optimal response. This is a challenging process to engage with, but one which is likely to have significant benefits to specific skills and your overall therapeutic effectiveness.

92

WRITING CLINICAL NOTES IN TA THERAPY

Effective note-keeping is an essential skill for therapists, and keeping and maintaining clear and accurate notes is a requirement in the code of ethics of almost all professional counselling and psychotherapy organizations. All therapists develop their own method of keeping notes over time, but it is worth periodically reviewing how you keep notes to make sure that the method used is the one which is most helpful, both for refreshing your memory and for treatment planning and tracking a client's progress. It is hard for a therapist to remember a lot of details about any given client, and with a full caseload, this becomes even more difficult.

Session notes are a reminder of the journey and process of the therapy. Notes keep track of the progress of your client, including improvements, deterioration or 'no change'. They are adjuncts to any notes you might have from intake and assessment regarding the client's history (see Point 31), your notes on diagnosis (such as the diagnosis checklist in Point 46) and your ongoing individualized treatment plan (see Points 56 and 57). Efficient notes should take no more than a few minutes to write up, and are best written up as soon as possible while the information is still fresh in your mind, ideally immediately after each session. Unless there are specific concerns around client risk, session notes do not need to be lengthy – a paragraph or two is usually sufficient. It is sensible to make more detailed records when the client is experiencing a crisis or there are safeguarding concerns. It is also wise to make a note of any homework tasks that have been agreed so these can be followed up in the next session.

 DOI: 10.4324/9781003375890-100

Various health professionals use the 'SOAP' formula for keeping clinical records (Weed, 1971). SOAP is an acronym:

S = subjective (report of client)
O = observation (of client)
A = analysis (in this instance, I suggest this is focused on a brief summary of the session themes and key interventions used)
P = plan (treatment plan).

This formula is easy to remember and keeps the therapist focused on what is observable. I have adapted this formula, which I present below with an example. I invite you to use this approach, and adapt it to suit your own purposes.

EXAMPLE: 'CLAIRE'

Session date: 1 September. Session number: 5

(*Subjective report of client*) Claire reports a fairly good week, with no further arguments with partner or family. Still rather upset over argument with son two weeks ago. Managing work stress fine. Scores from CORE-10 and GAD-7 show some improvement although PHQ-9 remains the same as previous week. (*Observation of client*) Client appeared to be upbeat and in fairly good spirits, although did appear emotional when discussing ongoing situation with son. (*Analysis of session: key areas of focus and interventions*) Session focused mostly on discussing family problems, with some problem-solving and discussion of assertiveness skills. Also discussing ways to reduce tension and avoid getting into arguments. Interventions largely empathic and supportive although some use of challenge around client passivity and of script beliefs around not being good enough. Some interpretation around repeating patterns from own childhood. (*Plan*) Monitor progress using outcome measures. Support client in developing assertiveness skills. Continue with ongoing emotional regulation work. Continue with challenging client script beliefs especially 'not being good enough'. Explore childhood relationship patterns with parents in later sessions.

93

STRENGTHENING THE ADULT BY CULTIVATING MINDFULNESS

Mindfulness is a concept and practice that has its origins in Buddhism. Essentially it involves a deep awareness of now. In practising mindfulness, the individual seeks a total immersion in the present moment, in their experiencing, but does so from a position of observing. For example, mindfulness can involve an awareness of the sensory input one is experiencing at any given moment. It can be practised in many situations, and requires no special equipment. Household chores can be approached mindfully, for example in washing the dishes, the water is felt on the hands, the plates are each felt and the different textures are noticed and appreciated. The smell of the detergent is noticed, together with the visual stimulus of the bubbles and the way that the light catches them. Another approach involves consciously directing one's attention to one's breathing. The breathing is not deliberately changed, but rather noticed: noticing the in-breath, and the little pause, and then the out-breath and then the next little pause before breathing in again. In mindfulness, one is not seeking to discover anything, or even do anything; one is just being.

As mindfulness practice involves a deep engagement with what is here and now, it is theoretically consistent to assume that mindfulness practice will by definition be something one does in one's Adult ego state. Regular mindfulness practice is also very likely to generally strengthen the Adult ego state and be a useful tool for decontamination. The cultivation of an attitude of acceptance implicit in mindfulness is also likely to have a beneficial impact in relation to promoting self-acceptance. In some respects, mindfulness is antithetical to the

DOI: 10.4324/9781003375890-101

goal-driven contractual approach to TA, in that, in mindfulness, there is no goal.

> When we let go of wanting something else to happen in this moment, we are taking a profound step toward being able to encounter what is here now. If we hope to go anywhere and develop ourselves in any way, we can only step from where we are standing. If we don't really know where we are standing – a knowing that comes directly from the cultivation of mindfulness – we may only go in circles, for all our efforts and expectations. So in meditation practice, the best way to get somewhere is to let go of trying to get anywhere at all.
>
> (Kabat-Zinn, 1994/2000: 15–16)

It is my view that practising mindfulness regularly is a deeply beneficial practice and one which enhances TA therapy, both for the therapist and for the client who begins regular mindfulness practice. I would recommend that TA therapists who want to integrate the use of mindfulness into their practice read the article by Žvelc, Černetič and Košak (2011).

Safran and Muran particularly recommend the use of mindfulness techniques in the training of relational psychotherapists:

> Trainees are instructed to observe the contents of their awareness without judgement and without letting themselves get caught up in or identified with any particular content of awareness … Trainees are instructed that the goal is not to eliminate thoughts or feelings, but rather to become more fully aware of them as they emerge on a moment-to-moment basis without judging them or pushing them away. Gradually, over time, this type of mindfulness work helps trainees to become more aware of subtle feelings, thoughts and fantasies emerging on the edge of awareness when working with their patients, which can subsequently provide an important source of information about what is occurring in the relationship. One of the most valuable by-products of this kind of mindfulness work is a gradual development of a more tolerant and accepting stance toward a full range of emotional experiences.
>
> (2003: 210)

It would make sense that similar processes also occur within clients who regularly practise mindfulness, including the deepening of self-awareness, and increased ability to observe the self (observing ego). Greater accounting of one's own process, sensory input and interoceptive processes will probably reduce discounting. Noticing one's own internal flow, and flow between ego states, is another potential outcome. The development of evenly suspended attention (Freud, 1912), without judgement and the accompanying increased awareness, also would logically enhance one's degree of autonomy (Berne, 1964).

94

SCRIPT DEVELOPMENT: AN ONGOING PROCESS

Some traditional views of TA consider the process of scripting to be complete by the time a person is in late childhood. Berne's own view on this was that scripting was largely complete by around 7 years old and in his last book he defined script as 'An unconscious life plan, made in childhood, reinforced by the parents, justified by subsequent events and culminating in a chosen alternative' (Berne, 1972: 445). Various TA sources indicate the period marking the end of scripting to be somewhere between 7 and 11 years old. Woollams and Brown share this view of script as being established in early life, as highlighted in their definition: 'A script is a personal life plan which an individual decides upon at an early age in reaction to her interpretation of both external and internal events' (1978: 151).

This view of script as a static, ossified phenomenon is not consistent with what we now understand from recent developments in both developmental theory and also from our understanding of adult learning theory. Viewing script as static does not account for the sometimes radical re-scripting that occurs in people who have experienced a severe and overwhelming trauma in adult life, for instance, rape or an assault. Various TA authors have questioned the inflexible and fixed view of script and have added in such definitions as: 'A life plan based on decisions made at any developmental stage which inhibit spontaneity and limit flexibility in problem solving and in relating to people' (Erskine, 1980). Erskine's definition does allow for later development, but maintains the position that script is a

 DOI: 10.4324/9781003375890-102

negative, limiting pattern and is not a view which supports the positive and adaptive aspects of script. Cornell (1988) critiques various theories of script, particularly the implication in much of script theory that the child is a passive recipient of script messages from their parents. Cornell emphasizes the creativity of children in finding influences from outside the family, and reminds transactional analysts of the importance of accounting for these influencing factors in script analysis.

Newton (2006) reviews script theory from the perspective of adult learning theory, and considers scripting to be an ongoing process. Newton insightfully uses the experiential learning cycle of Kolb (1984) to conceptualize this continuing process of scripting. Taking Kolb's model, Newton proposes that script is developed along similar lines: we experience something, we reflect upon the meaning of the experience, we develop script beliefs as a result of our reflection, and we then experiment with behaviours which either 'confirm' or 'refute' our beliefs. This process begins from our earliest experiences, whereby the infant is making sense of the world and developing a story, a sense of what happens and the reasons why it happens. Over time this story becomes coherent, consistent and is generalized by the infant's interactions with the world. This links to Stern's (1985) concept of representations of interactions that are generalized. The process continues, as Newton diagrams, in a spiral manner, with each experience paving the way for the next experience cycle. 'New experiences can thus provide updating evidence or can be interpreted through the theory, that is, filtered through the script' (Newton, 2006: 193).

Thus, more recent theories regarding script acknowledge the primary role of our early experiences in the formation of the self but also allow room for considering script as an ongoing developmental process. Perhaps more importantly for therapists, these theories provide a means by which we can understand the process of change and development. They also provide a reminder for the therapist of the sometimes cyclical nature of the change process, and how our clients need to 'go round the loop' many, many times, making small, incremental changes to the existing script before their script patterns are significantly changed to the extent that we might consider the person 'autonomous'. They also provide a challenge to concepts such as autonomy, suggesting that rather than becoming completely script-free, the individual simply develops a new more appropriate and flexible script.

HELPING CLIENTS IDENTIFY AND BUILD ON THEIR STRENGTHS

As therapists, we look for problems and spend a lot of time working out where and how things have gone wrong for our clients. We are perhaps less likely to help our clients look for their strengths and find out what is going right for them. Within TA, the psychotherapy field of application is focused on healing and change, whereas the counselling field of application is more focused on strengths and resources (see EATA, 2008: Section five). I believe that TA therapists can learn from this positive approach. As part of our goal to facilitate change, promote healing, engagement with life, and the finding of meaning, we can draw upon theories and methods that seek to promote positive engagement and self-actualization.

Martin Seligman, a leading figure in the positive psychology movement, has identified a series of personal character strengths (he refers to them as signature strengths) which include: curiosity, love of learning, critical thinking, creativity, social intelligence, perspective, courage, perseverance, genuineness, kindness, ability to give and receive love, fairness, leadership, self-control, prudence, humility, gratitude, appreciation of beauty, optimism, playfulness and enthusiasm (Seligman, 2002).

Seligman believes that when we identify our signature strengths and use them wisely, positive feelings are generated. It is interesting that his approach does not focus on weaknesses or encourage systematic development of areas where one is weak as areas for personal growth (ibid.). Instead, the focus is on helping clients identify their personal character

DOI: 10.4324/9781003375890-103

strengths and using these strengths in different aspects of their lives. A quick way to identify these strengths is to register with Seligman's website (www.authentichappiness. org) and complete the Values in Action Institute strengths survey. As therapists, we can assist in this process by looking for, noticing and highlighting our clients' strengths when we see them. This needs to be done clearly and in a manner which is direct and authentic. It is often worth asking the client if they can recognize that strength in their self. If they do not, this can be followed by asking them if they are prepared to accept that other people might see things in them that they are not yet able to see.

Positive psychology also seeks to encourage the experiencing of positive emotions towards our past (satisfaction, contentment, pride), the future (optimism, hope, confidence) and to promote pleasure, engagement and positive emotions about the present. It can sometimes be difficult to see how clients whose lives have been so full of pain and abuse can experience positive emotions about their past, but it is possible for them to reach a place of peace about their past. Furthermore, living a positive, productive and satisfying life will provide something one can look back on with satisfaction, and even pride in how one has overcome adversity.

A full life is considered to be one where the individual experiences a range of positive emotions in relation to their past, present and future, and regularly uses their signature strengths to engage with life, in relationships with others, and in the service of 'something larger' (perhaps the community, or a cause such as the environment).

The relevance of this to TA therapy is that these principles can be woven into our humanistic framework and the guiding values of our work. As part of the ongoing diagnostic process in therapy, we can pay attention to noticing our client's strengths and facilitate our client's discovery of their strengths. These strengths may be held in any of their ego states, and may indeed spring from how they adapted and developed in response to pain and adverse conditions in their past (for example, independence can be a great strength which is sometimes a product of a neglectful environment). In this sense, strengths can be a positive adaptation to the constraints of a sub-optimal environment and testament to the ingenuity and sometimes positive and useful nature of aspects of one's own script. We can also use the above principles to help guide our treatment planning, by considering how we can help the client heal their past pains, engage positively with the present, draw upon and apply their strengths, and begin constructing a positive future.

EXPLORING THE THERAPIST'S MOTIVATIONS

What is it that makes someone want to become a psycho-therapist? Even Freud, the father of psychotherapy, described it as an 'impossible' profession (Freud, 1937). The process of training is often deeply unsettling and involves sacrificing large amounts of time, energy and money. Practising as a psychotherapist involves sitting with people in the depth of their despair, and leaving ourselves open to feeling all kinds of unpleasant and disturbing emotions, and hearing first-hand stories of profound inhumanity and even torture. Why would someone want to do this? Maroda suggests:

> We are there because we want something that goes beyond earning a living and beyond a commitment to social service or intellectual inquiry. We seek to be healed ourselves and we heal our old 'afflicted' caretakers as we heal our patients.
>
> (1994/2004: 37–38)

Clearly, becoming a therapist is a deeply personal matter, and one which is influenced by our own life experiences and our script. The effective and ethical practice of psychotherapy requires that therapists repeatedly revisit their reasons for training as and becoming psychotherapists and examine honestly what of their own needs their work is seeking to meet, to reduce the potential for exploitation of clients. The therapist's experience, sensitivities and script can impact their work in many different ways, for example, therapists who came from volatile families, or even families where expression

DOI: 10.4324/9781003375890-104

of feeling was inhibited, may find it extremely difficult to tolerate and contain their client's anger.

McLeod (1993, 2003) discusses experiences common in the personal history of therapists that contribute to their career choice. He identifies three themes, of which at least one will have been present in the life of the therapist:

1. An experience of being in a caretaking role. This can include the role of 'peacemaker' in the family. Often a way of relating to others that involves a caring, helping role is a pattern in early life experiences of those who become therapists.
2. A period of intense personal distress or crisis. This generally includes experiences of loss in childhood or adolescence. Many therapists have also experienced episodes of depression. McWilliams (1994) also contends that a significant number of therapists have a depressive character type that predisposes them to working therapeutically. The 'wounded healer' model is a widely accepted archetype for therapists (Barnett, 2007). Extreme crisis in adolescence or early adulthood is also common, and it is possible that either the experience of having been helped or the absence of help has stimulated the desire to work as a therapist, in addition to providing a personal resource for understanding the deep distress and pain of others.
3. Experience of having been an 'outsider', with high levels of isolation or aloneness in childhood or adolescence. This includes experiences of prolonged illness, cultural differences, repeatedly moving home, or being the victim of bullying. McLeod suggests that 'these types of childhood experience can encourage the development in the young person of a rich "inner life", in compensation for the absence of companions and playmates, and a capacity to observe and speculate on the motives and behaviour of others' (McLeod, 1993: 3).

This is supported by Barnett (2007), who states:

> The two main themes that emerged ... concerned experiences of loss and deprivation, especially in early life, and the failure of

carers to meet the normal narcissistic needs of childhood. The resultant painful effects of early loss often lead to difficulties in respect of intimacy, dependency and separation, and where there has been narcissistic injury, to issues around control, selfless giving and a need to be needed. Resulting defences mask an underlying sense of vulnerability.

(ibid.: 259)

Clearly, personal therapy is a vital resource in the process of becoming a psychotherapist to minimize the potential for these issues to be acted out destructively in the therapist's own work.

Feelings of inferiority and experiences of humiliation may give rise to a need to feel loved and admired. Evaluation of trainee therapists' ability may feel like an evaluation of the self as a person (Wosket, 1999) and fear of 'failure' will affect the practice and inhibit their clients' use of them.

Situations in childhood may have contributed to an inability to tolerate gaps, uncertainties, periods of 'not-knowing', resulting in a therapist's desire to take charge of a session and steer the course of the therapy, rather than allowing adequate space for the client's own feelings and thought processes to emerge.

(Barnett, 2007: 261)

This is particularly relevant for the practice of transactional analysis and other therapeutic approaches that have models for the therapist working in a directive manner, or which encourage the therapist into an active, 'knowing' stance. The anxiety 'not knowing; can provoke can be deeply unsettling for therapists who have these underlying issues and can propel the therapist into working ever more actively and in an authoritarian manner to avoid the painful, unconscious experiences. Clearly, this is an example of acting destructively based on one's own script, rather than on clinical need.

The ethical and professional practice of transactional analysis psychotherapy requires that we undertake a thorough and lengthy personal therapy, and return to therapy periodically throughout our career to address these unconscious, 'scripty' motivations for our work. Beginning therapists are often unaware of the pervasive influence these forces have upon their motivation, and may react with outrage to requirements that they undertake personal therapy. It is questionable whether these issues will ever be truly resolved, and, in some respects, the practice of psychotherapy may reinforce some of them for individual therapists. Our work can be like repeatedly picking a scab off a wound, meaning it will not heal, or will not heal cleanly. It behoves therapists of all levels of training and experience to be open to awareness of how their experiences and script influence their work, and their choice of work.

USING SELF-DISCLOSURE
AND AUTHENTICITY

Self-disclosure is where the therapist reveals something of their own experience in the therapy with the client. Self-disclosure is one of the most controversial and potentially problematic interventions a therapist can use, and yet there is considerable research evidence that appropriate self-disclosure can enhance the therapy. Self-reflection is an essential precursor to effective and ethical self-disclosure. Yalom (2001) divides therapist self-disclosure into three different kinds: (1) disclosure on the mechanisms of therapy; (2) disclosure of the therapist's here-and-now feelings; and (3) disclosure of the therapist's personal life. He advocates full and frank disclosure regarding the processes of therapy in a way that most trans-actional analysts would identify as being part of a clear con-tracting phase at the outset of therapy, and as part of the orientation stage to assist clients in learning how to 'do therapy'. This process is ongoing in that the therapist may disclose their reasons for pursuing certain lines of enquiry, or may discuss aspects of their treatment plan and the rationale behind it with their client. Yalom goes on to advise the selective reporting of the therapist's here-and-now feelings in the therapy (linked to client diagnosis, presenting problem and whether it might help the client with exploring some aspect of their relational script), and cautious disclosure about the therapist's personal life. Generally, it is useful to reflect on how open you wish to be with your clients. There are argu-ments both for and against levels of openness and each therapist needs to determine what feels comfortable for them. For example, for me, it is important to be up-front and open

  DOI: 10.4324/9781003375890-105

with clients that I am a gay man. I make this clear from very early on in the intake process (although this information is already available online, and I suspect anyone who has seen videos of one of my talks on YouTube would likely already have guessed). The issue of whether to disclose one's sexual orientation is one which also has convincing arguments in favour of it and against. However, based on considerable reflection of my own stance and my own prizing of the importance of modelling authenticity, openness and self-acceptance and the rejection of shame for who one is in my work, I decided that being 'out' right from the outset is the right and congruent stance for me.

INITIAL SESSIONS

At the initial consultation, it is common for therapists to provide some basic information about themselves, their experience, and so forth for prospective clients. Nowadays, given that most therapists have online profiles with information about their training, experience and a little about who they are as a person, the need for therapists to provide clients with information has lessened considerably. Even so, it is still useful to check in with a client in the initial sessions if there is anything they need to know about the therapist. In many respects, how the therapist interacts with the client will be of more use to the client's decision-making process than lots of details about the therapist's background and experience (see Point 18).

METACOMMUNICATION

Part of therapy involves the therapist being aware of their own ongoing process, and being curious about the client's process and maintaining awareness of the unfolding and continually shifting interpersonal process happening between them in the room (Widdowson, 2008). In observing these processes, the therapist may use metacommunicative transactions as a means of disclosure about the here-and-now experience of the therapist (see Point 77).

MATCHING DISCLOSURE LEVEL TO CLIENT DIAGNOSIS

Greater levels of therapist self-disclosure are often needed with clients who are more profoundly disturbed. The distinction here is significant, in that clients who are more disturbed

> have such total, encompassing transferences that they can only learn about their distortions of reality when reality is painted in stark colours in front of them, while [less disturbed clients] have subtle and unconscious transferences that surface only when the therapist is carefully opaque.
>
> (McWilliams, 1994: 75)

BEING HONEST

According to Widdowson:

> Being honest with our clients can be extremely difficult. For example, having the courage to admit when we feel stuck can feel dreadfully exposing and deskilling for a therapist. Simply being honest and saying, 'I'm feeling stuck right now, and I am not sure where to take this' can be liberating and can open up a new avenue of exploration. Furthermore, our clients often know at some level when we feel stuck and are not being honest about it. Acting as if we know what is going on when we do not can feel (and is) false and disingenuous.
>
> (2008: 69)

RESPONDING TO DIRECT QUESTIONS FROM CLIENTS

Sometimes clients ask their therapists very direct questions about the therapist's personal life or life experiences. On occasions, these questions are fine and answering will not be particularly problematic, and answering can make the therapist more real and human to the client. Generally, I advise answering these honestly, directly and briefly. Although there are other times where the questions are not so clear-cut, and should not be taken at face value. Questions can have a hidden significance, and one which may be out of the client's awareness at the time of asking. If there is any doubt as to the potential significance of the question, the therapist can ask the client what the therapist's answer might mean to them.

A client once asked a very direct question regarding my personal experience and whether I had experienced a particular problem they were facing. I asked the client to tell me what it would mean to them if I said yes I had faced the same problem, and what it would mean if I said no, I hadn't. In the end, I decided not to answer my client's question. It became clear later on that the client was in effect asking me if I could understand their experiences and how painful they had been to them. I had a similar experience once with a religious client who experienced considerable shame and guilt which appeared to be related to the teachings of her church and bad experiences with religious leaders. In each session, she asked me about my own religious background and I refused to answer, as it was clear that whatever my answer was, it would affect the therapeutic relationship and so on this matter I chose to remain opaque. Refusal to answer a client's questions can also help the client articulate their fantasies about the therapist. This can be a very frustrating experience for clients, and it is important that, when refusing to answer, the therapist empathically acknowledges the client's frustration in response to their refusal. It can also be useful for the therapist to explain something of their rationale in their refusal to answer.

> When clients ask direct questions regarding what we are feeling (e.g., 'Are you irritated with me?'), these need to be taken seriously; it is worthwhile for the therapist to take a moment to reflect on whether there may a grain of truth in what the client is saying. The client's transaction is often a response to some transactional stimulus of which we may not be immediately aware ... One option is for the therapist to express his or her reaction to the question and to invite the client to explain some of the rationale behind the question (e.g., 'I am a little surprised by

your question and am wondering what you experienced that led you to ask it'). Again, the therapist needs to be truly receptive to hearing the client's response, which may result in uncomfortable feedback.

(ibid.: 69)

Often it is therapeutic to validate, and affirm out clients and provide them with confirmation of their experience (Erskine and Trautmann, 1996). This can be done by making comments such as 'Me too' or 'I would feel the same in that situation'. The final decision as to whether we should make a disclosure or not should be guided by our answer to the following question: 'To what extent will my disclosure be therapeutic for my client?'

THE ADULT EGO STATE REVISITED

The Adult ego state has been relatively neglected in the TA literature (Tudor, 2003). There seem to be conflicting thoughts about the nature of the Adult. Compare the following two descriptions of the Adult:

> The Adult functions as a probability-estimating computer. It appears not to be a fully autonomous ego state, but rather functions mostly at the request of one of the other ego states.
>
> (Woollams and Brown, 1978: 15)

> [The Adult is] a pulsating personality, processing and integrating feelings, attitudes, thoughts and behaviours appropriate to the here-and-now ... at all ages, from conception to death.
>
> (Tudor, 2003: 201)

Which of these descriptions do you prefer? Which seems to most accurately reflect your own subjective sense of your Adult ego state?

Often it seems that the Adult is identified by a process of elimination, by identifying Child and Parent ego states and determining that what is left is Adult. This is an approach that does not adhere to Berne's four methods and criteria for diagnosis of an ego state (Berne, 1961/1986). The Adult ego state can be defined as: the ego state which is present-centred, here-and-now and appropriate to the current situation. This definition can be operationally checked using all of Berne's four methods. In the light of this definition, to define the Adult as a 'probability-estimating computer' is unnecessarily restrictive and highly discounting of the range of here-and-now experiences we engage with. Furthermore, to describe the

DOI: 10.4324/9781003375890-106

Adult as not being 'a fully autonomous ego state' also seems grossly inaccurate; if the Adult is appropriate to the current situation and is based in the here and now, then, by definition, the Adult is only ever autonomous.

Erskine (1988) and Tudor (2003) draw on the description Berne gave of Parent and Child ego states as fixated ego states and identify Adult as being the part of our self that is (relatively) free and un-fixated. 'As the neopsychic Adult is in constant process, it may not be fixated either clinically or conceptually' (Tudor, 2003: 222). A number of TA authors posit that Child and, to some extent, Parent ego states are dynamic and changing throughout our lifespan (Blackstone, 1993). Differing views exist on whether these ego states are dynamic or static and fixated. However, the Adult ego state is by definition dynamic, vibrant, adaptive (in the true sense of the word) and malleable. The purpose, goal and signature characteristic of the Adult ego state, according to Tudor (2003), are integration (noun), and the Adult is considered to be continually engaged in integrating (verb). Although this is true, because of implicit memory and the nature and role of our unconscious, it is perhaps impossible to totally integrate all of our experiences into our Adult ego state.

There is a convention in TA that Parent and Child ego states are named in the plural as ego states whereas the Adult is named as a single state of the ego. This again seems to be restrictive and not accounting for the complexity and richness of the many processes and states we can engage with appropriately in the here and now. Perhaps it is more accurate to talk of Adult ego states, than the Adult ego state.

With our Adult ego states we compare, interpret, define, discriminate, apply, analyse, critique, differentiate and appraise. Although many of these words appear to be rather dull cognitive processes, they can also refer to Adult functioning in the affective realm. The Adult is also intuiting, creating, relating, feeling, being empathic, mentalizing and engaging. We can also use adverbs to describe how the Adult works in process, such as the Adult operates imaginatively, maturely, congruently, appropriately, reflectively.

The Adult ego states are also the source of adult sexuality. Sometimes sexuality is erroneously ascribed to the Child ego states. However, this is inaccurate as behavioural, social, historical and phenomenological diagnosis would not support locating an adult sexuality in the Child ego states. The Child ego states include sensuality, which of course has a part to play in sexuality and sexual expression but Adult ego states are the (age-appropriate) source of adult sexuality.

In the light of all of the above, an emphasis on growth is relevant to promoting development of Adult ego states. Although it is clinically useful to use our models of pathology and healing to clear away obstacles that inhibit full growth and use of Adult ego states, this approach is limited in that they simply clear away these obstacles and do not necessarily encourage growth. This can be likened to clearing away weeds in a garden to help the growth of our plants, but to help our plants truly flourish, we need to enrich the soil and increase their optimal growth conditions. The relatively new approach of positive psychology (Seligman, 2002) can provide therapists with theories and tools that can be used to enrich and optimize the growth conditions of the Adult ego states.

TA AS AN EXISTENTIAL PSYCHOTHERAPY

As a model of psychotherapy, people have claimed different philosophical allegiances for TA. I agree with Clarkson (1992a), who feels TA is part of the humanistic and existential tradition. Berne referenced, and was influenced by, existential authors, such as Kierkegaard (Berne, 1966/1994) and indeed in *Principles of Group Treatment* discusses links between transactional analysis and existential therapy (ibid.):

> Insofar as actual living in the world is concerned, transactional analysis shares with existential analysis a high esteem for and a keen interest in, the personal qualities of honesty, integrity, autonomy and authenticity, and their most poignant social manifestations in encounter and intimacy.

(ibid.: 305)

Although TA is a humanistic therapy, Berne retained the concept of mortido (Berne, 1969), thus accounting for destructive tendencies and placing TA within an existential framework as an approach to therapy, which is less certain of human goodness and accounts for destructive forces (Deurzen-Smith, 1997).

'Existential psychotherapy is a dynamic approach to therapy which focuses on concerns that are rooted in the individual's existence' (Yalom, 1980: 5). In existential psychotherapy conflict is seen to arise from an individual's confrontation with the 'givens of existence' (ibid.). The role of the therapist is to enable the client to come to terms with, and adjust to, these givens in their own unique manner. The process of coming to terms with

DOI: 10.4324/9781003375890-107

these givens is seen as one which will inevitably produce anxiety. However, this existential anxiety is different from the limiting, fearful anxiety with which many clients present to therapy. The goal of therapy is not the removal of existential anxiety, but of facilitating adjustment to it and the anxiety which is the product of an authentic, autonomous life.

The four existential givens, as identified by Yalom (ibid.), are:

- death
- freedom
- isolation
- meaninglessness.

Facing and accepting our mortality are clearly a process that will generate anxiety. Our scripts and magical thinking provide us with a means to avoid death anxiety, or even a blueprint about how we will die, thus creating the illusion of a sense of control over death. Existential approaches to psychotherapy, like TA, emphasize the importance of the client taking responsibility for their life. Existential approaches recognize that the taking of responsibility and claiming one's own freedom can paradoxically induce intense anxiety (Sartre, 1943). It is the realization that we truly are the masters of our own destiny and the weightiness of this realization that can induce terrible fear (Kundera, 2000a, 2000b). It is possible that our scripts and their limiting nature help us to avoid this anxiety. TA emphasizes personal responsibility and freedom – an approach which can trigger such anxiety reactions. The therapist is wise to explore this should their client experience unaccountable, free-floating anxiety following therapy sessions which focused on responsibility and freedom. The existential approach considers it is not desirable to seek to resolve this anxiety, but rather is it preferable to help the client live with the anxiety of uncertainty. The given of isolation means that ultimately we must face the world on our own. Again, our scripts can determine and give explanations that help us manage the anxiety of this isolation, but also maintain the isolation by preventing meaningful relating to others. Our scripts are our 'meaning-making mechanisms' and give us reasons for why we and others are the way we are. An existential approach to therapy seeks to uncover the process of meaning-making one uses, and how one construes the world, oneself and others. The realization that life, in and of itself, has no inherent meaning is a common source of torment for many of our depressed clients. Meaning cannot be given or generated but rather it is something that each individual has to find for themselves. Perhaps one of the tasks of the psychotherapist is to help our clients find their own meaning and purpose, just as we have done in our work of healing and service to others (even if this was called for in our scripts). The making of meaning is a central feature of most psychotherapy, as is coming to terms with events and experiences which are meaningless and for which we can find no explanation. Perhaps the approach of positive psychology, with its focus on using personal strengths, will be of use in facilitating meaning-making.

Being mindful of the four existential givens and their impact on the psyche and discussing these with clients can add great depth and poignancy to the therapy process. Pursuing the existential goal of authenticity is entirely compatible with the TA goal of promoting autonomy. Both require taking a conscious stance in relation to how one is choosing to live, as well as an awareness of how one perceives (Sartre, 1943) and examining one's values (Deurzen-Smith, 2002). Existential conflicts and tensions are not something to be avoided, but something to engage with and to dialogue with our clients about. The existential approach does not turn away from pain, suffering and ugliness, nor does it teach us how to avoid it, but rather it invites us to accept these things as a reality of life.

ANALYSING TRANSACTIONS

In several places throughout this book I have invited the reader to engage in analysis of transactions – a practice which inexplicably appears to have gone out of fashion among TA therapists. I finish this section on refining technique and the whole book by referring back to this potent yet basic TA method.

In turn, analyse your own transactional stimuli towards your client – at both the professional and personal level. What are you ostensibly seeking in each transactional stimulus? What is your intention? What is the significance of the transaction for you personally? What are the inner transactions you experience internally but do not voice? What influence do these internal transactions have on your work? What was the impact of your transaction? Did the impact match your intention? What was your client's response to your transactional stimuli? What happened for your client internally in response to your stimuli? What might they have held back from verbally expressing? What does their transactional response tell you about the impact of your stimuli? How does your client's response impact you in return? Go beyond the simple plotting of ego states and the transactional vectors between them to include the internal transactions that each person is experiencing simultaneously to the interpersonal transactions, and adopt a stance of curiosity in relation to them. A great deal of learning about one's self, and one's client can be gained through such a simple method. Account for the potentialities of the relationship. In analysing transcripts, speculate on what might have happened had the transactions been different in some way. What trajectory might the work have taken? What I am proposing is mindfulness in practice, a reflection in action (Schön, 1983).

DOI: 10.4324/9781003375890-108   365

Berne (1966/1994) was clear in his position: each transactional analyst should know what they are doing, and why they are doing it, in each moment of the therapy. If what we are doing with a client is exploring the unknown in an open-minded way and just being with the anxiety of uncertainty, or immersing ourselves in the present experience, this process should be intentional.

Above all, I invite you to be tentative. We can never truly be certain and, as I have discussed previously, certainty closes down the process of mentalizing. Finally, remember, transactions, like ego states (and arguably all psychotherapy theories), are just a fascinating fiction. A metaphor. A story we tell to bring order to our thoughts and experiences. A means of making sense, structure and meaning where there is none. A model for creating new narratives: a new angle on the past, a new experience of the present, and a set of new potentialities for the future.

REFERENCES

Abbass, A. (2015) *Reaching Through Resistance: Advanced Psychotherapy Techniques*. Kensington, MD: Seven Leaves Press.

Alexander, F., French, T. F. and Bacon, C. L. (1946) *Psychoanalytic Therapy: Principles and Application*. New York: Ronald Press.

Allen, J. and Allen, B. A. (1995) Narrative theory, redecision therapy and postmodernism. *Transactional Analysis Journal*, 25(4): 327–334.

Allen, J., Leeson, P., De Fruyt, F. and Martin, S. (2018) Application of a 10 week coaching program designed to facilitate volitional personality change: Overall effects on personality and the impacts of targeting. *International Journal of Evidence Based Coaching and Mentoring*, 16(1): 80–94.

Anderson, F., Howard, L., Dean, K., Moran, P. and Khalifeh, H. (2016) Childhood maltreatment and adulthood domestic and sexual violence victimisation among people with severe mental illness. *Social Psychiatry and Psychiatric Epidemiology*, 51(7): 961–970.

Anderson, T., Crowley, M. J., Himawan, L., Holmberg, J., and Uhlin, B. (2016) Therapist facilitative interpersonal skills and training status: A randomized clinical trial on alliance and outcome. *Psychotherapy Research*, 26: 511–529. doi: 10.1080/10503307.2015.1049671

Anderson, T., Ogles, B. M., Patterson, C. L., Lambert, M. J. and Vermeersch, D. A. (2009) Therapist effects: Facilitative interpersonal skills as a predictor of therapist success. *Journal of Clinical Psychology*, 65: 755–768. doi: 10.1002/jclp.20583

Anderson, T. and Patterson, C. (2013) *Facilitative inter-personal skill task and rating method*. Unpublished manuscript, Ohio University.

Angyal, A. (1939) The structure of wholes. *Philosophy of Science*, 6(1): 25–37.

APA (American Psychiatric Association) (2013) *Diagnostic and Statistical Manual of Mental Disorders (DSM-5)*. 5th edn. Washington, DC: American Psychological Association.

Ayres, A. (2006) The only way out: A consideration of suicide. *Transactions*, 4: 4–13.

Baker, J. and Widdowson, M. (2016) An inquiry into the experience of the dyslexic transactional analysis psychotherapist. *Transactional Analysis Journal*, 50(1): 24–40. doi: 10.1080/03621537.2019.1690236

Barnes, G. (ed.) (1977) *Transactional Analysis after Eric Berne: Teachings and Practice of Three TA Schools*. New York: Harper's College Press.

Barnett, M. (2007) What brings you here? An exploration of the unconscious motivations of those who choose to train and work as psychotherapists and counsellors. *Psychodynamic Practice*, 13(3): 257–274.

Barr, J. (1987) Therapeutic relationship model: Perspectives on the core of the healing process. *Transactional Analysis Journal*, 17(4): 134–140.

Barrow, G. and Marshall, H. (2023) Revisiting ecological transactional analysis: Emerging perspectives. *Transactional Analysis Journal*, 53(1): 7–20.

Bary, B. B. and Hufford, F. M. (1990) The six advantages to games and their use in treatment. *Transactional Analysis Journal*, 20(4): 214–220.

Baskerville, V. (2022) A transcultural and intersectional ego state model of the self: The influence of transcultural and intersectional identity on self and other. *Transactional Analysis Journal*, 52(3): 228–243. doi: 10.1080/03621537.2022.2076398

Bateman, A. W. and Fonagy, P. (2006) *Mentalization-Based Treatment for Borderline Personality Disorder: A Practical Guide*. Oxford: Oxford University Press.

Beck, A. T. and Beck, J. (1995) *Cognitive Therapy: Basics and Beyond*. New York: Guilford Press.

Beisser, A. (1970) The paradoxical theory of change. In J. Fagan and I. L. Shepherd (eds), *Gestalt Therapy Now: Theory, Techniques, Applications*. New York: Harper Colophon. Available at: http://www.gestalt.org/arnie.htm

Benjamin, L. S. (2003) *Interpersonal Diagnosis and Treatment of Personality Disorders*. New York: Guilford Press.

Benjamin, L. S. (2006) *Interpersonal Reconstructive Therapy: Promoting Change in Non-Responders*. New York: Guilford Press.

Berne, E. (1961/1986) *Transactional Analysis in Psychotherapy*. New York: Souvenir Press.

Berne, E. (1964) *Games People Play*. New York: Grove Press.

Berne, E. (1966/1994) *Principles of Group Treatment*. Menlo Park, CA: Shea Books.

Berne, E. (1968) *A Layman's Guide to Psychiatry and Psychoanalysis*. London: Penguin.

Berne, E. (1969) Minimal basic science curriculum for clinical membership in the ITAA. *Transactional Analysis Bulletin*, 8(32): 108–110.

Berne, E. (1970) *Sex in Human Loving*. New York: Penguin.

Berne, E. (1971) Away from a theory of the impact of interpersonal interaction on non-verbal participation. *Transactional Analysis Journal*, 1(1): 6–13.

Berne, E. (1972) *What Do You Say After You Say Hello?* London: Corgi.

Beutler, L., Edwards, C. and Someah, K. (2018) Adapting psychotherapy to patient reactance level: A meta-analytic review. *Journal of Clinical Psychology*, 74(11): 1952–1963. doi: 10.1002/jclp.22682

Bickman, L. (2005) A common factors approach to improving mental health services. *Mental Health Services Research*, 7(1): 1–4. doi:10.1007/s11020-005-1961-7

Bion, W. R. (1962) *Learning from Experience*. Lanham, MD: Jason Aronson.

Bion, W. R. (1970) *Attention and Interpretation: A Scientific Approach to Insight in Psycho-Analysis and Groups*. New York: Basic Books.

Blackstone, P. (1993) The dynamic child: Integration of second order structure, object relations and self psychology. *Transactional Analysis Journal*, 23(4): 216–234.

Blackwell, S., Browning, M., Mathews, A., Pictet, A., Welch, J., Davies J., Watson, P., Geddes, J. and Holmes, E. (2015) Positive imagery-based cognitive bias modification as a web-based treatment tool for depressed adults: A randomized controlled trial. *Clinical Psychological Science*, 3(1): 91–111. doi: 10.1177/216770261456074

Boliston-Mardula, J. (2001) Appetite path model: Working with escape hatch resolution with clients who use drugs and alcohol. *TA UK*, 61(Autumn): 9–14.

Bordin, E. S. (1979) The generalisability of the psychoanalytical concept of the working alliance. *Psychotherapy: Theory, Research and Practice*, 16(3): 252–260.

Bordin, E. S. (1994) Theory and research on the therapeutic working alliance. In O. Horvath and S. Greenberg (eds), *The Working Alliance: Theory, Research and Practice*. New York: John Wiley & Sons, Inc.

Bosch, M. and Arntz, A. (2021) Imagery rescripting for patients with posttraumatic stress disorder: a qualitative study of patients' and therapists' perspectives about the elements of change. *Cognitive and Behavioural Practice*. doi: 10. 1016/j.cbpra.2021.08.001

Bowers, C. and Widdowson, M. (2023) Transactional analysis psychotherapy for clients who are neurodivergent: Experiences and practice recommendations. *International Journal of Transactional Analysis Research and Practice*, 14(1). doi: 10.29044/v14i1pxx

Boyd, H. and Cowles-Boyd, L. (1980) Blocking tragic scripts. *Transactional Analysis Journal*, 10(3): 227–229.

Brehm, J. W. and Brehm, S. S. (1981) *Psychological Reactance: A Theory of Freedom and Control*. New York: Academic Press.

Breslau, N. and Kessler, R. C. (2001) The stressor criterion in DSM-IV posttraumatic stress disorder: An empirical investigation. *Biological Psychiatry*, 50(9): 699–704. 10. 1016/S0006-3223(01)01167-2

Burns, D. (2000) *The Feeling Good Handbook*. New York: Plume.

Byrd, K., Patterson, C. and Turchik, J. (2010) Working alliance as a mediator of client attachment dimensions and psychotherapy outcome. *Psychotherapy: Theory, Research, Practice, Training*, 47(4): 631–636. doi: 10.1037/a0022080

Castonguay, L., Constantino, M., and Beutler, L. (2019) *Principles of Change; How Psychotherapists Implement Research in Practice*. Oxford: Oxford University Press.

Chow, D. (2022) Parameters and samples for capturing weekly therapy learnings. Available at: www.darylchow.com/fromtiers/weeklytherapylearnings/

Clark, B. (1991) Empathic transactions in the deconfusion of the Child ego state. *Transactional Analysis Journal*, 21(2): 92–98.

Clarkin, J. F., Yeomans, F. E., and Kernberg, O. F. (2006) *Psychotherapy for Borderline Personality. Focusing on Object Relations*. Washington, DC: American Psychiatric Publishing.

Clarkson, P. (1988) Ego state dilemmas of abused children. *Transactional Analysis Journal*, 18(2): 85–93.

Clarkson, P. (1992a) *Transactional Analysis Psychotherapy: An Integrated Approach*. London: Routledge.

Clarkson, P. (1992b) In praise of speed, experimentation, agreeableness, endurance, and excellence: Counterscript drivers and aspiration. *Transactional Analysis Journal*, 22(1). doi: 10.1177/036215379202200103

Clarkson, P. (2003) *The Therapeutic Relationship*. London: Whurr Publishers.

Cook, R. (2012) Triumph or disaster?: A relational view of therapeutic mistakes. *Transactional Analysis Journal*, 42(1): 34–42. doi: 10.1177/036215371204200105

Cooper, M. (2019) *Integrating Counselling and Psychotherapy: Directionality, Synergy and Social Change*. Thousand Oaks, CA: Sage.

Cooper, M. and Norcross J. C. (2016) A brief, multi-dimensional measure of clients' therapy preferences:

The Cooper-Norcross Inventory of Preferences (C-NIP). *International Journal of Clinical and Health Psychology*, 16(1): 87–98.

Cornell, W. (1986) Setting the therapeutic stage: The initial sessions. *Transactional Analysis Journal*, 16(1): 4–10.

Cornell, W. (1988) Life script theory: Critical review from a developmental perspective. *Transactional Analysis Journal*, 18(4): 270–282.

Cornell, W. (1994) Shame: Binding affect, ego state contamination and relational repair. *Transactional Analysis Journal*, 24(2): 139–146.

Cornell, W. and Bonds-White, F. (2001) Therapeutic relatedness in transactional analysis: The truth of love or the love of truth. *Transactional Analysis Journal*, 31(1): 71–93.

Cornell, W. and Hargaden, H. (2005) *From Transactions to Relations: The Emergence of a Relational Tradition in Transactional Analysis*. Chadlington: Haddon Press.

Cornell, W. and Landaiche, M. (2006) Impasse and intimacy: Applying Berne's concept of script protocol. *Transactional Analysis Journal*, 36(3): 196–213.

Courtois, C. A. and Ford, J. D. (2009) *Treating Complex Traumatic Stress Disorders: An Evidence-Based Guide*. New York: Guilford Press.

Courtois, C. A., Ford, J. D. and Cloitre, M. (2009) Best practices in psychotherapy for adults. In C. A. Courtois and J. D. Ford (eds), *Treating Complex Traumatic Stress Disorders: An Evidence-Based Guide*. New York: Guilford Press, pp. 82–103.

Cowan, A. and Keltner, D. (2017) Self-report captures 27 distinct categories of emotion bridged by continuous gradients. *Proceedings of the National Academy of Sciences*, 114(38): E7900–E7909. doi: 10.1073/PNAS.1 702247114

Cox, M. (2000) A dynamic approach to treatment planning. Workshop presentation, Institute of Transactional Analysis Annual Conference, Canterbury, UK.

Cozolino, L. (2017) *The Neuroscience of Psychotherapy: Healing the Social Brain*. New York: W.W. Norton.

Crenshaw, K. (1989) Demarginalizing the intersection of race and sex: A black feminist critique of antidiscrimination doctrine, feminist theory and antiracist politics. *University of Chicago Legal Forum*, Issue 1, Article 8. Available at: https://chicagounbound.uchicago.edu/cgi/viewcontent.cgi?ar-ticle=1052andcontext=uclf

Crenshaw, K. (2019) "Reach everyone on the planet...": Kimberle Crenshaw and intersectionality. Lecture given at Gunda Werner Institute in the Heinrich Böll Foundation and the Centre for Intersectional Justice. Available at: https://www.boell.de/sites/default/files/crenshaw_-_reach_everyone_on_the_planet_en.pdf

Crits-Cristoph, P. and Gibbons, M. B. C. (2002) Relational interpretations. In J. C. Norcross (ed.), *Psychotherapy Relationships That Work: Therapist Contributions and Responsiveness to Patients*. Oxford: Oxford University Press, pp. 285–300.

Crossman, P. (1966) Permission and protection. *Transactional Analysis Bulletin*, 5(19): 152–154.

Daly, K. and Mallinckrodt, B. (2009) Experienced therapists' approach to psychotherapy for adults with attachment avoidance or attachment anxiety. *Journal of Counselling Psychology*, 56(4): 549–563. doi:10.1037/a0016695

Dashiell, S. (1978) The parent resolution process. *Transactional Analysis Journal*, 18(4): 289–294.

Davanloo, H. (1980) *Short-Term Dynamic Psychotherapy*. Lanham, MD: Jason Aronson.

Davies, J. M. and Frawley, M. G. (1994) *Treating the Adult Survivor of Childhood Sexual Abuse: A Psychoanalytic Perspective*. New York: HarperCollins.

Deurzen-Smith, E. (1997) *Everyday Mysteries: Existential Dimensions of Psychotherapy*. London: Sage.

Deurzen-Smith, E. (2002) *Existential Counselling and Psychotherapy in Practice*. London: Sage.

De Young, P. (2021) *Understanding and Treating Chronic Shame: Healing Right Brain Relational Trauma*. New York: Routledge.

Drego, P. (1983) The cultural parent. *Transactional Analysis Journal*, 13(4): 224–227.

Drew, B. L. (2001) Self-harm behavior and no-suicide contracting in psychiatric inpatient settings. *Archives of Psychiatric Nursing*, 15(3): 99–106.

Drye, R. (2006) The no-suicide decision: then and now. *The Script*, 36(6): 3–4 (reprinted in *ITA News*, 27: 1–6).

Drye, R., Goulding, R. and Goulding, M. (1973) No suicide decisions: Patient monitoring of suicidal risk. *American Journal of Psychiatry*, 130(2): 118–121.

Duncan, B. and Miller, S. (2000) The client's theory of change: Consulting the client in the integrative process. *Journal of Psychotherapy Integration*, 10(2): 169–187.

Dunning, D., Johnson, K., Ehrlinger, J. and Kruger, J. (2003) Why people fail to recognize their own incompetence. *Current Directions in Psychological Science*, 12(3): 83–87. doi:10.1111/1467-8721.01235

Dusay, J. (1972) Egograms and the constancy hypothesis. *Transactional Analysis Journal*, 2(3): 37.

EATA (2008) *EATA Training and Examinations Handbook*. Available at: www.eatanews.org

Ecker, B. (2018) Clinical translation of memory reconsolidation research: Therapeutic methodology for transformational change by erasing implicit emotional learnings driving symptom production. *International Journal of Neuropsychotherapy*, 6(1): 1–92. doi: 10.12744/ijnpt.2018.0001-0092

Ecker, B., Ticic, R. and Hulley, L. (2012) *Unlocking the Emotional Brain: Eliminating Symptoms at Their Roots Using Memory Reconsolidation*. New York: Routledge.

Eichfeld, C., Farrell, D., Matthess, M., Bumke, P., Sodemann, U., Nil, E., Phoeun, B., Direzkia, Y., Firmansyah, F., Sumampouw, N., and Matthess, H. (2019) Trauma stabilisation as a sole treatment for post-traumatic stress disorder in Southeast Asia. *Psychiatric Quarterly*, 90: 63–88. doi: 10.1007/s11126-018-9598-z

Ekman, P. (2004) *Emotions Revealed: Understanding Faces and Feelings*. New York: Times Books/Henry Holt & Co.

English, F. (1971) The substitution factor: Rackets and real feelings. *Transactional Analysis Journal*, 1(4): 225–230.

Elliott, R., Bohart, A., Watson, J. and Murphy, D. (2018) Therapist empathy and client outcome: An updated meta-analysis. *Psychotherapy (Chic)*, 55(4): 399–410. doi: 10.1037/pst0000175

Ernst, F. (1971) The OK corral: The grid for get-on-with. *Transactional Analysis Journal*, 1(4): 231–240.

Erskine, R. G. (1980) Script cure: Behavioral, intrapsychic and physiological. *Transactional Analysis Journal*, 10(2): 102–106.

Erskine, R. G. (1988) Ego structure, intrapsychic function and defense mechanisms: A commentary on Berne's original theoretical concepts. *Transactional Analysis Journal*, 18(4): 15–19.

Erskine, R. G. (1993) Inquiry, attunement and involvement in the psychotherapy of dissociation. *Transactional Analysis Journal*, 23(4): 184–190.

Erskine, R. G. (1994) Shame and self-righteousness: Transactional analysis perspectives and clinical interventions. *Transactional Analysis Journal*, 24(2): 87–102.

Erskine, R. G. (1998) The therapeutic relationship: Integrating motivation and personality theories., *Transactional Analysis Journal*, 28(2): 132–141.

Erskine, R. G., Moursund, J. P. and Trautmann, R. L. (1999) *Beyond Empathy: A Therapy of Contact-in-Relationship*. New York: Brunner-Routledge.

Erskine, R. G. and Trautmann, R. L. (1996) Methods of an integrative psychotherapy. *Transactional Analysis Journal*, 26(4): 316–328.

Erskine, R. G. and Zalcman, M. (1979) The racket system: A model for racket analysis. *Transactional Analysis Journal*, 9(1): 51–59.

Eubanks, C. F. and Goldfried, M. R. (2019) A principle-based approach to psychotherapy integration. In J. Norcross and M. Goldfried (eds), *Handbook of Psychotherapy Integration* 3rd edn. Oxford: Oxford University Press.

Eubanks, C. F., Muran. C. and Safran, J. (2018) Alliance rupture repair: A meta-analysis. *Psychotherapy*: 55(4): 508–519. doi: 10.1037/pst0000185.

Evans, A. and Koenig Nelson, J. (2021) The value of adapting counseling to client's spirituality and religion: Evidence-based relationship factor. *Religions*, 12(11): 951. doi: 10.3390/rel12110951

Fairbairn W. R. (1952). *Psychoanalytic Studies of the Personality*. New York: Routledge.

Feldman Barrett, L. (2006) Valence is a basic building block of emotional life. *Journal of Research in Personality*, 40(1): 33–55. doi: 10.1016/j.jrp.2005.08.006

Felitti, M. D., Anda, R. F., Nordenberg, M. D. et al. (1998) Relationship of childhood abuse and household dysfunction to many of the leading causes of death in adults: The Adverse Childhood Experiences (ACE) Study. *American Journal of Preventative Medicine*, 14(4): 245–258.

Flückiger, C., Del Re, A., Wampold, B. E., and Horvath, A. O. (2018) The alliance in adult psychotherapy: A meta-analytic synthesis. *Psychotherapy (Chic)*, 55(4): 316–340. doi: 10.1037/pst0000172.

Fowlie, H. and Sills, C. (eds) (2011) *Relational Transactional Analysis: Principles in Practice*. New York: Karnac.

Freud, S. (1912) Recommendations to physicians practising psychoanalysis. In *Complete Psychological Works*, Standard Edition, vol. 12. London: Hogarth Press, pp. 109–120.

Freud, S. (1937) Analysis terminable and interminable. In *Complete Psychological Works*, Standard Edition, vol. 23. London: Hogarth Press, pp. 216–253.

Gentelet, B. and Widdowson, M. (2014) Paradoxical alliances in transactional analysis for anxiety: A systematic adjudicated case study. *Transactional Analysis Journal*, 46(3): 182–194.

Gill, M. M. (1979) The analysis of the transference. *Journal of the American Psychoanalytic Association*, 27: 263–288.

Gobes, L. (1985) Abandonment and engulfment issues in relationship therapy. *Transactional Analysis Journal*, 15(3): 216–219.

Goldberg, S. B., Rousmaniere, T., Miller, S. D., Whipple, J., Nielsen, S. L., Hoyt, W. T. and Wampold, B. E. (2016) Do psychotherapists improve with time and experience? A longitudinal analysis of outcomes in a clinical setting. *Journal of Counseling Psychology*, 63(1): 1–11. doi:10.1 037/cou0000131

Goulding, M. M. and Goulding, R. L. (1979) *Changing Lives Through Redecision Therapy*. New York: Grove Press.

Goulding, R. L. and Goulding, M. M. (1978) *The Power Is in the Patient*. San Francisco: TA Press.

Grover, S., Avasthi, A. and Jagiwala, M. (2020) Clinical practice guidelines for practice of supportive psychotherapy. *Indian Journal of Psychiatry*, 62(Suppl. 2), published online. doi: 10.4103/psychiatry.IndianJPsychiatry_768_19

Guistolise, P. G. (1996) Failures in the therapeutic relationship: Inevitable and necessary? *Transactional Analysis Journal*, 26(4): 284–288.

Hahn, A. (2004) The borderline personality disorder. In J. F. Masterson and A. R. Liebermann (eds), *A Therapist's Guide to the Personality Disorders: A Handbook and Workbook*. Phoenix, AZ: Zeig Tucker.

Hansen, N. B., Lambert, M. J. and Forman, E. M. (2002) The psychotherapy dose-response effect and its implications for treatment delivery services. *Clinical Psychology: Science and Practice*, 9(3): 329–343.

Hargaden, H. (2007) Love and desire in the therapeutic relationship: Transformation or betrayal? *Transactions*, 6: 4–14.

Hargaden, H. and Sills, C. (2002) *Transactional Analysis: A Relational Perspective*. New York: Brunner-Routledge.

Hargaden, H. and Sills, C. (2003) Who am I for you? The Child ego state and transferential domains. In C. Sills and H. Hargaden (eds), *Ego States*. London: Worth Publishing.

Harvey, A., Watkins, E., Mansell, W. and Shafran, R. (2004) *Cognitive Behavioural Processes across Psychological Disorders: A Transdiagnostic Approach to Research and Treatment*. Maidenhead: Open University Press.

Herman, J. (1992) *Trauma and Recovery: The Aftermath of Violence—From Domestic Abuse to Political Terror*. New York: Basic Books.

Holloway, W. H. (1973) Shut the escape hatch. In *The Monograph Series, Numbers I–X*. Ohio: Midwest Institute for Human Understanding Inc.

Holmes, J. (2001) *The Search for the Secure Base: Attachment Theory and Psychotherapy*. New York: Routledge.

Horvath, A. and Greenberg, L. (1994) *The Working Alliance: Theory, Research and Practice*. New York: Wiley.

International Transactional Analysis Association Education Committee. (1969) Minimal basic science curriculum for clinical membership in the ITAA. *Transactional Analysis Bulletin*, 8: 108–110.

Jacobs, A. (1994) Theory as ideology: Reparenting and thought reform. *Transactional Analysis Journal*, 24(1): 39–55.

Jacobs, M. (1988) *Psychodynamic Counselling in Action*. London: Sage.

James, M. (1974) Self-reparenting: Theory and process. *Transactional Analysis Journal*, 4(3): 32–39.

James, M. (1981) *Breaking Free: Self Re-Parenting for a New Life*. Reading, M: Addison-Wesley.

James, M. (2002) *It's Never Too Late to Be Happy! Reparenting Yourself for Happiness*. Sanger, CA: Quill Driver Books.

James, M. and Jongeward, D. (1971) *Born to Win: Transactional Analysis with Gestalt Experiments*. Reading, MA: Addison-Wesley.

Kabat-Zinn, J. (1994/2000/2004) *Wherever You Go, There You Are*. London: Piatkus.

Kabat-Zinn, J. (2001) *Full Catastrophe Living: Using the Wisdom of Your Body and Mind to Face Stress, Pain and Illness*. New York: Delta.

Kahler, T. (1975) Drivers: The key to the process of scripts. *Transactional Analysis Journal*, 5(3): 280–284.

Karpman, S. (1968) Fairy tales and script drama analysis. *Transactional Analysis Bulletin*, 7(26): 39–43.

Karpman, S. (1971) Options. *Transactional Analysis Journal*, 1(1): 79–87.

Kellogg, S. (2015) *Transformational Chair Work: Using Psychotherapeutic Dialogues in Clinical Practice*. Lanham, MD: Rowman & Littlefield.

Kernberg, O. F. (1976) *Object Relations Theory and Clinical Psychoanalysis*. Lanham, MD: Jason Aronson.

Kernberg, O. F. (1980) *Internal World and External Reality: Object Relations Theory Applied*. Lanham, MD: Jason Aronson.

Kernberg, O. F. (1984) *Severe Personality Disorders: Psychotherapeutic Strategies*. New Haven, CT: Yale University Press.

Kernberg, O. F. (2004) *Contemporary Controversies in Psychoanalytic Theory, Techniques, and Their Applications*. New Haven, CT: Yale University Press.

Kernberg, O. F. (2012) *The Inseparable Nature of Love and Aggression: Clinical and Theoretical Perspectives*. Washington, DC: American Psychiatric Association.

Kessler, R., Aguillar-Gaxiola, S., Alonso, J., Benjet, C., Bromet, E., Cardoso, G. ... et al. (2017) Trauma and PTSD in the WHO World Mental Health Surveys. *European Journal of Psychotraumatology*, 8(Suppl. 5). doi: 10.1080/20008198.2017.1353383

Kirca, A., Malouff, J. and Meynadier. J. (2023) The effect of expressed gratitude interventions on psychological wellbeing: A meta-analysis of randomised controlled studies. *International Journal of Applied Positive Psychology*, 10.1007/s41042-023-00086-6

Kohut, H. (1984) *How Does Analysis Cure?* Chicago: University of Chicago Press.

Kolb, D. A. (1984) *Experiential Learning: Experience as the Source of Learning and Development*. Englewood Cliffs, NJ: Prentice-Hall.

Korn, D. and Leeds, A. (2002) Preliminary evidence of efficacy for EMDR resource development and installation in the stabilization phase of treatment of complex post traumatic stress disorder. *Journal of Clinical Psychology*, 58(12): 1465–1487.

Kundera, M. (2000a) *The Unbearable Lightness of Being*. London: Faber and Faber.

Kundera, M. (2000b) *Immortality*. London: Faber and Faber.

Kupfer, D. and Haimowitz, M. (1971) Therapeutic interventions Part 1. Rubberbands now. *Transactional Analysis Journal*, 1(1): 10–16.

Lammers, W. (1992) Using the therapist's kinesthetic responses as a therapeutic tool. *Transactional Analysis Journal*, 22(4): 216–221.

Lapworth, P. and Sills, C. (2011) *An Introduction to Transactional Analysis: Helping People Change*. London: Sage.

Lapworth, P., Sills, C. and Fish, S. (1993) *Transactional Analysis Counselling*. Oxford: Winslow Press.

Lazarus, G. and Fisher, A. (2021) Negative emotion differentiation predicts psychotherapy outcome: Preliminary findings. *Frontiers in Psychology*, 12. doi: 10.3389/fpsyg.2021.689407

Leader, D. (2008) *The New Black: Mourning, Melancholia and Depression*. London: Hamish Hamilton.

Lee, A. (1997) Process contracts. In C. Sills (ed.), *Contracts in Counselling*. London: Sage.

Lee, A. (1998) The drowning man (diagram). In T. Tilney (ed.), *Dictionary of Transactional Analysis*. London: Wiley Blackwell.

Lee, A. (2003) The mirror exercise: Creating new ego states now – a constructivist approach. In C. Sills and H. Hargaden (eds), *Ego States*. London: Worth Publishing.

Leppännen, J., Milders, M., Bell, S., Terriere, E. and Hietanen, J. (2004) Depression biases the recognition of emotionally neutral faces. *Psychiatry Research*, 128(2): 123–133. doi: 10.1016/j.psychres.2004.05.020.

Levin-Landheer, P. (1982) The cycle of development. *Transactional Analysis Journal*, 12(2): 129–139.

Lindquist, K. and Feldman Barrett, L. (2008) Emotional complexity. In M. Lewis, J. Haviland-Jones and L. Feldman Barrett (eds), *Handbook of Emotions*, 3rd edn. New York: Guilford Press.

Little, R. (2013) The new emerges out of the old: An integrated relational perspective on psychological development, psychopathology and therapeutic action. *Transactional Analysis Journal*, 43(2): 106–121.

Lovelock, J. (1979) *Gaia: A New Look at Life on Earth*. Oxford: Oxford University Press.

Luborsky, L. (1984) *Principles of Psychoanalytic Psychotherapy: A Manual for Supportive-Expressive Treatment*. New York: Basic Books.

Luborsky, L. and Crits-Cristoph, P. (1990) *Understanding Transference: The Core Conflictual Relational Theme Method*. Washington, DC: American Psychological Association.

Lutz, W., de Jong, K., Rubel, J. and Degadillo, J. (2021) Measuring, predicting and tracking change in psychotherapy. In M. Barkham, W. Lutz and L. G. Castonguay (eds), *Bergin and Garfield's Handbook of Psychotherapy and Behaviour Change*, 7th edn. New York: Wiley.

Malan, D. (1979) *Individual Psychotherapy and the Science of Psychodynamics*. Oxford: Butterworths.

Maroda, K. (1994/2004) *The Power of Countertransference: Innovation in Analytic Technique*. Hillsdale, NJ: Analytic Press.

Masterson, J. (1981) *The Narcissistic and Borderline Disorders: An Integrated Developmental Approach*. Hillsdale, NJ: Analytic Press.

Masterson, J. and Lieberman, A. R. (2004) *A Therapist's Guide to the Personality Disorders*. Phoenix, AZ: Zeig Tucker.

Matze, M. G. (1988) Reciprocity in script formation: A revision of the concept of symbiosis. *Transactional Analysis Journal*, 18(4): 304–308.

McConnell Lewis, L. (2007) No harm contracts: A review of what we know. *Suicide and Life-Threatening Behaviour*, 37(1): 50–57.

McCormick, P. and Pulleyblank, E. (1985) Stages of redecision therapy. In L. Kadis (ed.), *Redecision Therapy: Expanded*

Perspectives. Watsonville, CA: Western Institute for Group and Family Therapy.

McLaughlin, C. (2007) *Suicide-Related Behaviour: Understanding, Caring and Therapeutic Responses*. Oxford: Wiley-Blackwell.

McLeod, J. (1993) The counsellor's journey. Unpublished paper. Keele University.

McLeod, J. (2003) *An Introduction to Counselling*, 3rd edn. Maidenhead: Open University Press.

McLeod, J. (2022) How students use deliberate practice during the first stage of counsellor training. *Counselling and Psychotherapy Research*, 22(1): 207–218. doi: 10.1002/capr.12397

McNeel, J. (1976) The parent interview. *Transactional Analysis Journal*, 6(1): 61–68.

McNeel, J. (2010) Understanding the power of injunctive messages and how they are resolved in redecision therapy. *Transactional Analysis Journal*, 40(2): 159–169. doi:10.1177/036215371004000211

McNeel, J. (2022) Friends of the injunctive messages charts. Available at: https://www.aspiringtokindness.com/redecision-therapy

McWilliams, N. (1994) *Psychoanalytic Diagnosis*. New York: Guilford Press.

Mellacqua, Z. (2016) When spirit comes to mind. *Transactional Analysis Journal*, 46(2): 149–163.

Mellor, K. (1980) Impasses: A developmental and structural understanding. *Transactional Analysis Journal*, 10(3): 213–222.

Mellor, K. and Schiff, E. (1975) Discounting. *Transactional Analysis Journal*, 5(3): 295–302.

Meyer, I. H. (1995) Minority stress and mental health in gay men. *Journal of Health and Social Behavior*, 36: 38–56.

Miller, S., Bargmann, S., Chow, D. and Seidel, J. (2016) Feedback-Informed Treatment (FIT): Improving the outcome of psychotherapy one person at a time. In W. O'Donohue and A. Maragakis (eds), *Quality Improvement in Behavioral Health*. New York: Springer.

Miller, S., Duncan, B., Brown, J., Sorrell, R. and Chalk, M. (2007) Using formal client feedback to improve retention and outcome. *Journal of Brief Therapy*, 5: 19–28.

Miller, S. D., Hubble, M. A. and Chow, D. (2020) *Better Results: Using Deliberate Practice to Improve Therapeutic Effectiveness.* Washington, C: American Psychological Association. doi: 10.1037/0000191-000

Miller, W. R. and Rollnick, S. (2013) *Motivational Interviewing: Helping People to Change,* 3rd edn. New York: Guilford Press.

Minikin, K. (2018) Radical relational psychiatry: Toward a democracy of mind and people. *Transactional Analysis Journal*, online, pp. 111–125. doi: 10.1080/03621537.2018.1429287

Mirowsky, J. and Ross, C. E. (1989) *Social Causes of Psychological Distress.* Berlin: Aldine de Gruyter.

Mobbs, D., Marchant, J. L., Hassabis, D., Seymour, B., Tan, G., Gray, M., Petrovic, P., Dolan, R. J. and Frith, C. D. (2009) From threat to fear: The neural organization of defensive fear systems in humans. *Journal of Neuroscience*, 29(39): 12236–12243. doi: 10.1523/JNEUROSCI.2378-09.2009

Moiso, C. (1984) The feeling loop. In E. Stern (ed.), *TA: The State of the Art.* Dordrecht: Foris Publications, pp. 69–76.

Moiso, C. (1985) Ego states and transference. *Transactional Analysis Journal*, 15(3): 194–201.

Mothersole, G. (1996) Existential realities and no-suicide contracts. *Transactional Analysis Journal*, 26(2): 151–159.

Müller, U. and Tudor, K. (2001) Transactional analysis as brief therapy. In K. Tudor (ed.), *Transactional Analysis Approaches to Brief Therapy.* London: Sage, pp. 19–44.

Nathanson, D. (1994) Shame transactions. *Transactional Analysis Journal*, 24(2): 121–129.

Newton, T. (2006) Script, psychological life plans, and the learning cycle. *Transactional Analysis Journal*, 14(1): 186–195.

Norcross, J. and Lambert, M. (2019a) *Psychotherapy Relationships That Work.* Vol. 1: *Evidence-Based*

Therapist Contributions, 3rd edn. Oxford: Oxford University Press.

Norcross, J. and Wampold, B. (2019b) *Psychotherapy Relationships That Work*. Vol. 2: *Evidence-Based Therapist Responsiveness*, 3rd edn. Oxford: Oxford University Press.

Novellino, M. (1984) Self-analysis of countertransference. *Transactional Analysis Journal*, 24(2): 121–129.

Novellino, M. (2003) On closer analysis: A psychodynamic revision of the rules of communication within the framework of transactional psychoanalysis. In C. Sills and H. Hargaden, H. (eds), *Ego States*. London: Worth Publishing.

Nutall, J. (2006) The existential phenomenology of transactional analysis. *Transactional Analysis Journal*, 33(3): 214–227.

Oates, S. (2021) What if my "I'm OK, You're OK" is different from yours? Could the inherent optimism in transactional analysis be a form of compulsory ableism? *Transactional Analysis Journal*, 51(1): 63–76.

O'Brien, M. and Houston, G. (2007) *Integrative Therapy: A Practitioner's Guide*. London: Sage.

O'Connor, R. and Kirtley, O. (2018) The integrated motivational–volitional model of suicidal behaviour. *Philosophical Transactions of the Royal Society*, 373(1754). doi: 10.1098/rstb.2017.0268

Ogden, T. (1982) *Projective Identification and Psychotherapeutic Technique*. Lanham, MD: Jason Aronson.

Oller Vallejo, J. (1986) Withdrawal: A basic positive adaptation in addition to compliance and rebellion. *Transactional Analysis Journal*, 16(2): 114–119.

Papalini, S., Beckers, T. and Vervliet, B. (2020) Dopamine: From prediction error to psychotherapy. *Translational Psychiatry*, 10(164). doi: 10.1038/s41398-020-0814-x

Parlett, M. (1991) Reflections on field theory. *The British Gestalt Journal*, I: 69–81.

Paulsen, S. (2021) Where there are no words: Working with pre-verbal trauma. Workshop presentation.

Pedeira, M., Pérez-Cuesta, L. and Maldonado, H. (2002) Mismatch between what is expected and what actually occurs triggers memory reconsolidation or extinction. *Learning and Memory*, 11(2004): 579–585.

Pennebaker J. W. (1997) Writing about emotional experiences as a therapeutic process. *Psychological Science*, 8: 162–166.

Perls, F. (1969) *Gestalt Therapy Verbatim*. Moab, UT: Real People Press.

Petriglieri, G. (2007) Stuck in a moment: A developmental perspective on impasses. *Transactional Analysis Journal*, 37(3): 185–194.

Pine, F. (1985) *Developmental Theory and Clinical Process*. New Haven, CT: Yale University Press.

Racker, H. (1968) *Transference and Countertransference*. Madison, CT: International Universities Press.

Rockliff, H., Gilbert, P., McEwan, K., Lightman, S. and Glover, D. (2008) A pilot exploration of heart-rate variability and salivary cortisol responses to compassion-focused imagery. *Clinical Neuropsychiatry*, 5(3): 132–139.

Rogers, C. (1957) The necessary and sufficient conditions of therapeutic personality change. *Journal of Consulting Psychology*, 21: 95–103.

Rogers, C. (1980) *A Way of Being*. Boston: Houghton-Mifflin.

Rook, J. (In press) Working with religion and the cultural parent.

Rothschild, B. (2000) *The Body Remembers: The Psychophysiology of Trauma and Trauma Treatment*. New York: Norton.

Rousmaniere, T. G. (2016). *Deliberate Practice for Psychotherapists: A Guide to Improving Clinical Effectiveness*. New York: Routledge.

Rousmaniere, T. G. (2018). *Mastering the Inner Skills of Psychotherapy: A Deliberate Practice Handbook*. New York: Gold Lantern Press.

Roszak, T. (1992) *Voice of the Earth: An Exploration of Eco-Psychology*. New York: Phanes Press.

Roszak, T. and Gomes, M. (eds) (1995) *Ecopsychology: Restoring the Earth, Healing the Mind*. New York: Counterpoint.

Safran, J. D. and Muran, C. J. (2003) *Negotiating the Therapeutic Relationship: A Relational Treatment Guide*. New York: Guilford Press.

Sambin, M. and Scotta, F. (2018) *Intensive Transactional Analysis Psychotherapy: An Integrated Model*. New York: Routledge.

SAMHSA. (2015) *Trauma-Informed Care in Behavioral Health Services; Quick Guide for Clinicians*. Washington, DC: U.S. Department of Health and Human Services, Substance Abuse and Mental Health Services Administration.

Sartre, J-P. (1943) *Being and Nothingness: An Essay on Phenomenological Ontology* (trans. H. Barnes. 1956). New York: Philosophical Library.

Schiff, A. and Schiff, J. (1971) Passivity. *Transactional Analysis Journal* 1(1): 71–78.

Schiff, J., Schiff, A., Mellor, K., Schiff, E., Fishman, J., Wolz, L., Fishman, C. and Momb, D. (1975) *The Cathexis Reader: Transactional Analysis Treatment of Psychosis*. New York: Harper and Row.

Schlegel, L. (1998) What is Transactional Analysis? *Transactional Analysis Journal*, 28(4): 269–287.

Schmidt, N. B. and Woolaway-Bickel, K. (2000) The effects of reatment compliance on outcome in cognitive-behavioral therapy for panic disorder: Quality vs. quantity. *Journal of Consulting and Clinical Psychology*, 68: 13–18.

Schön, D. A. (1983) *The Reflective Practitioner: How Professionals Think in Action*. London: Temple Smith.

Seligman, M. (2002) *Authentic Happiness*. London: Nicholas Brealey.

Shadbolt, C. (2004) Homophobia and gay affirmative transactional analysis. *Transactional Analysis Journal*, 34(2): 113–125.

Shadbolt, C. (2012) The place of failure and rupture in psychotherapy. *Transactional Analysis Journal*, 42(1): 5–16.

Shapiro, F. (2018) *Eye Movement Desensitization and Reprocessing (EMDR) Therapy: Basic Principles, Protocols, and Procedures*, 3rd edn. New York: Guilford Press.

Shivanath, S. and Hiremath, M. (2003) The psychodynamics of race and culture. In C. Sills and H. Hargaden (eds), *Ego States*. London: Worth Publishing.

Siegel, D. (2007) *The Mindful Brain: Reflection and Attunement in Cultivating Wellbeing*. New York: Guilford Press.

Siegel, D. (2020) *The Developing Mind: How Relationships and Brain Interact to Shape Who We Are*, 3rd edn. New York: Guilford Press.

Sills, C. and Hargaden, H. (2003) *Ego States*. London: Worth Publishing.

Singer, J. (1998) Odd people in: The birth of community amongst people on the autism spectrum: a personal exploration of a new social movement based on neurological diversity. Thesis, the University of Technology, Sydney.

Singer, J. (1999) Why can't you be normal for once in your life?: From a "Problem with No Name" to a new category of disability. In M. Corker and S. French (eds), *Disability Discourse*. Maidenhead: Open University Press.

Skottnik, L. and Linden, D. (2019) Mental imagery and brain regulation: New links between psychotherapy and neuroscience. *Frontiers in Psychiatry*, 10: 779. doi: 10.3389/fpsyt.2019.00779

Stark, M. (2000) *Modes of Therapeutic Action*. Lanham, MD: Jason Aronson.

Steiger, M., Flückiger, C., Rüegger, D. and Allemand, M. (2021) Changing personality traits with the help of a digital personality change intervention. PNAS, 118(8): e2017548118. 10.1073/pnas.201754811

Steindl, C., Jonas, E., Sittenhaler, S., Traut-Mattausch, E. and Greenberg, J. (2015) Understanding psychological reactance: New developments and findings. *Zeitschrift für Psychologie*, 223(4): 205–214. doi: 10.1027/2151-2604/a000222

Steiner, C. (1966) Script and counterscript. *Transactional Analysis Bulletin*, 5(18): 133–135.

Steiner, C. (1968) Transactional analysis as a treatment philosophy. *Transactional Analysis Bulletin*, 5(18): 133–135.

Steiner, C. (1971) The stroke economy. *Transactional Analysis Journal*, 1(3): 9–15.

Steiner, C. (1974) *Scripts People Live: Transactional Analysis of Life Scripts*. New York: Grove Press.

Steiner, C. and Perry, P. (1999) *Achieving Emotional Literacy*. New York: Avon Books.

Stern, D. (1985) *The Interpersonal World of the Infant*. New York: Basic Books.

Stern, D. (2004) *The Present Moment: In Psychotherapy and Everyday Life*. New York: W.W. Norton.

Stewart, I. (1992) *Eric Berne*. Thousand Oaks, CA: Sage.

Stewart, I. (1996) *Developing Transactional Analysis Counselling*. Thousand Oaks, CA: Sage.

Stewart, I. (2007) *Transactional Analysis Counselling in Action*, 2nd edn. Thousand Oaks, CA: Sage.

Stewart, I. and Joines, V. (1987) *TA Today: A New Introduction to Transactional Analysis*. Nottingham: Lifespace.

Stewart, I. and Joines, V. (2012) *TA Today: A New Introduction to Transactional Analysis*, 2nd edn. Nottingham: Lifespace.

Stiles, W. B., Barkham, M., and Wheeler, S. (2015). Duration of psychological therapy: Relation to recovery and improvement rates in UK routine practice. *The British Journal of Psychiatry*, 207(2): 115–122. 10.1192/bjp.bp.114.145565

Summers, G. (2011) Dynamic ego states: The significance of nonconscious and unconscious patterns, as well as conscious patterns. In H. Fowlie and C. Sills (eds), *Relational Transactional Analysis: Principles in Practice*. New York: Routledge, pp. 59–67.

Summers, G. and Tudor, K. (2000) Co-creative transactional analysis. *Transactional Analysis Journal*, 30(1): 23–40.

Summers, G. and Tudor, K. (2005) Introducing co-creative TA. Available at: www.co-creativity.com

Swede, S. (1977) *How to Cure: How Eric Berne Practiced Transactional Analysis*. Berkeley, CA: Southey Swede.

Terlato, V. (2001) The analysis of defence mechanisms in the transactional analysis setting. *Transactional Analysis Journal*, 31(2): 103–113.

Thomson, G. (1983) Fear, anger and sadness. *Transactional Analysis Journal*, 13(1): 20–24.

Tryon, G. S., Birch, S. E. and Verkuilen, J. (2019) Goal consensus and collaboration. In J. C. Norcross and M. J. Lambert (eds), *Psychotherapy Relationships That Work: Evidence-Based Therapist Contributions*. Oxford: Oxford University Press, pp.167–204. doi: 10.1093/med-psych/9780190843953.003.0005

Tryon, G. S. and Winograd, G. (2001). Goal consensus and collaboration. *Psychotherapy*, 38(4): 385–389.

Tudor, K. (1995) What do you say about saying goodbye? Ending psychotherapy. *Transactional Analysis Journal*, 25(3): 228–233.

Tudor, K. (2003) The neopsyche: The integrating adult ego state. In C. Sills and H. Hargaden (eds), *Ego States*. London: Worth Publishing.

Tudor, K. (2011a) Understanding empathy. *Transactional Analysis Journal*, 41(1): 39–57.

Tudor, K. (2011b) Empathy: A co-creative perspective. *Transactional Analysis Journal*, 41(4): 322–335. doi: 10.1177/036215371104100409

Tudor, K. (2019) Religion, faith, spirituality, and the beyond in transactional analysis. *Transactional Analysis Journal*, 49(2): 71–87.

Tudor, K. and Widdowson, M. (2008) From client process to therapeutic relating: A critique of the process model and personality adaptations. *Transactional Analysis Journal*, 38(3): 218–232.

Tyrer, P. (2018). *Taming the Beast Within: Shredding the Stereotypes of Personality Disorder*. New York: Sheldon Press.

Van der Kolk, B. (2015) *The Body Keeps the Score: Brain, Mind and Body in the Healing of Trauma*. New York: Penguin.

Van Poelje, S. (2022) Workshop presentation, PTAT Conference, Poznan, Poland.

Vos, J. and Van Rijn, B. (2021) The transactional analysis review survey: An investigation into self-reported practices and philosophies of psychotherapists. *Transactional Analysis Journal*, 51(2): 111–126.

Walker, M., Brakefield, T., Hobson, R. and Stickgold, H. (2003) Dissociable stages of human memory consolidation and reconsolidation. *Nature*, 42(2003): 616–620.

Waller, G. and Turner, H. (2016) Therapist drift redux: Why well-meaning clinicians fail to deliver evidence-based therapy, and how to get back on track. *Behaviour Research and Therapy*, 77: 129–137.

Wampold, B., Norcross, J. and Lambert, M. (2019) *Psychotherapy Relationships That Work*. Vol, 1: *Therapist Contributions*. Oxford: Oxford University Press.

Ware, P. (1983). Personality adaptations (doors to therapy). *Transactional Analysis Journal*, 13(1): 11–19.

Weed, L. L. (1971) *Medical Records, Medical Education and Patient Care*, 5th edn. Cleveland, OH: The Press of Western Reserve University.

Weekers, L., Hutsebaut, J. and Kamphuis, J. (2018) The Level of Personality Functioning Scale- Brief Form 2.0: Update of a brief instrument for assessing level of personality functioning. *Personality and Mental Health*, 13(1): 3–14. doi: 10.1002/pmh.1434

WHO (World Health Organisation) (2019) *International Classification of Diseases (ICD-11)*. Eleventh Revision. Geneva: WHO. Available at: https://icd.who.int/browse11

Widdowson, M. (2008) Metacommunicative transactions. *Transactional Analysis Journal*, 38(1): 58–71.

Widdowson, M. (2013) The process and outcome of transactional analysis psychotherapy for the treatment of depression: An adjudicated case series. PhD thesis, University of Leicester.

Widdowson, M. (2014) Transactional analysis psychotherapy for a case of mixed anxiety and depression: A pragmatic adjudicated case study 'Alastair'. *International Journal of Transactional Analysis Research*, 5(2): 66–76. doi: 10.29044/v5i2p66

Widdowson, M. (2016) *Transactional Analysis for Depression: A Step-by-Step Treatment Manual.* London: Routledge.

Widdowson, M. (2021) Mind the gap. Public lecture for TEDx Larissa. Available at: https://www.youtube.com/watch?v=okRAdjS8oeY

Widdowson, M. (2022) TA for the 21st century. Keynote speech at the Ellesmere Counselling and Psychotherapy Conference, Hull, UK, and the Polish TA Association conference, Poznan, Poland.

Widiger, T. and McCabe, G. (2020) The Alternative Model of Personality Disorders (AMPD) from the perspective of the five-factor model. *Psychopathology*, 53(3–4): 149–156. doi: 10.1159/000507378

Willcox, G. (1982) The Feeling Wheel: A Tool for Expanding Awareness of Emotions and Increasing Spontaneity and Intimacy. *Transactional Analysis Journal*, 12(4): 274–276.

Winkler, C., Koval, P., Philips, L. and Felmingham, K. (2022) Does prediction error during exposure relate to clinical outcomes in cognitive behavior therapy for social anxiety disorder? A study protocol. *Frontiers in Psychiatry*, 13. doi: 10.3389/fpsyt.2022.1000686

Winnicott, D. W. (1946/1987). Hate in the countertransference. In D. W. Winnicott, *Through Paediatrics to Psychoanalysis.* London: Hogarth Press.

Winnicott, D. W. (1960a/1965a) Psychiatric disorder in terms of infantile maturational processes. In D. W. Winnicott, *The Maturational Processes and the Facilitating Environment.* Madison, CT: International Universities Press, pp. 230–241.

Winnicott, D. W. (1960a/1965b) The theory of the parent-infant relationship. In D. W. Winnicott, *The Maturational Processes and the Facilitating Environment.* Madison, CT: International Universities Press, pp. 37–55.

Winnicott, D. (1971) *Playing and Reality.* London: Tavistock Publications.

Woods, K. (1996) Projective identification and game analysis. *Transactional Analysis Journal*, 26(3): 228–231.

Woods, K. (2000) The defensive function of the game scenario. *Transactional Analysis Journal*, 30(1): 94–97.

Woollams, S. and Brown, M. (1978) *Transactional Analysis*. Dexter: Huron Valley Institute.

Wosket, V. (1999) *The Therapeutic Use of Self: Counselling Practice, Research and Supervision*. New York: Routledge.

Yalom, I. (1980) *Existential Psychotherapy*. New York: Basic Books.

Yalom, I. (2001) *The Gift of Therapy: An Open Letter to a New Generation of Therapists and Their Patients*. New York: HarperCollins.

Yeomans, F. E., Clarkin, J. F. and Kernberg, O. F. (2015) *Transference-Focused Psychotherapy for Borderline Personality Disorder: A Clinical Guide*. Washington, DC: American Psychiatric Publishing, Inc.

Yoon, K. L. and Zinbarg, R. E. (2008) Interpreting neutral faces as threatening is a default mode for socially anxious individuals. *Journal of Abnormal Psychology*, 117(3): 680–685. doi: 10.1037/0021-843X.117.3.680.

Zivkovic, A. (2022) Introduction to Interpretative Dynamic TA Psychotherapy (IDTAP). Lecture at Metanoia Institute, London, 7 June.

Žvelc, G., Černetič, M. and Košak, M. (2011) Mindfulness-based transactional analysis. *Transactional Analysis Journal*, 41(3): 241–254.

INDEX

Note: Locators in *italic* indicate figures, in **bold** tables and in ***italic-bold*** boxes.

'5, 4, 3, 2, 1' technique 265–266

accounting for diversity in therapeutic relationship 77–80
Adapted Child 133, *134*; Rebellious Adapted Child 198
Adapted Child responses, indicator of alliance rupture 87–88; adaption/compliance 88; deflection, redefinition 88–89; rebellion/confrontation 88; withdrawal 88
Adult ego states 359–361, *134*, ***171***; available 121, 242, 269, 304–305; contamination, decontamination 12, 14, 279, 280; vs Child ego dominance 264, 266; concept, definition 1, 359–360; escape-hatch closure 164–165; mindfulness practice 341; phenomenological diagnosis 124–125; purpose 360; redecision school 16; sexuality 361; sufficient 48, 133–134, 269, 302; therapeutic letter writing (Adult to Child ego) 321–322
Adverse Childhood Experiences (ACEs) 116, 220, 221, 222, 230
affect: attunement 74; vs cognition 275; deepening 267–270; regulation, tolerance 56, 266, 301
alienation 28–30
Anderson, T. 335
Angyal, A. 33
assessment, diagnosis: accounting for: cultural and religious parent 141–144; accounting for: internal ego state dialogue 138–141; accounting for: intersectionality and opression 145–149; accounting for: neurodiversity 149–151; Berne four diagnosis methods 122–125; checklist, diagnosis 171–176, ***171–176***; conversational interview techniques 126–128; drivers, exploring 157–159; ego states, functional/structural analysis 133–137; escape hatches 163–166; games, analysing 160–162; intake assessment, structured 115–118;

observation, importance 111–114; pro-formas for rapid script diagnosis 129–132; script systems, building up 152–156; suicidal ideation 167–170; TA therapy suitability assessment 119–121
attentional bias 325
attunement: affective 73, 74, 75; integrative TA 38, 40–41
authenticity 354–358
awareness 233–234

Baker, J. 150
Barkham M. 239–240
Barnes, G. 7
Barnett, M. 351–352
Barrow, G. 32–33
Bary, B. B. 140
Baskerville, V. 77
behavioural diagnosis, ego state 122–123
Berne, E. **210**; autonomy 233; awareness 233–234; classical school, TA 11–13, 14–15; confrontation 329; contracting 181, 185, 193; deconfusion, decontamination 279–281; ego states / ego states diagnosis 36, 122–125, 133, **171**, 261, 279, 359–360; eight therapeutic operations 14, 58, 72; games / games analysis 98, 99, 160, 161, 293; individualized treatment plans **210**; observation 111–112; *Principles of Group Treatment* 362; psychodynamic TA 43–44, 50; redecision school 16, 17; script development 344; six categories of time structuring

82; social diagnosis 82; 'splinter,' 'bent penny' analogies 230–232; sweatshirts 97–98; TA concept development 1, 7; therapy endings, types 105–106; transactions, transactional analysis 82, 96–97, 112, 138; *What Do You Say After You Say Hello?* 147
Bickman, L. 331
Boliston-Mardula, J. 165
bonds, work alliance 85, 86
Bonds-White, F. 26
borderline personality disorder 25, 270, 328
Bordin, E. S. 84
Bowers, C. 150
Boyd, H 163
Brown, M. 183–184, **210**, 344, 359

Cathexis Institute 22, 23, 24, 25, 26
cathexis school 22–27, 89; background 22–23; critique 25–27; key theoretical concepts 23–24; methods 25; philosophy, approach 23
Černetič, M. 342
chair work techniques 17, 19, 313–317, 322; development 313; ending 317; external dialogues 314; facilitating 316; impasse resolution 311; initiating 315–316; internal dialogues 314–315; transference 17; types 314–316
challenge-support balance 259–260

checklist, diagnosis 171–176,
    171–176
Child ego states 133, *134*, **171**;
    behavioural, historical,
    phenomenological diagnosis
    122–123, 125; cathexis school
    23, 25; concept and concept
    alternatives 56–57, 122;
    deconfusing 43, 76, 261, 279;
    development 23; diagnosis
    124, 125; Free Child, capacity
    133; Hargaden and Sills model
    56; vs Parent ego state conflict
    51, 272, 310, *310*, 313, 315;
    Rebellious Adapted Child ego
    state 198; redecision school 16,
    17; sexuality 361; soothing
    264–267, 318–319; therapist-
    Child ego state alliance 45;
    trauma resolving 321–323;
    variations 137
Chow, D. 278, 331
Clark, B. 73, 76, 272
Clarkson, P. 102–103, 106, 158,
    210, 250, 329, 362
classical school, TA 8, 11–15;
    background 11; critique 15;
    key theoretical concepts
    12–13; methods 14–15;
    philosophy, approach 11–12
client, direct questioning,
    reacting to 356–358
client feedback 333
client identity help 347–349
client protection 303–305
client strength building 347–349
client tracking (openness,
    closeness) in therapy 274–275
clients contracting: client ability
    121; unsure clients 190–192;
    see also contracting

client-therapist psychological
    mindedness 120–121
clinical effectiveness, evaluating
    331–333
clinical effectiveness, measuring
    tools 332–333
clinical note writing 338–340,
    339–340
co-creative TA approach:
    background 60–61; guiding
    principles: present-centred
    development 61–62; guiding
    principles: shared responsibility
    61; guiding principles:
    'we-ness' 61; theoretical
    concepts: reflections for practice
    62–63; theoretical concepts: two
    types of relating 62–63
cognitive bias 324–327;
    attentional bias 325;
    confirmation bias 325;
    egocentric bias 325;
    fundamental attribution error
    326; naïve realism 325;
    negativity bias 318, 326;
    planning fallacy 326; spotlight
    effect 325; transparency
    effect 325
common pitfall, avoiding:
    directionality, avoiding
    therapy drift 242–244;
    iatrogenic shaming, risk
    reduction 245–248;
    marshmallowing, avoiding
    253–256; 'racket OKness,'
    avoiding 249–252; treatment
    length, realism 239–241
comparative treatment
    sequences 209–211, **210**
conceptualizing therapeutic
    relationship 81–83

confirmation bias 325

conflict preparation, contracting 204–206

confrontation 328–330

contact, concept 28, 37–38, 39

contracting 14; goal-orientated TA therapy 182–184; 'good-enough' contract 201–203; homework, behavioural contracts 193–195; process orientated TA therapy 182–184; resistance, non-compliance 196–200; standard written contract 185–189; therapy tasks and goals 179–181; unsure clients 190–192

conversational interview techniques 126–128

Cooper-Norcross Inventory of Preferences (C-NIP) 68, 180, 214

Core Conflictual Relational Themes (CCRT) 94, **95**

Cornell, W. 26, 67, 294–295, 311, 345

COVID-19 pandemic 34–35

Cowles-Boyd, L. 163

Critical Parent, Internal 138–139, **171**

Critical Parent (or Persecutor) 29, 30, 31, 52

Cultural Parent 141–144

'culture of excellence,' psychotherapists 331–332

deconfusion 43, 50, 51, 62, 76, *176*, **210**, 272; vs decontamination 209, 279–282; using alliance rupture and repair 286–289

decontamination 14, 72, 209, **210**, 246, 279–282, 329

deficit model 23, 37, 82

deliberate practice for skill enhancement 334–337; areas 335; interpersonal skills 335; therapeutic skills 335–336

diagnosis checklist 171, *172–176*

directionality 242

discounting, incorporating cognitive bias 324–327

diversity, accounting for 77–80

Drego, P. 141

drift avoidance, therapy 243–244

drivers, exploring 157–159

Drye, R. 164, 300

Dunning-Kruger effect 331–332

Eco-script 34

eco-TA approach: background 32–33; critique 35; key theoretical concepts 33; methods 34–35

ego state diagnosis 122–125, 133, *171*; behavioural 122–123; historical 123–124; phenomenological 124–125; social 123

ego states, functional/structural analysis 133–137; abstraction levels 134–135; Adult Ego states 133–134; Child ego states (*see under own heading*); ego states model 133, *134*; Parent Ego state 51; third-order structural model 134, *135*

egocentric bias 325

Ekman, P. 262, 271

embodiment and the environment, eco-TA 34

emotion expression, healthy 271–273
emotion regulation techniques and skills 222, 264–266, 319
emotional awareness and granulation 261–263
empathy: centrality in TA therapeutic relationships 73–76; confrontation 328, 330; diagnosis checklist **174–175**; 'easy' vs 'difficult' 79–80; empathic failure 247–248; empathic transactions 52, 280, 281; IDTAP 52; integrative TA as empathic therapy 40, 41; interpretative intervention 44; juxtaposition 39; one-and-a-half-person psychology 73–76
enactment, relational/game 160, 161, 287, 291, 292–293
ending, TA therapy 105–107; accidental 105; enforced 106; resistant 106; therapeutic 106
enquiry, integrative TA 40
enquiry, therapeutic 71–72
Erikson, E. 44
Erskine, R. G. 36–37, 38–39, 41, 71, 83, 153, 344–345, 360
escape hatches 163–166
escape-hatch closure 163, 164–165, 300–302
Existential Psychotherapy (Yalom) 169
experiential disconfirmation 224–229, 283, 284–285
Eye Movement Desensitization and Reprocessing (EMDR) therapy 318–319

Federn, P. 44

feelings wheel 262–263
Fowlie, H. 54–56
Free Child 133
Freud, S. 350
functional/structural analysis of ego states 133–137
fundamental attribution error 326

Gaia theory 33
game: analysing 98, 99, 160–162; diagnosis checklist **172**; enactment 160, 161, 291, 292–293; evolvement 101; nature 98, 99; psychological roles in (drama triangle) 99; therapy 290–293; transference/countertransference 98
General Data Protection Regulation (GDPR) 186, 188, 189
goal-orientated TA therapy 182–184
goals: contracting for 179, 181, 190–191, 201, 342; work alliance 84, 85, 116–117
'good enough' contract 201–203
Gouldings, B. / Gouldings, M. 16, 17, 20, 21, 294–295, 309, 311, 318
granulation and emotional awareness 261–263
gratitude journals 195, 266
group therapy 15, 30–31, 101

Hahn, A. 328
Hargaden, H. 53, 56, 58, 59, 60, 103, 179, 250, 272, 280
Harvey, A. 231–232
'Hate in the

countertransference' (Winnicott) 250
Herman, J. 222
Hiremath, M. 77, 79, 142, 143
historical diagnosis, ego state 123–124
Holmes, J. 294
homework, behavioural contracts 193–195
homonomy 33–34, 235
honesty 356
Hubble, M. A. 331–332
Hufford, F. M. 140

iatrogenic illness 245
iatrogenic shaming, risks 245–248, 259; contracting 245–246; decontamination through exhortation 246; discounting 247; examining client-therapist experience 248; game analysis 246–247; 'pollyanna-ing' 247–248
identity categorization 145; see also intersectionality and oppression
impasse, diagnostic checklist 176
impasse theory 18, 176, 309–312, 310; Gouldings' model 20, 309; impasse acceptance 311–312; impasse clarification 18; impasse resolution 310–311; impasse vs feeling 'stuck' 309; type one, two, three 309–310, 310
incorporating cognitive bias, discounting 324–327
individual and group therapy 30–31
individualized treatment plans 210, 212–215

Information Commissioner's Office 188, 189
initial session 67–70
injunction, injunctive messages 129, 150, 169, 175, 226–227; 'don't (do anything)' 299; 'don't be a child' 298; 'don't be important' 175, 213, 214, 217, 226–227, 284, 297–298; 'don't be well'/'don't be sane' 299; 'don't exist' 150, 165–166, 167, 296–297; 'don't feel' 299; 'don't grow up' 298; 'don't succeed' 150, 298; 'don't think' 150, 299; Gouldings' list 294–295; intervention and approaches 296–299; therapy of injunctions 294–295; see also scripts / script beliefs
intake assessment, therapist suitability (skills, experience) 115–118
integrative TA approach: background 36; critique 41–42; key theoretical concepts 37–39; methods 40–41; philosophy, approach 36–37
Intensive Transactional Analysis Psychotherapy (ITAP): background 47; methods 47–49
interconnectedness, eco-TA 33, 235
internal ego states: dialogue, accounting for 138–141; Internal Critical Parent 133, 138–141, 171
International Association for Relational TA 54
International Transactional

Analysis Association (ITAA) 43
Interpretive Dynamic Transactional Analysis Psychotherapy (IDTAP): background 50–51; methods 51–52
intersectionality and oppression 145–149; cultural references 146; intersectional identity acknowledgement (client, therapist) 145–146; intersectionality, term 145; language patterns 146; sexual orientation, gender identity, LGBTQ+ 146–148; societal inequalities 146
intervention: affect-deepening 269–270, 270; categories, classical school 14, 15; chair work 314; confrontation 329; empathic transaction 58; initial session 67, 69; injunction, injunctive messages 296–299; interpretative 44; metacommunication 289–290; needs, minimising through enquiry 71–72, 75; observation 111; Ware sequence 274
interview techniques, conversational 126–128
intimacy 235
involvement, integrative TA 40, 41

Jacobs, A. 26
Jacobs, M. 44
James Game Plan / James, M. 11, 160, 321

Joines, V. 2
journaling for self-awareness/ reflection 195, 266, 276–278
juxtaposition 39

Kabat-Zinn, J. 342
Kahler, T. 158
Kellogg, S. 314
Kohut, H. 38, 103–104
Kolb, D. A. 345
Košak, M. 342

Landaiche, M. 311
Lapworth, P. 2
Leader, D. 267
Lee, A. 129, *130*, 157, 182, 322
Levin, P. 24, 26
LGBTQ+ 147
lies/discounts and alienation 30
life position **176**
Luborsky, L. 94, 269, 291
Lutz, W. 239, 332

Malan, D. 47, 48
Malan's triangles, concept 47
Maroda, K. 250, 250–251, 252, 292, 350
Marshall, H. 32–33
marshmallowing, avoiding 253–256
Masterson, J. F. 328
McLeod, J. 351
McNeel, J. 295, 296, 313
McWilliams, N. 78, 307–308, 351, 356
metacommunication 355–356
metacommunicative transactions 289–290
Miller, S. D. 331–332, 333
mindfulness cultivation 341–343
Moiso, C. 103, 273

monitoring, revising 216–219
mortido concept 362
Moursund, J. P. 36
Muran, C. J. 87, 88, 286–287, 288, 342

naïve realism 325
Natural Child *134*
negative automatic thoughts (NATS) 139–140
negativity bias 318, 326
neurodiversity 149–151
Newton, T. 345
no-harm contracts 164, 300, 301–302
Nurturing Parent, internal 133, 139, **171**, **210**
Nurturing Parent (or Rescuer) 52, *134*

observation, importance 111–114
Occam's razor 136, 233
Ogden 251
'OKness,' sense of 157, 249–250, 252
one-and-a-half-person psychology 9
one-person psychology 9

parasympathetic nervous system 265
parent ego state: Critical Parent / Internal Critical Parent 133, 138–139, **171**; Cultural Parent 141–144; Nurturing Parent, internal / Nurturing Parent (Rescuer) 52, 133, *134*, 139, **171**, **210**, 319; Religious Parent 141–144; Structuring Parent 133, *134*, 319
Parlett, M. 60
passivity **175–176**
Patterson, C. 335
Pennebaker, J. 277
Pennebaker, J. W. 277
Perls, F. 16, 309
permission 306, 307–308
permission transaction 14
personality functioning **174–175**
personality traits **173–174**
Petriglieri, G. 310–311
phenomenological diagnosis, ego state 124–125
physis 163, 242, 268
Pig Parents 29; *see also* Critical Parents (or Persecutor)
planning fallacy 326
Post-Traumatic Stress Disorder (PTSD) 220, 241
potency 12, 235, 306–307
present-centred development, co-creative TA 61–62
principle of parsimony 136
Principles of Group Treatment (Berne) 362
process orientated TA therapy 182–184
pro-formas use, rapid script diagnosis 129–132; drowning person diagram (Lee) 129, *130*; negative script beliefs 129, **131–132**
projective identification 98, 104, 251
psychodynamic TA 1 approach: background 43–44; critique 46; methods 44–46

psychodynamic TA 2 approach: Intensive Transactional Analysis Psychotherapy (ITAP): background 47; methods 47–49, 51–52

psychodynamic TA 3 approach: Interpretive Dynamic Transactional Analysis Psychotherapy (IDTAP), background 50–51

psychological mindedness, client-therapist 120–121

Psychotherapy Relationships That Work (Norcross, Lambert) 17

'racket OKness,' avoiding 249–252

radical psychiatry school 28–31; background 28; critique 31; key theoretical concepts, methods 29–31m; philosophy, approach 28–29

rapid script diagnosis, pro formas use 129–132; drowning person diagram (Lee) 129, *130*; negative script beliefs 129, **131–132**

redecision **210**, 224, 283, 295, 336

redecision school, TA 17–21, 41, 140, 267; background 17; critique 20–21; key theoretical concepts 18; methods 19–20, 295; philosophy and approach 17–18

reflections for practice, co-creative TA 62–63

reflective journals 276–277

relational TA approach: background 53; critique 59; key theoretical concepts 56–57; methods 58–59; philosophy, approach 53–56; principles 54–56

Religious Parent 141–144

resistance/non-compliance, contracting for 196–200

Rogers, C. 37, 74

Rook, J. 143

Rousmaniere, T. 334–335, 336–337

rubber banding 97

rupture and repair, therapeutic alliance 90–93; adapted Child responses as rupture indicator 87–88; deconfusuion 286–288; due to therapist attitudes 92; miscommunications (mistakes, responsibility) 92–93; preventive direction change 92; relational affective significance of rupture 91; as therapist-client game enactment 291, 292, 293

Safran, J. D. 87, 88, 286–287, 288, 342

Sambin, M. 47

San Francisco Transactional Analysis Seminars 7

Schiff, A. 23–24, 26, 27

Schiff, J. 22, 23–24, 26, 27

Scotta, F. 47

script antithesis 15

script beliefs 129–130; attunement and cumulative trauma 38; disconfirming 224, 226, 227, 229, 283–285, *339–340*; individualized treatment plans 213, 214–215, **217–218**; negative script

beliefs 129, *130*, **131–132**, 150, 157, 248
script development, ongoing 344–346
script system, analysis *172–173*
script system, integrative TA 39
script systems, building 152–156, **153**; reinforcing memories 155–156; scripty beliefs 152–153 (*see also under own heading*); scripty displays 153–154
self-awareness 77, 101, 123, 276–278
self-disclosure 354–358
self-reflection 276–278, 354
Seligman, M. 347–348
Session Rating Scale, Miler's 333
Session Rating Scale (Miller) 333
Shadbolt, C. 79, 146–147
shaming; *see* iatrogenic shaming, risk
shared responsibility, co-creative TA 61
Shivanath, S. 77, 79, 142, 143
Sills, C. 53, 54–56, 58, 59, 60, 103, 179, 250, 272, 280
Singer, J. 149
'SOAP' formula, record keeping 339
social diagnosis 96
social diagnosis, ego state 123
'splinter,' 'bent penny' tackling 230–232
spontaneity 234–235
spotlight effect 325
standard written business contract: cancellation policy

186; confidentiality 186–187; document title/name 185–186; fees 186; GDPR compliance privacy statement 188–189
Stark, M. 8–10, 75, 79–80, 82–83, 251, 292
Stark's three modes of therapeutic action: one-and-a-half-person psychology 9; one-person psychology 9; two-person psychology 10
Steiner, C. 28, 85, 272
Stern, D. 56, 73, 74, 345
Stern, E. 345
Stewart, I. 2, 164–165, 233, 300, 305
Stiles, W. B. 239–240
strengthening working alliance: bonds 86; goals 85; tasks 84–85
stroke economy 30, *172*
Structuring parent 133, *134*, 319
suicidal ideation 164, 165, 167–170, 301–302, 303, 304
suitability assessment, TA therapy 119–121; Adult ego state, availability 121; contract, ability to enter 121; practitioner limitations 119; psychological mindedness 120–121; resources 119–120; service, availability limitations 120
Summers, G. 60
support-challenge balance 259–260
sustainability, sufficiency, eco-TA 35
sweatshirts 97–98
Swede, S. 268

TA therapy suitability assessment; *see* suitability assessment, TA therapy

tasks: contracting for 180–181, 182; homework and behavioural contracts 194–195, 196–197, 198; work alliance 84–85

Terlato, V. 161

therapeutic alliance, rupture: adapted Child responses as indicator 87–88; adaption/compliance 88; deconfusion 286–289; deflection, redefinition 88–89; direction change to avoid 92; miscommunications, mistakes and responsibility 92–93; rebellion/confrontation 88; relational affective significance 91; therapist attitudes 92; withdrawal 88

therapeutic enquiry 71–72

therapeutic relationship: accounting for diversity in 77–80; conceptualizing 81–83; empathy, centrality of 73–76; ending 105–107; initial session 67–70; strengthening working alliance (tasks, goal, bonds) 84–88; therapeutic alliance: adapted Child responses as rupture indicator 87–88; therapeutic alliance: rupture, repair 90–93; therapeutic enquiry 71–72; transference/countertransference: aide-mémoire of TA models 102–104; transference/

countertransference: understanding 94–98

therapeutic skills, refining: Adult ego state 359–361; affect deepening 267–270; analysing transactions 365–366; authenticity 354–358; chair work, guidelines 313–317; challenge-support balance 259–260; Child ego state, soothing 264–267; Child ego state, trauma resolving 321–323; client tracking (openness, closeness) 274–275; client identity, help 347–349; client protection 303–305; client strength building 347–349; clinical effectiveness, evaluating 331–333; clinical note writing 338–340; confrontation 328–330; deconfusion, alliance rupture and repair 286–289; decontamination vs deconfusion 279–282; deliberate practice for 334–337; disconfirming script beliefs 283; discounting, incorporating cognitive bias 324–327; emotion expression, healthy 271–273; emotional awareness, granulation 261–263; escape-hatch closure 300–302; impasse theory 309–312; injunction/injunction messages, therapy of 296; journaling, encouraging to 276–278; metacommunicative transactions 289–290;

mindfulness cultivation, Adult 341–343; potency and permission 306–308; script development, ongoing 344–346; self-disclosure, using 354–358; TA as existential psychotherapy 362–364; therapist's motivation, exploring 350–353; therapy of games 290–293; therapy of injunctions 294–295; visualization and mental imagery 318–320

therapist-client psychological mindedness 120–121

therapist's motivation 350–353

therapy of games 290–293

therapy of injunctions 294–295, 296–299

therapy of injunctive messages, John McNeel; *see* injunction, injunctive messages

therapy tasks and goals 179–181, 182–184

Thomson, G. 273

therapy drift, avoiding 242–244

'Three Ps' (potency, protection, permission) 12, 235, 306–308

Townsend, F. 191

Transactional Analysis Journal 262

Transactional Analysis (TA) approaches: co-creative 60–63; eco-TA 32–35; integrative TA 36–42; psychodynamic TA 43–52; relational TA 53–59; *see also under own headings*

Transactional Analysis (TA), methods/interventions: categories of interventions 14;

contracting 14; decontamination 14; group therapy 15; permission transaction 14; script antithesis 15

Transactional Analysis (TA) schools: cathexis school 22–27; classical 11–15; radical psychiatry 28–31; redecision school 16–21

Transactional Analysis (TA) theory: cognitive bias 324–327; escape-hatch closure 163, 164–165, 300–302; physis concept 163, 242

transactions 96–97

transference/ countertransference: aide-mémoire of TA models 102–104; chair work techniques 17, 313–317; drama triangle 99–101, *100*; games 98; negative transference preparation, contracting 204–206; projective identification 98, 104, 251; rubberbanding 97; social diagnosis 96; sweatshirts 97–98; transactions 96–97; understanding 94–98, **95**

Transference-Focused Psychotherapy (TFP) 50

transparency effect 325

trauma: and attunement 38; defining 220–221; identifying, PCL-5 measure 117; impact monitoring 220–223; relational 36, 82; trauma-informed, being 220–221; treatment: Child ego state

321–323; treatment: imagery techniques 318; treatment: tri-phasic model 222
Trautmann, R. L. 36, 38–39
treatment, trauma 222, 318, 321–323
treatment length, realism 239–241
treatment plan tracker 217, **217–218**
treatment planning: awareness 233–234; comparative treatment sequences 209–211; experiential disconfirmation 224–229; homonomy 235; individualized treatment plans 212–215; intimacy 235; monitoring, revising 216–219, **217–218**; 'splinter,' 'bent penny' tackling 230–232; spontaneity 234–235; trauma impact, monitoring 220–223
treatment sequences, comparative 209–211, **210**
tri-phasic model, trauma treatment 222–223
Tryon, G. S. 193
Tudor, K. 62–63, 106, 141, **210**, 274, 359, 360–360
two-chair dialogue 17, 322
two-person psychology 10
types of relating, co-creative TA 62–63

unsure clients and contracting 190–192

valence-arousal circumplex chart 262, 263
van Poelje, S. 135–136
visualization and mental imagery 318–320

walk and talk therapy, eco-TA method 34–35
Ware sequence / Ware, P. 274–275
Weiss, E. 44
'we-ness,' co-creative TA 61
What Do You Say After You Say Hello? (Berne) 147
Wheeler, S. 239–240
Widdowson, M. 141, 150, **210**, 224, 274, 289, 356
Winnicott, D. W. 250
Winograd, G. 193
Woollams, S. 183–184, **210**, 344
working alliance, strengthening bonds 86; goals 85; tasks 84–85; *see also* therapeutic relationship
writing, use in therapy 276–277

Yalom, I. 69, 169, 354, 362, 363

Zalcman, M. 39, 152, 153
Zivkovic, A. / Zivkovic's model 50–51, 52
Žvelc, G. 342

Printed in the United States
by Baker & Taylor Publisher Services